SEPTEMBER 11, 2001

P9-CRP-036

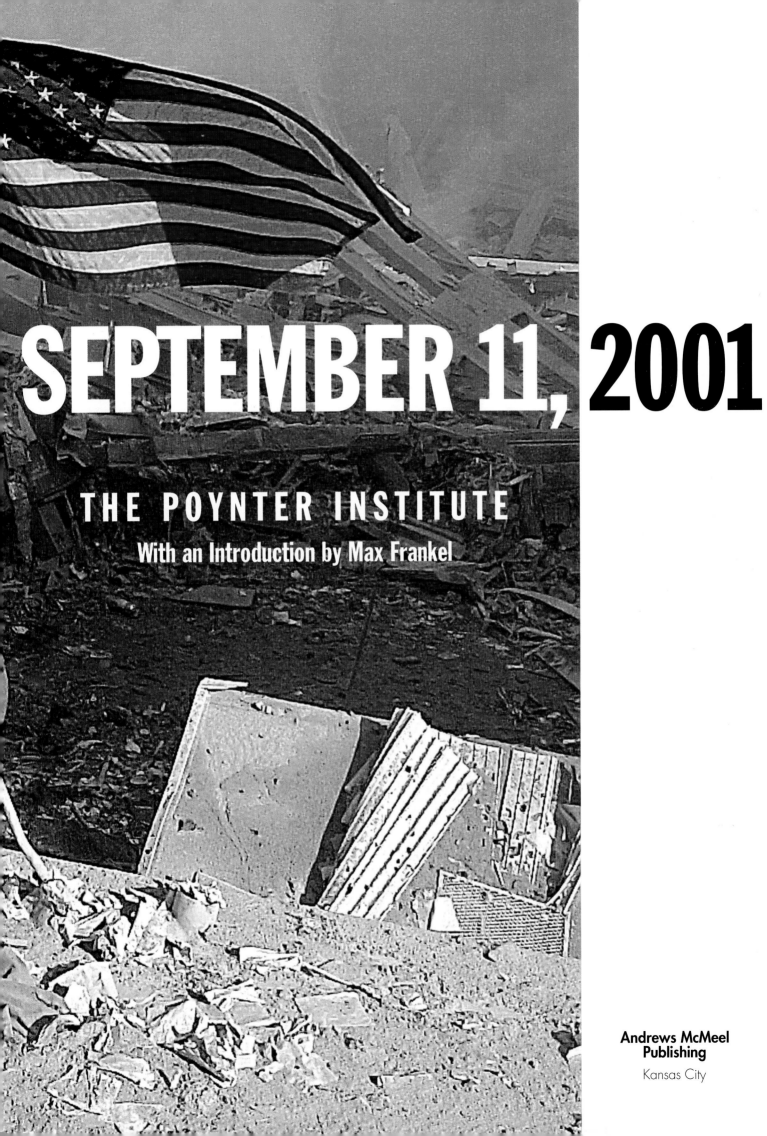

SEPTEMBER 11, 2001

THE POYNTER INSTITUTE

With an Introduction by Max Frankel

Andrews McMeel
Publishing

Kansas City

SEPTEMBER 11, 2001

Copyright © 2001 by The Poynter Institute. All rights reserved.
Printed in the United States of America. No part of this book may be used
or reproduced in any manner whatsoever without written permission except
in the case of reprints in the context of reviews. For information,
write Andrews McMeel Publishing, an Andrews McMeel Universal company,
4520 Main Street, Kansas City, Missouri 64111.

02 03 04 05 RDW 10 9 8 7 6 5 4

ISBN: 0-7407-2492-4

Library of Congress Control Number: 2001097006

—————— **Attention: Schools and Businesses** ——————

Andrews McMeel books are available at quantity discounts with bulk purchase for educational,
business, or sales promotional use. For information, please write to: Special Sales Department,
Andrews McMeel Publishing, 4520 Main Street, Kansas City, Missouri 64111.

Dedicated to the victims
of the terrorist attacks on September 11, 2001

Contents

CONTENTS

PREFACE

Moments Frozen in Time

For each of us, there are occasions—a wedding, a child's birth, a family tragedy—so compelling that details are forever etched in memory. Few events define all of us.

September 11, 2001, did.

We all gaped, horrified, as the second passenger plane collided with the second tower. We all watched the wedge of destruction carved into the Pentagon. We all peered into the desolate crater on a field in Pennsylvania. We all looked eagerly for more ghostly survivors to trudge, holding one another, out of the concrete soot that clouded the remains of collapsed twin towers.

Not since the assassination of John F. Kennedy has one event so transfixed a nation, a world.

The Poynter Institute, a school that teaches skills and ethics to professional journalists in St. Petersburg, Florida, had no plan to memorialize these frozen moments in time.

The school merely posted a notice on its Web site inviting news editors who design front pages to send us an electronic copy of how they told this urgent story. Within a day, hundreds of front pages were recorded on our Web site. And all over the world people were turning to the school as another place to connect themselves to the record of these terrible events, and thus to one another. Our computers nearly sank beneath the weight of witnesses to these pages.

It was then that the school decided to publish representative front pages. We have three purposes: to provide a more permanent record as a memorial to the dead, the bereaved, the heroic; to take the occasion, as Max Frankel, the retired executive editor of *The New York Times*, does with unflinching insight, to remind Americans—especially media corporations—of the purpose of a free press; and to help provide funds for the victims.

The Poynter Institute, the newspapers who have allowed their pages to be republished, and Andrews McMeel Publishing will receive no profits from this book. They will go instead to The September 11th Fund, administered by the United Way. Domtar Industries, Inc., Montreal, Quebec, Canada, and Lindenmeyr Book Publishing Papers, Chicago, furnished paper below cost for the printing of this book, and the R. R. Donnelley and Sons plant in Willard, Ohio, provided book manufacturing services.

May these pages serve to remind all of us how much we rely on the goodwill of each of us.

Andrew E. Barnes
Chairman, The Poynter Institute
Chairman & CEO, St. Petersburg Times

INTRODUCTION

The Oxygen of Our Liberty

By Max Frankel

Here lies a souvenir of horror, a blazing obituary of American innocence.

But you are also holding a testament to news, tangible evidence that urgent and reliable news is no more obsolete than hate and heroism, fear and favor. Here atop the rubble lies a reminder that news remains the oxygen of our liberty.

Can you imagine September 11, 2001, without the oft-scorned "media"?

Some might argue that the world's great communications network served to invite this nightmare, that the terrorists were looking not only to kill random thousands but also to produce a spectacle whose imagery would instantly humble the strong and empower the weak.

But only honest and reliable news media could instruct the world in its vulnerability, summon Americans to heroic acts of rescue, and ignite the global search for meaning and response. Only trusted news teams could discern the nation's anxiety, spread words of hope and therapy, and help to move us from numbing fear toward recovery.

Here, then, lies above all the ultimate demonstration of the danger that Americans invited when they lost their interest in the world beyond the self and in serious news coverage of those other realms. Another generation has been awakened, summoned to recognize that dependable news occupies a precious but vulnerable place in our society.

Every page of this book proves that news is no mere rendering of lifeless facts. (Facts galore inhabit the phone book, but not a shred of understanding.) News is the portrayal and ordering of information in vivid image and narrative. News is the transformation of facts into stories so that they can be understood and remembered in ways that inform and instruct, even as they delight or dismay. News not only portrays events, it ranks them in some order of importance as defined by public needs and interests. And besides recounting events, meaningful news digs to discover their causes and to assess their consequences.

News is not neutral. Like literature, the most important news dwells on stories of conflict, on the rivalries and casualties of life. Yet while conflict is universal, so is the human desire to avoid and reduce it. And so news also serves the armies of reform and implicitly holds out hope and a faith in progress. Since a free and open society is, by definition, a constantly self-correcting organism, it is constantly nourished by news that exposes flaws and failures and so stimulates debate about how to overcome them. News is the enemy of certainty, and therefore of tyranny.

This precious news does not, however, grow wild, like poisonous rumor. It must be expensively harvested and effectively distributed. News, therefore, is a dependent of technology, the product of an industry. And there's the rub: the paradox that a most vital public service needs to be sustained by private profit.

Time and again in American history, that industry's pursuit of profit has threatened to overwhelm its capacity for service. The years before September 11, 2001, were such a time.

Journalists grow up with the idea of serving the public. They assume it to be their duty to arm the citizenry with the information it needs to select its leaders, define its problems, and grope for remedies. But most of the costs of good journalism, on television or paper, are borne by advertisers and investors whose commercial interests often diverge from those who gather the news. Investors demand profits and require advertisers who demand large audiences, crowds that may respond more readily to entertaining theater than to informative news. And as Russell Baker once put it, when the citizenry is deemed to be merely an audience, the journalist becomes a hustling barker, "like the guy who used to stand outside tents working his mouth to draw a crowd."

When in the '90s Americans found themselves liberated from hot and cold wars, they rapidly shifted attention from sober news to facile entertainments. And our great media companies indulged them without shame.

Television had become the nation's principal medium of information, but news ceased to be its proudest product. Indeed, as television companies were swallowed by ever larger corporations, their news departments became ever weaker cogs in the enterprise. Pressed to show a profit, they largely withdrew from the world and treated five billion people beyond our borders as inconsequential and irrelevant. Blaming the audience for these choices, they lavished money and attention on sports and celebrities, petty scandals, and crowd-pleasing fictions that they cynically defined as "reality."

Many newspapers followed the television trail toward the trivial. Unable to command the attention of young readers, the papers blamed young people's loss of interest in public affairs instead of their own failure to make the important interesting. And the many papers that were gobbled up by large media corporations were too often forced to reduce their staffs and ambitions to enhance the income of distant masters. Editors trained to be teachers were hounded into becoming marketers.

Technology accelerated these trends. Cable, satellite, and Internet transmissions carved audiences into "niche" markets that undermined all sense of community. Impatience with public service drove political news almost off the tube. Documentaries about great national issues totally disappeared. Foreign correspondents were brought home and given parachutes to cover an occasional coup or royal funeral. And even at home, candidates for public office were given short shrift and forced to sell their souls to pay for crude and canned campaign commercials. On the eve of the World Trade Center attack, media mavens had begun to wonder how long the major networks would bother to retain prime-time news programs.

Did the terrorists change all that in a single blow? Will important news once again take precedence over commercial interests as it did so dramatically on September 11 and successive weeks? Will instructing the public about remote and perplexing affairs take the place of beclouding the screen with shouted opinions?

Journalists were quick to return to their roots and assert their claims. The terror attack "helped all of us regain our focus," said Walter Isaacson, the former editor of *Time* magazine and new chairman of CNN. "It's injected a note of real seriousness. And the things we think of doing to chase ratings now pale in comparison to the importance of doing this story seriously and reliably."

But other stories? Erik Sorenson, the president of CNN's all-news rival MSNBC, blamed the decline of seriousness on "a national fog of materialism and disinterest and avoidance" and seemed unsure how long our present clarity would last.

Fear is the great engine of news. It focuses minds. It demands a ranking of dangers. It searches near and far for paths to safety. That is why news of terror trumps the fear of growing fat or losing the pennant, and why as fear recedes so will the thirst for relevant news. Still, an informed intelligence should also want to discern the risks and benefits that lie beyond the horizon. It wants to inspect the ground that breeds a terrorist long before he crashes cruelly into our lives.

After we have sung the hymns to heroes who dig in the rubble and wage war, where will we find the media heroes who will sacrifice some profit to nourish us with news?

TUESDAY, SEPTEMBER 11, 2001

The Huntsville Times

Huntsville, Alabama

Final edition, **50**

Attack on America

■ Coordinated airplane attacks strike the World Trade Center and the Pentagon.

■ Huntsvillians are in limbo as FAA shuts down all airports across the country.

■ Arafat is horrified, but Palestinian crowds chant 'God is great' and pass out candy.

■ Pain of Oklahoma comes crashing back.

■ A nightmarish scene at Ground Zero.

PAGES A6 and A7

1

Forecast: *Sunny, dry after a clear night.* **Page B10**

 60 *The low tonight*

 86 *The high Wednesday*

Did today's horror touch you? Tell us: **536-9999,** *then category* **1005.**

EXTRA
THE ARIZONA REPUBLIC

TUESDAY • SEPTEMBER 11, 2001   az central.com   50 CENTS

U.S. ATTACKED

2

Jets crash into Trade Center, Pentagon

■

Bush rushed to military base

■

Planes grounded nationwide

■

Sky Harbor, state dams, buildings closed

■

Bin Laden suspected in attacks

■

Log on to azcentral.com throughout the day and night for extensive coverage of the attack:
■ The latest coverage from The Arizona Republic newsroom.
■ Video of the attack from 12 News and NBC News.
■ Photos of the attack and aftermath.
■ Details of the unfolding investigation.
■ Information on previous attacks.

Arizona Daily Star

50¢
One dollar
in Mexico
. .

SERVING TUCSON SINCE 1877 · WEDNESDAY, SEPTEMBER 12, 2001 ★★

UNTHINKABLE

Terrorists use knives, box cutters to hijack four planes; World Trade Center destroyed, Pentagon damaged

> *We will make no distinction between the terrorists who committed these acts and those who harbor them.*

President Bush
In an address to the nation

MOMENT OF HORROR *Huge, flying bomb zeros in for its assault on the second World Trade Center tower as the first burns with a fatal fury.*

The Associated Press

Death toll seen in thousands; rescue delayed

FROM WIRE REPORTS

A pall of smoke, dust and sadness settled over lower Manhattan at nightfall Tuesday as rescue workers, police and firefighters pressed their desperate search for survivors of the worst terrorist attack in United States history, a coordinated airborne assault that destroyed the twin towers of the World Trade Center and left a portion of the Pentagon in Washington in smoking ruins.

In New York alone, it was feared the death toll could reach the thousands. Officials said at least 300 firefighters and 78 police officers were missing and presumed dead at midday. Upwards of 50,000 people worked in the 110-story World Trade Center towers, reduced by explosions and fire to ruins within hours of the initial attack.

Speaking Tuesday evening from the White House, President Bush evoked a biblical message in saying the United States was walking "through the valley of the shadow of death" but still feared no evil. He described the attack as a mass murder that had ended the lives of thousands of people and called on the nation to remember the victims in its prayers.

Amid reports that investigators were focusing their attention on renegade Saudi exile Osama bin Laden, believed to be in exile in Afghanistan, Bush promised all the government's resources would be used to find and punish the perpetrators of the attack.

"Today, our nation saw evil," Bush said.

Said Adm. Robert J. Natter, commander of the U.S. Atlantic Fleet: "We have been attacked like we haven't since Pearl Harbor."

SEE **DISASTER / A7**

Bin Laden links start to emerge

By Karen Gullo and John Solomon
THE ASSOCIATED PRESS

WASHINGTON — U.S. officials began piecing together a case linking Osama bin Laden to the worst terrorist attack in U.S. history, aided by an intercept of communications between his supporters and harrowing cellphone calls from victims aboard the jetliners before they crashed on Tuesday.

Barbara Olson, *a victim, called from a hijacked plane.*

Authorities were focusing some of their efforts on possible bin Laden supporters in Florida based on the identification of a suspected hijacker on one of the manifests of the four jets that crashed, law enforcement officials said.

The FBI was preparing to search locations in Broward County in South Florida and the Daytona Beach area in Central Florida, Florida Department of Law Enforcement spokesman Rick Morera said.

The locations had links to the suspected bin Laden supporter on the jet manifest, officials said.

Among the passengers was Barbara Olson, the wife of a top Justice Department official, who called her husband as the hijacking took place.

U.S. intelligence intercepted communications between bin Laden supporters discussing the attacks on the World Trade Center and Pentagon, according to

SEE **BIN LADEN / A7**

OVERWHELMING TASK *In a scene right out of a disaster movie, firefighters make an early, tentative probe of the World Trade Center rubble.*

The Associated Press

THE PENTAGON

Reports suggest that as many as 800 people died in attack on defense headquarters. Still, says top official, "The Pentagon is functioning."

PAGE A2

NEW YORK CITY

Scenes of devastation, panic and fear unfolded as thousands fled the city on foot.

PAGE A3

TWIN TOWERS

The engineer who designed the World Trade Center said the towers could take a 707 hit.

PAGE A4

THE ECONOMY

Fed official speaking in Tucson says the nation's financial system is in no danger.

PAGE A10

IN TUCSON

Residents join in widespread prayer; followers of Islam are target of anger; Red Cross seeks blood donations.

PAGE A15

On StarNet
www.azstarnet.com

A PULITZER NEWSPAPER
Vol. 160, No. 255

Get Star stories from Tuesday and today, or watch local and national video coverage.
azstarnet.com/attack

7 50136 00001 5

THE DAILY CALIFORNIAN

Established 1871. Independent Student Press Since 1871.

BERKELEY, CALIFORNIA   WEDNESDAY, SEPTEMBER 12, 2001   WWW.DAILYCAL.ORG

'OUR NATION SAW EVIL'

HIJACKED AIRPLANES RAM INTO WORLD TRADE CENTER, PENTAGON; AIRWAYS, STOCK MARKETS SHUT DOWN AS BUSH VOWS RETALIATION

4

UC Stays Open, Labs on Heightened Alert; Gov. Davis Closes All State Buildings

By ELIOT RAMIREZ
and STEVE SEXTON
DAILY CAL STAFF WRITERS

The effects of the devastating collapse of the World Trade Center in New York rippled across the country to California and the Bay Area yesterday, where those around its aftermath fell to state and local governments shut down for the day.

Gov. Gray Davis ordered all state buildings close and called on California men to remain calm and united.

"This horrible moment of many men people will be around for a very horror and a whole forever," Davis said in a radio address Tuesday. "Californians have always pulled in times of crisis and we will do so again now."

All federal and local government buildings in Oakland and San

See PERSONAL, page 3

Campus Community Reacts with Shock, Sorrow

by ERIN McLAUGHLIN,
RACHEL METZ
and ELIOT RAMIREZ
DAILY CAL STAFF WRITERS

Prof. Marmatko sat nervously their smoking at 11 a.m. Tuesday morning on the steps of Sproul Plaza.

He got a phone call at 5:00 a.m. from his father who told him to turn on the television and keep calling witnesses.

Marmatko, a UC Berkeley senior, has an aunt who works in the World Trade Center. As of a ten-year-old, he had not heard whether she is safe.

"I just want to know if my aunt is okay," he said. "I don't know what to think. You don't expect something like that to happen to our country."

her but still shocked."

UC Berkeley students and faculty reacted with shock and horror yesterday to news that the World Trade Center in New York was gone and that part of the Pentagon collapsed Tuesday after hijackers apparently crashed airliners into the building.

Professors solemnly told their students about the tragedy as they walked into class Tuesday morning. Some instructors canceled classes, others talked about the situation, and some proceeded with lectures when a crowd discussing a deepening sense of chaos.

The Free Speech Movement Cafe settled in the heart of the campus, was packed yesterday with students, staff and faculty glued to the

See CAMPUS, page 6

COUNTRY STRUGGLES TO GRASP SCOPE OF CATASTROPHE

President Estimates Death Toll to be in Thousands

by RACHEL METZ
and STEVE SEXTON
DAILY CAL STAFF WRITERS

The day after the World Trade Center and a portion of the Pentagon collapsed, Americans are grappling with the magnitude of an event so overwrought that air traffic was frozen and financial markets shut down.

And with no easy grasp as the number of people presumed dead.

"Thousands of lives were suddenly ended by evil, despicable acts of terror," President Bush said in a televised address to the nation Tuesday evening.

"Today, our nation saw evil, the

See ATTACKS, page 8

INSIDE

EDITORIAL Have we lost our innocence, or grown closer to it? *See page 5*

DAMAGE Experts explain how the trade towers likely collapsed. *See page 6*

CENTERSPREAD Images emotions and reactions *See pages 8-9*

EXTRA ★ EXTRA ★ EXTRA

The Fresno Bee

www.fresnobee.com   CENTRAL CALIFORNIA'S LEADING NEWSPAPER FOR 78 YEARS   50 CENTS

TUESDAY, SEPTEMBER 11, 2001

American horror

Terrorists hijack, crash jetliners; thousands feared dead

CHAO SOI CHEONG — ASSOCIATED PRESS

Smoke, flames and debris erupt from one of the World Trade Center towers in New York City as a plane strikes it this morning. The first tower already was burning following a terror attack minutes earlier. Terrorists crashed hijacked airliners into the two buildings and both towers collapsed.

5

Pentagon hit in Arlington, Va.	Valley goes on police alert	U.S. in shock over attacks
Airplane crash leaves a gaping hole in the five-story building. **PAGE 4**	Airport, government buildings are kept under tight security. **PAGE 8**	Editorial: Bombings signal an end to American innocence. **PAGE 11**

CALIFORNIA STATE UNIVERSITY, FULLERTON

The Daily TITAN

EXTRA SPECIAL ISSUE

VOLUME 73, ISSUE 4 — WEDNESDAY — SEPTEMBER 12, 2001

Angels Take Flight

As every major city in America evacuates, Los Angeles, a city that thrives in business commerce is a ghost town.

— See Page 4

Putting Faith to the Test

Images of Armageddon and thought s of a higher power – religious believers pray that faith will see them through.

— See Page 4

OC Supports the Cause

Local Red Cross stations overflow with blood donators as nation-wide tragedy strikes and the need is anticipated to rise.

— See Page 6

September 11, 2001
TERROR

ATTACK TIMELINE

8:45 a.m. EDT
American Airlines Flight 11 plunges into the north World Trade Center tower. A second plane, United Airlines Flight 175 crashes into the south WTC tower 18 minutes later.

9:30 a.m. EDT
President George W. Bush, speaking in Florida, said the country has suffered an "apparent terrorist attack."

Bush

9:40 a.m. EDT
The Federal Aviation Association halts all U.S. flight operations for the first time in history.

9:43 a.m. EDT
American Airlines Flight 77 crashes into the defense part of the Pentagon. White House begins evacuating immediately.

10:05 a.m. EDT
The south tower of the WTC collapses throwing ash and debris into the New York City skyline.

10:10 a.m. EDT
United Airlines Flight 93 crashes in Somerset County just southeast of Pittsburgh, PA.

10:28 a.m. EDT
The north WTC tower collapses throwing more gray ash and debris into the air.

2:00 p.m. EDT
The FBI tells CNN it believes all four planes were hijacked as part of a terrorist attack.

8:30 p.m. EDT
President Bush returns to the White House to address nation.

Timeline compiled by Naomi Ulloi, Daily Titan Staff Writer, based on information provided by www.cnn.com and other news services.

Robyn Harney and Brittany L'Hommedieu express emotion as they watch developments unfold on television sets in the Titan Student Union.
MAYRA BELTRAN/Daily Titan

Kamikaze attacks rock the country

■TRAGEDY: Government agencies tighten security all over the state in response to lower Manhattan's mass destruction

BY SAMANTHA GONZAGA
Daily Titan Managing Editor

Twenty-year-old Michael Crea woke up to clear blue skies in his home- town of New Hyde Park in New York. About half an hour away, that same sky was gray as falling rubble punctuated the decimation of the World Trade Center.

"It's not sinking in yet," he said. "It's so unreal."

Early Tuesday morning two planes plummeted into one of the building's two towers.

Both were commercial flights bound for Los Angeles . All those aboard American Airlines flight 11 and United Airlines flight 175 perished in the suicide dive.

The Pentagon now bears a hole the size of a football field where American Airlines flight 77 crashed. Though Pentagon officials say that the structure was actually made stronger by a recent renovation, it did nothing to save the lives of the plane passengers.

Another commercial plane smashed a few miles away from Pittsburgh, PA in the city of Somerset. Pennsylvania houses Camp David, a presidential retreat.

Over the airwaves, New York Mayor Rudolph Guiliani could only express his shock at the aftermath of each crash.

"I didn't think anything like this would happen, "Guiliani said. "I saw people jumping out of the [tower] as it was falling...it is an unbelievable sight."

On the other side of the nation, 34-year-old Jean Reynosa's TWA flight to Seattle, WA was interrupted by an announcement from its pilot.

"We were in the air for about 20 minutes and the pilot told us 'We're heading back,'" Reynosa said. "Back at San Francisco, everyone told us what happened."

Undeterred by the lockdown of air traffic, Reynosa has taken to the ground: "I'm driving up to Seattle.

The Federal Aviation Administration (FAA), under instructions from the government has shut down air traffic systems all over the United States. Flights bound for California from the East Coast have been suspended. Airports all over California are likewise closed off. Evacuation orders have been issued, leaving travelers from airports as big as the Los Angeles International Airport outside.

Traffic congestion in Southern California freeways formed, as government and county employees working in off-site buildings were instructed to evacuate.

"As far as I know county-wide, a lot of county buildings were closed," said Christine Mendez, who works at the Los Angeles Department of Health Services. "L.A is a big county, a lot of people are being asked to leave. Hospitals are on stand-by alert."

A bomb squad was deployed in the city as well. Ports and bridges quickly issued closures. The CSU Chancellor's Office issued an email stating its decision to close all 23 of

ATTACKS/ 8

COURTESY OF CNN.COM
Two commercial planes slammed into the World Trade Center in New York early Tuesday, throwing ash and debris above the skyline.

6

ATTACK ON AMERICA | SPECIAL SECTION INSIDE

 # Daily News

WEATHER
Cloudy
Highs: 73-80
Lows: 56-62
Back of Sports

Online: dailynews.com ★   WEDNESDAY, SEPTEMBER 12, 2001   50 Cen
DESIGNATED AREAS HIG

HORROR!

Thousands feared dead in terrorist attack

Flames, smoke and debris hurtle outward from the south tower of the World Trade Center after a hijacked airliner hit the 110-story building Tuesday in New York.

Kristen Brochmann/The New York Times

Nation stunned, on alert

By Serge Schmemann
The New York Times

NEW YORK — Hijackers rammed jetliners into each of New York's World Trade Center towers Tuesday morning, toppling both in a hellish storm of ash, glass, smoke and leaping victims, while a third jetliner crashed into the Pentagon in Virginia.

There was no official count, but President Bush said thousands had perished, and in the immediate aftermath the calamity was already being ranked as the worst and most audacious terror attack in American history.

The attacks seemed carefully coordinated. The hijacked planes were all en route to California, and therefore gorged with fuel, and their departures were spaced within an hour and 40 minutes. The first, American Airlines Flight 11, a Boeing 767 out of Boston for Los Angeles, crashed into the north tower at 8:48 a.m. Eighteen minutes later, United Airlines Flight 175, also headed from Boston to Los Angeles, plowed into the south tower. Then an American Airlines Boeing 757, Flight 77, left

► Should the U.S. blow the terrorists to hell?
See below

See ATTACK / Page 8

SPECIAL SECTION PAGE 2: President Bush reassures the nation as he deals with a crucial test of his leadership.

Washington's Dulles International Airport bound for Los Angeles, but instead hit the western part of the Pentagon, the military headquarters where 24,000 people work, at 9:40 a.m. Finally, United Airlines Flight 93, a Boeing 757 flying from Newark to San Francisco, crashed near Pittsburgh, raising the possibility that its hijackers had failed in whatever their mission was.

There were indications that the hijackers on at least two of the planes were armed with knives. Attorney General John Ashcroft told reporters in the evening that the suspects on Flight 11 were armed that way. And Barbara Olson, a television

Firefighters raise a flag at the World Trade Center.
Thomas E. Franklin/The Reco

Volume 90, Number 255

Copyright 2001, Daily News of Los Angeles, Los Angeles Daily News

TO REACH US
Circulation: (818) 713-3131; Burbank, Glendale, East Valley: (818) 546-1624. From 805 and 661: (800) 562-3360. To reach NIE: (818) 713-3199. To run a classified ad: (818) 713-3711. For other numbers, see Page 4.

LOTTO
Fantasy Five numbers picked Tuesday. Complete results on Page 4

1   17
21
31   32

Q: Should the U.S. blow the terrorists to hell?
Cast your vote by 5 p.m. by calling (818) 883-6397, category code 3636. This is not a scientific poll.

Do you think the Valley is a good place to retire?
YES 20%   NO 80%
Responses: 121

For continual updates on the attack, go to our Web site.

online **EXTR** dailynews.co AOL Keyword Daily News

NATIONAL EDITION

Los Angeles Times

On The Internet: WWW.LATIMES.COM   WEDNESDAY, SEPTEMBER 12, 2001   COPYRIGHT 2001 $1.00 Designated Areas Higher

8

TERRORISTS ATTACK NEW YORK, PENTAGON

Thousands Dead, Injured as Hijacked U.S. Airliners Ram Targets; World Trade Center Is Destroyed

AP photos / CARMEN TAYLOR via KHBS/KHOG-TV

United Flight 175, left, heads for the south tower of the World Trade Center, then explodes on impact while the north tower burns from an attack 20 minutes earlier.

Tragedy: Assault leaves Manhattan in chaos. Three of the flights were en route to L.A., one to San Francisco. President Bush puts military on highest alert, closes borders and vows to 'find those responsible.'

By GERALDINE BAUM
and MAGGIE FARLEY
TIMES STAFF WRITERS

NEW YORK—Terrorists struck at the preeminent symbols of America's wealth and might Tuesday, flying hijacked airliners into the World Trade Center and the Pentagon, killing and injuring thousands of people.

As a horrified nation watched on television, the twin towers of the World Trade Center in lower Manhattan collapsed into flaming rubble after two Boeing 767s rammed their upper stories. A third airliner, a Boeing 757, flattened one of the Pentagon's famed five sides.

A fourth hijacked jetliner crashed in western Pennsylvania. Authorities said the hijackers might have been trying to crash the plane at the presidential retreat at Camp David, Md.

The assaults, which stirred fear and anxiety across the country and evoked comparisons to Pearl Harbor, were carefully planned and coordinated, occurring within 50 minutes. No one claimed responsibility, but official suspicion quickly fell on Saudi fugitive Osama bin Laden.

Addressing the nation Tuesday night, President Bush vowed to "find those responsible and bring them to justice." This country, he said, would retaliate against "those behind these evil acts" and any country that harbors them.

Altogether, the four downed planes carried 266 people.Scores of people jumped to their deaths or died in fires and the collapsing superstructure at the World Trade Center. New York Mayor Rudolph W. Giuliani said earliest reports counted 2,100 people injured, about 150 of them in critical condition.

Estimates of the death toll at the Pentagon ranged from 100 to 800.

Please see ATTACK, A10

Special Coverage

The buildings: Terrorists struck the World Trade Center towers at their most vulnerable spot, structural engineers say, **A2**

Washington: In the nation's crippled capital, dazed people flee federal buildings and wander the streets as the Pentagon burns, **A5**

Pittsburgh crash: A passenger aboard United jet calls 911 to report a hijacking. Moments later, the plane plunges to earth, **A8**

Planes grounded: For the first time, the FAA halted all U.S. air traffic. Stricter security measures are expected, **A15**

The suspects: Preliminary evidence indicates that Osama bin Laden is behind the attacks, U.S. officials say, **A16**

The victims: At least three people aboard the hijacked jets make cell phone calls to alert others of the danger, **A20**

NEWS ANALYSIS

President Shoulders Historic Weight

By RONALD BROWNSTEIN
and DOYLE McMANUS
TIMES STAFF WRITERS

WASHINGTON—The greatest challenge any American president can face is war—and George W. Bush, who won the presidency at a moment of peace and prosperity, is abruptly facing a sterner test than anyone expected.

Tuesday's attacks on New York and Washington were almost certain to rank as the most damaging ever against U.S. territory, with the final death toll expected to exceed Japan's 1941 attack on Pearl Harbor.

Bush's initial response—after an awkward day, dictated by security concerns, in seclusion on military bases—was a brief statement pledging "to find those responsible and to bring them to justice."

"We will make no distinction between the terrorists who committed these acts and those who harbor them," Bush said, warning countries such as Afghanistan that they can no longer count on U.S. restraint.

But the real test of the new president's leadership will come in the weeks to come: Can he unify the nation in grief and anger? Can he choose an effective military response? And can he find ways to prevent another attack from occurring?

Please see BUSH, A6

A Struggle to Escape Fiery Chaos

Scene: For those who got out of the burning towers, it was a day of fear and heroism.

By GERALDINE BAUM
and PAUL LIEBERMAN
TIMES STAFF WRITERS

NEW YORK—People likened it to a bomb, to midnight, to a hurricane and, finally, when the air was choked with soot and smoke, to hell.

In the aftermath of the explosions Tuesday morning that shook the twin towers of the World Trade Center, thousands struggled to escape. Some were lucky and fast enough to find elevators still functioning. Others walked

and crawled and groped their way down hundreds of stairs.

Many, no one yet knows their number, could not escape, blocked by fire or fear. Experts said blazing jet fuel inside the building would have driven temperatures to beyond 1,400 degrees Fahrenheit, hot enough to melt steel, which it did, and hot enough to kill, which it did as well. Some people, unable to withstand the flames, jumped or were sucked out into the high empty air, their bodies tumbling like dolls all the way to the ground.

At 8:45 a.m., Robert Lipiak had just unlocked the door to Cosmos Service America on the 89th floor of the north tower, the first to be struck and the second to collapse. He still had his key in the lock when the explosion rocked the

building, sending him flying across the office, crashing into a desk. Others came in and he made them lie on the floor and covered them with towels.

Then he gathered them up and herded them toward the stairwell, which was locked. Police arrived, unlocked the exit and Lipiak's people joined what would become a throng on the route down.

Four floors below, Geoffrey Heineman, managing partner of a law firm on the 85th floor of One World Trade Center, had taken an early train from his home in Garden City, N.Y., because it was "a special day," his oldest son's 11th birthday, "and I wanted to get home for the party."

The firm's offices take up more than half the 85th floor, with spectacular views of New York Harbor

and the Statue of Liberty. Ohrenstein & Brown has 90 people at peak hours, but only the early wave had arrived, maybe 15 in all. Heineman was the first in and, by 8:20, had already finished his first phone conference of the day, about a case in New Jersey, when he heard the thud and felt the building sway.

"There was a big bang, an explosion. The building has always swayed in windy weather, but it was nothing like that," he said. "Then it swayed back. I came out of my office, and said, 'Let's round up the people.'"

He figured a helicopter or small plane had accidentally struck the tower because, as he explained, "we often see small planes flying by, below the top of the tower."

Please see DESCENT, A12

Associated Press

A woman watches the World Trade Center burn. Both towers collapsed within two hours of the first hit by a hijacked jet.

The Choreography of Carnage Was Precisely Timed, FBI Says

Terrorism: The hijackers penetrated susceptible security systems before authorities could react to impending disaster.

By RICHARD A. SERRANO
and DAVID WILLMAN
TIMES STAFF WRITERS

WASHINGTON—The air attacks Tuesday morning in New York and Washington and a jetliner crash in Pennsylvania were the work of a conspiracy that deftly skirted a beleaguered U.S. airport security system and placed terrorists on four planes, senior

FBI officials believe.

Authorities suspect that the terrorists had help from airport ground crews, that they chose cross-country flights because the planes would be heavily loaded with fuel, and that their ranks included hijackers who could fly planes.

But what investigators found most surprising was the timing. They marveled at how teams of hijackers working in at least three cities simultaneously overpowered commercial planes in the air before federal authorities could shut down all flights across the country.

In doing so, the terrorists penetrated an airport security net that many have warned previ-

ously is inadequate.

Lewis Schiliro, who as head of the FBI office in New York helped oversee investigations into the explosion aboard TWA Flight 800 and an earlier bombing at the World Trade Center, was left in utter disbelief by what he saw unfold Tuesday morning.

"I've been chilled by a lot of things," Schiliro said. "But this is something I just can't begin to comprehend. They put this together very, very neatly."

In the past, terrorist acts in the U.S. have been marked by disarray. Even the last attack on the World Trade Center in 1993, which killed six people, failed to deliver the carnage intended.

Please see PROBE, A16

The Sacramento Bee

FOUNDED 1857

WEDNESDAY September 12, 2001 ✦✦✦ · · · · Final edition **50 cents**

www.**sacbee**.com

ATTACK ON AMERICA

| Hijacked jets crash into World Trade Center. Thousands are killed. | Another airliner crashes into the Pentagon. Hundreds feared dead. | White House, Capitol evacuated. Financial markets shut down. | Federal investigators focus on terrorist leader Osama bin Laden. |

New York Times/Kelly Guenther

The second of two hijacked airliners that destroyed the World Trade Center approaches the center's south tower, then explodes into it.

Bush vows to punish 'evil' acts of terror

Agence France-Presse/Doug Kanter

Amid the massive rubble of the collapsed 110-story towers of the World Trade Center in New York City, a man calls out, seeking anyone who might be in need of help.

Huge search for the plotters

By Sam Stanton
BEE STAFF WRITER

In the deadliest and most ruthless assault ever leveled at the United States, terrorists hijacked four airliners Tuesday morning, leveling New York's World Trade Center towers and destroying part of the Pentagon in Washington.

The carefully timed attacks in the two cities hit just as the workday was starting on the East Coast and apparently killed thousands of Americans, although it may be weeks before an accurate estimate can be made.

The calamity shook the nation from coast to coast, paralyzing transportation and communications systems and sending President Bush traveling to secret locations to ensure his safety.

When he reappeared in Washington to address the nation at 5:30 p.m. West Coast time, Bush denounced the "evil, despicable acts of terror" and promised retaliation.

"Today, our fellow citizens, our way of life, our very freedom, came under attack in a series of deliberate and deadly terrorist acts," the president said, adding that the attacks had created "a quiet, unyielding anger" in the nation.

"This is the second Pearl Harbor; I don't think that I can overstate it," said Sen. Chuck Hagel, R-Neb.

Other political leaders denounced the attacks as an act of war, and said they supported the president's call for action against those responsible.

"The search is under way for

► ATTACK, page A14

sacbee

For more information
For the latest Sacramento Bee coverage of the terror attacks, including local and state developments, please go to:
► www.sacbee.com

A shaken nation asks: How could it happen?

By Steve Wiegand, Stuart Leavenworth and Mareva Brown
BEE STAFF WRITERS

While the nation reeled Tuesday from the worst terrorist attacks in its history, three questions were foremost in the minds of many: Who did it, how did they succeed, and what is going to be done about it?

"We've never seen anything of this magnitude in the United States," said Miki Vohryzek-Bolden, a criminal justice professor at California State University, Sacramento, and co-author of a new book on domestic terrorism.

"Oklahoma City stunned us," she said, referring to the 1995 bombing of the federal building there, "but this has left us speechless."

Although federal investigators declined Tuesday to publicly point fingers at suspects in the atrocities, much of their attention seemed to be focused on the terrorist group al Qaeda (the Base) and its leader, Osama bin Laden.

The group, a nebulous collection of committees affiliated with other terrorist organizations, is believed to have been responsible for a number of high-profile terrorist acts, including the 1998 bombings of two U.S. embassies in Africa.

A senior government official told the Washington Post that the probability was "in the high 90s" that bin Laden, who is believed to be hiding in Afghanistan, was

► TERRORISM, page A15

Reuters/Shannon Stapleton

Rescue workers hurry a man from one of the World Trade Center towers. An adjacent 47-story building also collapsed several hours after the terrorist attack.

---

7 12499 30303 5

Recession looming?
The terrorist attacks are likely to push an already shaky economy over the edge, many economists say.
► Page A2

INSIDE THE BEE

Clear message
President Bush, in a terse warning, says nations that give shelter to murderers will be held equally guilty.
► Page A4

Moving on, carefully
Even as intense security precautions are put into place statewide, officials prepare to resume normal operations. ► Page A6

SPORTS ►C1
Pro baseball, other sports cancel games

BUSINESS ►D1
Commerce virtually halts in Sacramento

BUSINESS ►D2
World markets plummet on news of terror

EXTRA: AMERICA UNDER ATTACK

The San Diego
Union-Tribune.

TUESDAY
SEPTEMBER 11, 2001

EXTRA EDITION
35¢

DEVASTATION

Thousands feared dead as terrorist attacks hit New York, Washington and spread fear across U.S.

TIME LINE OF TERROR

(all times are Eastern Standard Time this morning)

8:42 A Boeing 767 en route to Los Angeles with 56 passengers crashes into the north tower of the World Trade Center in Manhattan, rattling the 110-story landmark.

9:03 A Boeing 757 flying from Washington, D.C., to Los Angeles with 58 passengers crashes into the World Trade Center's south tower, sending flames out the other side.

9:40 Federal authorities close all domestic airports.

9:45 An aircraft plane of undetermined size crashes into the Pentagon, sparking a fire that collapses part of the massive office building.

10:00 The 110-story World Trade Center's south tower crumbles to the street. The north tower collapses minutes later.

10:05 White House evacuated.

10:48 A third airliner, carrying 38 passengers from Newark, N.J. to San Francisco crashed southeast of Pittsburgh.

VOICES

"This is the second Pearl Harbor. I don't think that I overstated it."

CHUCK HAGEL,
Republican senator from Nebraska

"Make no mistake, we will show the world we will pass this test."

PRESIDENT BUSH

"I have a sense it's a horrendous number of lives lost."

RUDOLPH GIULIANI,
New York Mayor

"They flew the planes themselves. No pilot, even with a gun to his head, is going to fly into the World Towers."

GENE POTEAT, Association of Former Intelligence Officers

"I just hoped and hoped for all these years that we would never have anything worse than what happened in Oklahoma City."

ROB RODDY, survivor of 1995 Oklahoma City bombing

A COPLEY NEWSPAPER
6 sections   94 pages

Smoke and flames poured from World Trade Center towers in Manhattan this morning after two airliners smashed into the 110-story landmarks. The airliners, carrying a total of 156 people, hit the towers 18 minutes apart. The buildings ultimately crashed to the street below. Authorities have not yet begun to estimate the casualties, which could run into the thousands. *Kelly Guenther / New York Times News Service*

Rescue workers removed an injured man from the World Trade Center this morning after the attack. Many of the still-uncounted injured were badly burned. *Shannon Stapleton / Reuters*

Coordinated air attacks on trade towers and Pentagon

Hijacked commercial airliners used as weapons

By Jerry Schwartz, ASSOCIATED PRESS

NEW YORK — In a horrific sequence of destruction, terrorists hijacked two airliners and crashed them into the World Trade Center in a coordinated series of attacks this morning that brought down the twin 110-story towers. A plane also slammed into the Pentagon, raising fears that the seat of government itself was under attack.

"This is the second Pearl Harbor. I don't think that I overstate it," said Sen. Chuck Hagel, R-Neb.

High-ranking New York City police officials said the number of people killed or injured could be in the thousands.

Authorities in New York had been trying to evacuate those who work in the twin towers, but many were thought to have been trapped. About 50,000 people work at the trade center. American Airlines said its two aircraft were carrying a total of 156 people.

"Today we've had a national tragedy," President Bush said in Sarasota, Fla., where he quickly cut short his visit. He added, "Terrorism against our nation will not stand."

The White House, the Pentagon and the Capitol were evacuated along with other federal buildings in Washington and New York. Foreign embassies were shut down.

There was no word from federal officials on who was responsible for the attacks. Bush ordered a full-scale investigation to "hunt down the folks who committed this act."

Within the hour, the Pentagon took a direct, devastating hit from an aircraft. The fiery crash collapsed one side of the five-sided structure.

Pentagon spokesman Glenn Flood said all the Defense Department's leaders were safe, including Secretary Donald Rumsfeld. Senior officials staffed the agency's National Military Command

SEE Terror, Extra 4

San Diego airport, office buildings closed; military bases on high alert

By James Steinberg
STAFF WRITER

All flights were grounded at Lindbergh Field this morning as the nation's airline system was shut down in the wake of what appeared to be coordinated terrorist attacks in New York and Washington. Security was heightened at government and military facilities around the county, and some downtown office buildings were evacuated.

San Diego police activated the department's emergency operations center and took a number of measures within minutes of the multiple tragedies in the East, which occurred starting around 6 a.m. local time. The department also activated a plan to secure all key buildings in the city, which it did not specify, Police Department spokesman Dave Cohen said.

Police dispatched units to Lindbergh Field to assist Harbor Police with gridlocked traffic and to local military installations to assist with traffic control.

Police Chief David Bejarano was scheduled to hold a closed-door briefing for the mayor, City Council and other officials at 9:30 a.m.

San Diego's border crossings with Mexico remained open, but security was increased to Level 1, the highest, said U.S. Customs Service spokesman Kevin Bell.

Local military bases were under armed guard this morning, and all vehicles, including those with base privileges, were stopped and all occupants had their identification checked.

At most bases, long lines of cars and trucks formed on nearby streets because

SEE Local, Extra 6

UNION-TRIBUNE

AMERICA UNDER ATTACK

San Francisco Chronicle

NORTHERN CALIFORNIA'S LARGEST NEWSPAPER

★★★★★•• WEDNESDAY, SEPTEMBER 12, 2001 415-777-1111 23 CENTS PLUS TAX

SPORTS FINAL

Terrorists mount their most brazen and devastating attack in history as hijackers turn four passenger planes into bombs — and change America forever

NIGHTMARE

The South Tower collapsed, and when it was over, dust and debris covered streets around the World Trade Center and a mushroom cloud floated above it.

AMY SANCETTA / Associated Press

EXPANDED COVERAGE

Associated Press

Attacks stun the nation
Terrorists crash hijacked jetliners into the World Trade Center in New York City and the Pentagon near Washington. **A3**

Joan Ryan
The tragedy lets us know that our sense of security is as illusory as a Hollywood set. **A2**

Test of the president
Bush is confronted with worst act of aggression against the U.S. since Pearl Harbor. **A4**

Frantic call from S.F.-bound jet
San Ramon man phones his wife seconds before his United flight goes down in Pennsylvania. **A5**

Bay Area in shock
As events unfold, residents feel like it is all a dream. **A17**

Business toll
Big names in U.S. and international business suffer serious casualties. **BUSINESS, B1**

John Carman
Television struggles to find its way in the face of such tragedy. **DATEBOOK, E1**

Sports world reacts
Sporting events virtually shut down in response to terrorist attacks. **SPORTS, D1**

On the Web
For news updates, additional photos, videos and a discussion group, go to sfgate.com

SPECIAL EDITION

S A N   F R A N C I S C O

The Examiner.

Wednesday, September 12, 2001   Keeping San Francisco a two-newspaper town.   (Including tax) **25 cents**

BASTARDS!

12

KRISTEN BROCHMANN/The New York Times

A CHANGED AMERICA

ATTACK ON AMERICA 30-PAGE SPECIAL REPORT

San Jose Mercury News

SERVING NORTHERN CALIFORNIA SINCE 1851   WWW.BAYAREA.COM   THE NEWSPAPER OF SILICON VALLEY

35 CENTS | FINAL EDITION | ....   SEPTEMBER 12, 2001 | WEDNESDAY

'ACTS OF WAR'

THOUSANDS FEARED KILLED IN WORST U.S. TERRORIST STRIKE

HIJACKED PLANES HIT TRADE TOWERS, PENTAGON

KRISTEN BROCHMANN — NEW YORK TIMES

A fireball engulfs the upper South Tower of the World Trade Center after a second airliner slammed into the complex Tuesday. The center's twin 110-story towers eventually collapsed. Thousands presumed dead.

COPING WITH THE NEWS

A LONG DAY OF DREAD

Dazed Americans struggling with a new, harsher world

By Patrick May and Julia Prodis Sulek
Mercury News

The explosions were a continent away, yet the country suddenly seemed so small and fragile, lashed together by shock and dread.

Never before had the United States felt so totally at the mercy of terrorists. Wrenched by the horror that thousands may have died, the nation added another grim defining moment to its list: Pearl Harbor, the Kennedy assassination, the Oklahoma City bombing.

And now this.

By late morning, Californians were feeling dreadfully connected to the chaos: All four hijacked planes had been destined for the West Coast, three to Los Angeles and one to San Francisco. Surely, among the casualties on those planes or in the buildings would be, at the very least, a friend of a friend.

Many in the Bay Area attempted to carry on their normal day, getting dressed for work, battling

See **DAY**, *Page 27A*

KELLY GUENTHER — NEW YORK TIMES

THE ATTACK: Two hijacked airliners slam into World Trade Center in New York, a third hits the Pentagon, and a San Francisco-bound flight crashes in Pennsylvania.

THE CASUALTIES: Total unknown. About 50,000 work in the skyscrapers, 20,000 in the Pentagon; 266 aboard the airliners are presumed dead. PAGES 5A, 9A, 10A

THE BLAME: The United States gathers evidence that points to Osama bin Laden's terrorist network. The information is not definitive. PAGE 6A

THE RESPONSE: President Bush vows to punish those "behind these evil acts," and any country that harbors them. Military is on highest alert. PAGES 3A, 7A, 10A

THE S.F.-BOUND FLIGHT: The crash may have followed resistance by a doomed pilot or a struggle by a Bay Area passenger. PAGE 4A

ONLINE: For continuous coverage throughout the day, go to **www.bayarea.com/mercurynews**

THE ATTACKS

Unparalleled assaults shock, paralyze nation

BUSH PLEDGES TO PROSECUTE 'ACTS OF MASS MURDER'

By Steven Thomma
Mercury News Washington Bureau

WASHINGTON — The United States came to a virtual halt Tuesday as terrorists unleashed a suicidal assault on the citadels of American military and financial might, hijacking four commercial jets and then flinging them into the World Trade Center in New York and the Pentagon. One jet fell short of its Washington target, crashing into the Pennsylvania countryside.

It was by far the most devastating terrorist operation in American history, killing possibly thousands of people. Authorities estimate the death toll in the Pentagon attack at 100 to 800.

It was the most dramatic attack on American soil since Pearl Harbor. The attacks created indelible scenes of carnage and chaos, obliterating the World Trade Center's twin 110-story towers from their familiar perch in

Manhattan's skyline, grounding the domestic air traffic system for the first time, closing stock markets and businesses, and plunging the entire nation into an unparalleled state of anxiety.

U.S. military forces at home and around the world were put on a "go to war" footing, the highest state of alert next to actual military action. The Pentagon deployed a loose air defense network of warships along the west and east coasts, as well as an unspecified number of interceptor and reconnaissance aircraft to hunt for unauthorized planes and missiles.

The terrorists hijacked four California-bound flights from three airports on the Eastern seaboard, suggesting a well-financed, well-coordinated plot.

First, two jets slammed into the World Trade Center. Then an American Airlines flight out of Dulles Inter-

See **ATTACKS**, *Page 29A*

KNIGHT RIDDER   INFORMATION FOR LIFE

16

VOL. 93 NO. 316 SEPT. 12, 2001 GREELEY, COLO. 50 CENTS

Greeley Tribune

WEDNESDAY

The Greeley Daily Tribune
Original script by Horace Greeley

"Even though I walk through the valley of the shadow of death, I will fear no evil ..."

Psalm 23:4

'OUR NATION SAW EVIL'

A shell of New York's World Trade Center rises above the rubble that remains after both towers were destroyed in a terrorist attack.

ASSOCIATED PRESS

Thousands feared dead in attacks

WIRE REPORTS

NEW YORK — In the most devastating terrorist onslaught ever waged against the United States, knife-wielding hijackers crashed two airliners into the World Trade Center on Tuesday, toppling its twin 110-story towers. The deadly calamity was witnessed on televisions throughout the world as another plane slammed into the Pentagon, and a fourth crashed outside Pittsburgh.

"Today, our nation saw evil," President Bush said in an address to the nation Tuesday night. He said thousands of lives were "suddenly ended by evil, despicable acts of terror."

Said Adm. Robert Natter, commander of the U.S. Atlantic Fleet: "We have been attacked like we haven't since Pearl Harbor."

Establishing the U.S. death toll could take weeks. The four airliners alone had 266 people aboard and there were no known survivors. At the Pentagon, about 800 people were believed dead.

In addition, a firefighters union official said he feared an estimated 300 firefighters had died in rescue efforts at the trade center — where 50,000 people worked — and dozens of police officers were believed missing.

"The number of casualties will be more than most of us can bear," a visibly distraught Mayor Rudolph Giuliani said.

No one took responsibility for the attacks that rocked the seats of finance and government. But federal authorities identified Osama bin Laden, who has been given asylum by Afghanistan's Taliban rulers, as the prime suspect.

Aided by an intercept of communications between his supporters and harrowing cell phone calls from at least one flight attendant and two passengers aboard the jetliners before they crashed, U.S. officials began assembling a case linking bin Laden to the devastation.

See **ATTACKS**, Page A12

inside

www.greeleytrib.com

September 12, 2001

50 cents

WEDNESDAY

DAILY TIMES-CALL

LONGMONT AND THE ST. VRAIN VALLEY, COLORADO

No. 255

SHATTERED

Thousands of Americans killed in attacks aimed at nation's soul

AP photo

Firefighters make their way through the rubble of the World Trade Center on Tuesday. Perhaps 300 firefighters, including New York's fire chief, perished in the towers.

By Michael Grunwald
The Washington Post

Terrorists unleashed an astonishing air assault on America's military and financial power centers Tuesday morning, hijacking four commercial jets and then crashing them into the World Trade Center in New York, the Pentagon and the Pennsylvania countryside.

It was by far the most devastating terrorist operation in American history, killing at least hundreds and possibly thousands of people. It was also the most dramatic attack on American soil since Pearl Harbor.

The attacks created indelible scenes of carnage and chaos, obliterating the World Trade Center's twin 110-story towers from their familiar perch above Manhattan's skyline, grounding the domestic air traffic system for the first time and plunging the entire nation into an unparalleled state of anxiety.

bin Laden

Page D6:

■ Investigation quickly centers on Osama bin Laden

U.S. military forces at home and around the world were put on a "go to war" footing, the highest state of alert next to actual military action. The Pentagon deployed a loose air-defense network of warships along the West and East coasts, as well as an unspecified number of interceptor and reconnaissance aircraft to hunt for unauthorized planes and missiles.

The terrorists hijacked four California-bound flights from three airports on the Eastern Seaboard, suggesting a well-financed, well-coordinated plot.

First, two jets slammed into the World Trade Center. Then an American Airlines flight out of Dulles International Airport ripped through the newly renovated walls of the Pentagon, probably the world's most secure office building. A fourth plane crashed 80 miles southeast of Pittsburgh shortly after it was commandeered and turned in the direction of Washington.

None of the 266 people aboard the four planes survived. There were even more horrific but still uncounted casualties in the World Trade Center and the Pentagon, which together provided office space for more than 60,000 people. The spectacular collapse of the Trade Center's twin towers as well as a third skyscraper while the rescue operations were going on caused even more bloodshed; about 300 New York firefighters and at least 78 police officers are presumed dead.

■ See TERROR / A2

AP photo by Chao Soi Cheong

The second World Trade Center tower explodes after being hit by a passenger jet Tuesday morning in the deadliest attack against Americans since World War II. Both of the twin towers — symbols of American commercial power — collapsed. Thousands are feared dead in New York and simultaneous attacks in Washington and Pennsylvania.

Victims say goodbye from doomed plane

By Marc Fisher and Don Phillips
The Washington Post

WASHINGTON — There was not even the grace of instant death. Instead, there was time to call from the sky over Virginia to loved ones, fingers pumping cell phones, voices saying quick, final goodbyes.

Herded to the back of the plane by hijackers armed with knives and box-cutters, the 64 passengers of American Airlines Flight 77 — including the wife of Solicitor General Theodore Olson, a Senate staffer, three D.C. schoolchildren and three teachers on an educational field trip, and a suburban family of four headed to Australia for a two-month adventure — were ordered to call relatives to say they were about to die.

About an hour after takeoff from Dulles International Airport on Tuesday morning, Flight 77, a Boeing 757 headed for Los Angeles, became a massive missile aimed at the White House. The target would change suddenly, but the symbolism was equally devastating.

By 9:45 a.m., when the diving plane carved out a massive chunk of the Pentagon, its passengers had experienced unspeakable terror, untold dozens died and the nation's greatest symbol of security lay shattered, thick plumes of smoke camouflaging a gaping hole in its heart.

Barbara Olson, the former federal prosecutor who became a prominent TV commentator during the impeachment of President Clinton, called her husband twice in the final minutes.

■ See PLANE / A2

AP photo

An emergency worker carries a woman injured in the attack on New York's World Trade Center on Tuesday morning.

Inside

A2	President weighs retaliatory options
A2	Pilot was from Denver
A3	Chronology of a horrific morning
A4	Editorial: Terror can't cripple nation
A5	FBI stunned by planning of attacks
A7	Secretary of defense predicted attack
A8	President Bush's remarks
B1	Coloradans rush to donate blood
B3	Schools remain open
C6	Governor, senators, citizens speak out
C8	Federal Reserve promises to supply banking system
D1	The day in pictures
D5	Attacks could cripple stock markets
D6	Inside the mind of a terrorist

Phone call brings home tragedy

LONGMONT — I got the call as many did — 8 a.m. Tuesday, still in my pajamas.

"Turn on the news," he said.

Asking no questions, I did.

To think at the time, my greatest fear was I had missed a big story.

The unfortunate truth was that I hadn't. Even worse, it was still going on.

Sitting cross-legged on the floor, not knowing which foot was where, I sat and stared.

Like you, I saw the smoke, I saw the fire.

I saw the emblem of our nation's financial strength and freedom fall to the ground.

Dan Rather was saying this was the worst attack the United States had ever seen — that there were no words to describe the destruction.

But I, a 25-year-old optimist, had them.

I, having never lived in a war-torn country, was naive enough to think they mattered.

Erin Laspa

The Daily Times-Call

■ See CALL / A2

E1	Classifieds
D4	Features
B4	Local news
D3	Obituaries
C1	Sports

No Cuisine page

To accommodate extra news coverage, there is no Cuisine page today. Local news can be found on Page B4.

How to help or check on a loved one

Bonfils Blood Center-Boulder: **303-442-0577**
American Red Cross, Boulder: **303-442-0577**
United Methodist Committee on Relief: **1-800-554-8583**

Pentagon personnel
Army: **1-800-984-8523** or **703-428-0002**
Navy and Marines: **1-877-663-6772**
Air Force: **1-800-253-9276**

American Airlines: **1-800-245-0999**
Morgan Stanley: **1-888-883-4391**
United Airlines: **1-800-932-8555**

Justice Department's Family Assistance: **1-800-331-0075**
Federal Emergency Management Agency: **www.fema.gov**
New York City information: **www.nyc.gov**

Visit the Times-Call online at **www.LongmontFYI.com**

LOVELAND DAILY

REPORTER-HERALD

Wednesday, September 12, 2001　　　www.lovelandfyi.com　　　50 cents No. 255

| Hijackers crash planes into World Trade Center | Others strike Pentagon, farmland in Pennsylvania | Thousands feared dead; America reeling with shock |

'EVIL ACTS OF TERROR'

ATTACKERS THROW U.S. INTO CHAOS

President vows American resolve will not be dented, and those responsible will be punished

NEW YORK (AP) — In the most devastating terrorist onslaught ever waged against the United States, knife-wielding hijackers crashed two airliners into the World Trade Center on Tuesday, toppling its twin 110-story towers. The deadly calamity was witnessed on televisions across the world as another plane slammed into the Pentagon, and a fourth crashed outside Pittsburgh.

"Today, our nation saw evil," President Bush said in an address to the nation Tuesday night. He said thousands of lives were "suddenly ended by evil, despicable acts of terror."

With smoke still pouring out of rubble in Washington and New York, Bush declared: "These acts shattered steel, but they cannot dent the steel of American resolve."

Said Adm. Robert J. Natter, commander of the U.S. Atlantic Fleet: "We have been attacked like we haven't since Pearl Harbor."

"We will make no distinction between the terrorists who committed these acts and those who harbor them," Bush said.

Establishing the U.S. death toll could take weeks. The four airliners alone had 266 people aboard, and there were no known survivors. At the Pentagon, about 100 people were believed dead.

In addition, a firefighters union official said he feared an estimated 300 firefighters had died in rescue efforts at the trade center — where 50,000 people worked — and dozens of police officers were believed missing.

"The number of casualties will be more than most of us can bear," a visibly distraught Mayor Rudolph Giuliani said.

No one took responsibility for the attacks that rocked the seats of finance and government. But federal authorities identified Osama bin Laden, who has been given asylum by Afghanistan's Taliban rulers, as the prime suspect.

Aided by an intercept of communications between his supporters and harrowing cell phone calls from at least one flight attendant and two passengers aboard the jetliners before they crashed, U.S. officials began assembling a case linking bin Laden to the devastation.

U.S. intelligence intercepted communications between bin Laden supporters discussing the attacks on the World Trade Center and Pentagon, according to Utah Sen. Orrin Hatch, the top Republican on the Senate Judiciary Committee.

The people aboard planes who managed to make cell phone calls each described similar circumstances: They indicated the hijackers were armed with knives, in some cases stabbing flight attendants. The hijackers then took control of the planes.

At the World Trade Center, the dead and the doomed plummeted from the skyscrapers, among them a man and woman holding hands.

Shortly after 5 p.m. MDT, crews began heading into ground zero of the attack to search for survivors and recover bodies. All that remained of the twin towers by then was a pile of rubble and twisted steel that stood barely two stories high, leaving a huge gap in the New York City skyline.

"Freedom itself was attacked this morning, and I assure you freedom will be defended," said Bush, who was in Florida at the time of the catastrophe. As a security measure, he was shuttled to a Strategic Air Command bunker in Nebraska before leaving for Washington.

"Make no mistake," he said. "The United States will hunt down and pursue those responsible for these cowardly actions."

More than nine hours after the U.S. attacks began, explosions could be heard north of the Afghan capital of Kabul, but American officials said the United States was not responsible.

"It isn't us. I don't know

■ See Attack/Page A-2

The Associated Press/CHAO SOI CHEONG
Smoke, flames and debris erupt from one of the World Trade Center towers Tuesday as the second of two planes strikes the second building. The first tower was already burning following a terror attack minutes earlier. Both towers collapsed soon after, and a third building in the complex fell Tuesday evening.

The Associated Press
A helicopter flies over the burning Pentagon on Tuesday in Arlington, Va. The Washington Monument can be seen at right, through the smoke. The White House roof is visible in the trees of Washington at left.

Colorado mobilizes aid efforts

BY FELICIA JORDAN
Reporter-Herald Staff Writer

Northern Colorado residents who wanted to help terrorist-attack victims crowded blood-donation centers Tuesday in Greeley and Fort Collins.

Because Loveland has no permanent donation site, local residents had to go elsewhere to donate.

Many did.

"We are overwhelmed with donors," said Dr. Joe Chaffin, medical director of blood services at North Colorado Medical Center in Greeley. "It's a wonderful response.

"Unfortunately, we have such a limited staff, people are having to wait awhile."

The staff extended its normal 8 a.m.-5 p.m. hours until 6:30 p.m. to accommodate people who wanted to donate. The blood bank likely will remain open late again today, Chaffin said.

He expected the hospital to collect at least 100 units of blood Tuesday.

At Poudre Valley Hospital, so many people came to donate that staff members set up extra beds. They asked people who have not yet donated to call to set up appointments for later in the week.

"You don't have to donate today or even tomorrow to help with this catastrophe," said Robert Carpenter, director of the hospital's clinical laboratory, in a release. "Your blood will still be as valuable two days from now or even next week."

Poudre Valley Hospital staff members will offer surplus blood supplies to Bonfils Blood

■ See Aid/Page A-2

HOW TO HELP

How to help victims of the World Trade Center and Pentagon terrorist attacks:

■ North Colorado Medical Center, 1801 16th St. in Greeley, is accepting blood donations 8 a.m.-5 p.m. Monday through Friday, with extended hours likely today. Appointments are not needed; however, people can call ahead to find out how long their waits might be, at (970) 350-6100.

■ Poudre Valley Hospital, Garfield Street and South Lemay Avenue in Fort Collins, is accepting blood donations. Staff members there are asking people who have not donated already to call ahead for an appointment at 495-8705.

■ Contributions to help the American Red Cross assist disaster victims may be mailed to Centennial Chapter, American Red Cross, 120 Saturn Drive, Fort Collins, 80525. Call 226-5728 for more information.

■ The United Way of America has set up the National Response Fund to help victims. Donations may be made through the United Way of Loveland-Berthoud-Estes Park, 315 E. Seventh St., Loveland, 80537. Call 669-1450 for more information.

Hartford ✠ Courant.

America's Oldest
Continuously
Published Newspaper

WEATHER
Mostly Sunny, Highs
In The Mid-70s. B10

VOLUME CLXIII, NUMBER 255   COPYRIGHT 2001, THE HARTFORD COURANT CO.   WEDNESDAY, SEPTEMBER 12, 2001   15★ New Haven County/Shoreline   NEWSSTAND 50¢

ACT OF WAR

WITH CHILLING PRECISION, TERRORISTS DELIVER DEATH AS AMERICA WATCHES HELPLESSLY

AFP

ARMED WITH NOTHING but a fire extinguisher, an unidentified man makes his way through the rubble of the twin towers of the World Trade Center, shouting for victims who needed assistance. The towers disappeared from the Manhattan skyline Tuesday after being hit by hijacked passenger airplanes.

BY EDMUND MAHONY / COURANT STAFF WRITER

America's sense of security was smashed with apocalyptic fury Tuesday when the most destructive and meticulously planned terror attack in history shattered two of the country's most potent symbols.

Shortly after leaving Boston, American Airlines flight 11 to Los Angeles banked south near Albany and raced down the Hudson River Valley. It plummeted from a crystal blue bowl of morning sky and punched a hole through the north tower of the World Trade Center, the heart of the nation's financial nerve center in lower Manhattan.

It was 8:45 a.m., the start of a series of calamitous attacks that brought the nation face to face with its vulnerability. With the twin towers toppled in New York, the Pentagon burning, a jetliner down in Pennsylvania, the morning's cruel work ended the nation's normalcy.

"Today, our nation saw evil," a grim-faced President Bush said Tuesday night during his first prime-time address from the Oval Office. He promised that the United States will avenge its thousands of terror victims by retaliating against "those behind these evil acts," and any country that harbors them.

There were four planes hijacked by presumed terrorists Tuesday, and four accompanying disasters that caused unfathomable carnage. Rescue experts would only speculate that the death toll could reach well into the thousands. The four planes alone carried 266 people, and

PLEASE SEE **A NATION**, PAGE A3

"If you can do this to the USA and get at two symbols of the strength of America, that tells you essentially we are at war."

- SEN. CHUCK HAGEL, R-NEB.

Nowhere To Run

Photos, video reports and updates:

ctnow.com

10912
6 04209 00050 4

The Day

EDNESDAY, SEPTEMBER 12, 2001, NEW LONDON   SERVING EASTERN CONNECTICUT SINCE 1881   VOL. 121, No. 73   52 PAGES   **50 CENT**

20

TERROR AT HOME

ACTS OF WAR

ATTACKS ON WORLD TRADE CENTER, PENTAGON STUN WORLD; DEATHS EXPECTED TO BE IN THE THOUSANDS

A massive fireball erupts from the upper floors of the south tower of the World Trade Center after a second hijacked airliner hit the complex Tuesday morning.

KRISTEN BROCHMANN/The New York Times

U.S. Naval Submarine Base Among Installations on Wartime Alert

Military installations in the region were put on wartime alert, increasing patrols by boat on the river and on foot along fences. See **A3**

Impact Of Disaster Hits Home With Deaths Of Local Residents

A young man who grew up in Stonington and a mother and young daughter from New London are believed to be victims of the attack in New York. See **A5**

Experts Fear Attack On United States May Spur A Global Depression

While the immediate impacts on the financial world were obvious in closed markets and disrupted transportation, the worldwide effect is likely to be much deeper. See **C9**

Running For Their Lives

PAUL HAWTHORNE/Associated Press

Pedestrians scramble for safety in front of New York City Hall as the first World Trade Center tower collapses after being hit by an airliner in a terrorist attack Tuesday. See **A3**

Weather

Today: *Sunny, pleasant.*
High 82. Low 60.
Thursday: *Mostly sunny.*
High 82. Low 56.

Details, Page B10

The Washington Post

FINAL

Inside: **Food, Classified**
Today's Contents on Page A2

25¢

111TH YEAR No. 281   M2   DM VA

WEDNESDAY, SEPTEMBER 12, 2001

Prices may vary in areas outside metropolitan
Washington. (See box on Page A4).

Terrorists Hijack 4 Airliners, Destroy World Trade Center, Hit Pentagon; Hundreds Dead

Bodies Pulled From Pentagon; Troops Patrol District Streets

By Steve Twomey and Arthur Santana
Washington Post Staff Writers

Rescuers fought through tons of debris in quest of victims at the Pentagon last night after terrorists seized an airliner outbound from Dulles International Airport and plunged it into the heart of American military power, killing an estimated several hundred people.

Hampered by fires that still raged as evening fell, emergency teams had carried out only six bodies, but they were preparing to remove many more, and rescuers were using dogs and listening devices to search for people they believed might be trapped alive.

Precise figures were hard to come by because portions of the building were under construction, and many of the military and civilian personnel had been temporarily relocated, according to Arlington Fire Chief Edward P. Plaugher.

Coming less than an hour after two hijacked passenger jets slammed into the twin towers of New York's World Trade Center, the assault on the Pentagon began an unprecedented day of office and school closings, panicked phone calls, wild rumor and extraordinary security in the Washington area.

Last night, downtown streets were largely deserted as D.C. National Guard units joined police in patrolling the city. D.C. Mayor Anthony A. Williams (D), Maryland Gov. Parris N. Glendening (D) and Virginia Gov. James S. Gilmore III (R) declared states of emergency that broadened their power to govern without legislative authority.

Most of the region's school systems will be closed today, although President Bush announced that the federal government would reopen, after having shut down within an hour of yesterday's Pentagon attack.

At a late-evening news conference, D.C. Police Chief Charles H. Ramsey said that the attacks here and in New York would forever change security operations in Washington and that there was no longer such a thing as "business as usual" here.

Originally headed for Los Angeles, the American Airlines Boeing 757—carrying 64 people and loaded with 30,000 pounds of fuel for the long flight to the West Coast—

See PENTAGON, A14, Col. 1

BY SETH McALLISTER—AGENCE FRANCE-PRESSE

Minutes after an American Airlines plane crashed into the World Trade Center in New York City, a United airliner is about to hit the complex.

BY RICH LIPSKI—THE WASHINGTON POST

Firefighters battle blazes at the Pentagon, which was hit by a plane that had been hijacked after taking off from Dulles International Airport.

Bush Promises Retribution; Military Put on Highest Alert

By Michael Grunwald
Washington Post Staff Writer

Terrorists unleashed an astonishing air assault on America's military and financial power centers yesterday morning, hijacking four commercial jets and then crashing them into the World Trade Center in New York, the Pentagon and the Pennsylvania countryside.

There were no reliable estimates last night of how many people were killed in the most devastating terrorist operation in American history. The number was certainly in the hundreds and could be in the thousands.

It was the most dramatic attack on American soil since Pearl Harbor, and it created indelible scenes of carnage and chaos. The commandeered jets obliterated the World Trade Center's twin 110-story towers from their familiar perch above Manhattan's skyline and ripped a blazing swath through the Defense Department's imposing five-sided fortress, grounding the domestic air traffic system for the first time and plunging the entire nation into an unparalleled state of anxiety.

U.S. military forces at home and abroad were placed on their highest state of alert, and a loose network of Navy warships was deployed along both coasts for air defense.

The terrorists hijacked four California-bound planes from three airports on the Eastern Seaboard; the airliners were loaded with the maximum amount of fuel, suggesting a well-financed, well-coordinated plot. First, two planes slammed into the World Trade Center. Then an American Airlines plane out of Dulles International Airport ripped through the newly renovated walls of the Pentagon, perhaps the world's most secure office building. A fourth jet crashed 80 miles southeast of Pittsburgh, shortly after it was hijacked and turned in the direction of Washington.

None of the 266 people aboard the four planes survived. There were even more horrific but still untallied casualties in the World Trade Center and the Pentagon, which together provided office space for more than 70,000 people. At just one of the firms with offices in the World Trade Center, the Marsh & McLennan insurance bro-

See ATTACK, A13, Col. 1

Washington

On Flight 77: 'Our Plane Is Being Hijacked'

By Marc Fisher
and Don Phillips
Washington Post Staff Writers

There was not even the grace of instant death. Instead, there was time to call from the sky over Virginia, fingers pumping cell phones, terrified passengers talking to loved ones for one final time.

Herded to the back of the plane by hijackers armed with knives and box-cutters, the passengers and crew members of American Airlines Flight 77—including the wife of Solicitor General Theodore Olson, a Senate staffer, three D.C. schoolchildren and three teachers on an educational field trip and a University Park family of four headed to Australia for a two-month adventure—were ordered to call relatives to say they were about to die.

About an hour after takeoff from Dulles International Airport yesterday morning, Flight 77, a Boeing 757 headed for Los Angeles with 64 people aboard, became a massive missile aimed at the White House. The target would change suddenly, but the symbolism was equally devastating.

By about 9:40 a.m., when the diving plane carved out a massive chunk of the Pentagon, its passengers had experienced unspeak-

BY JAMES A. PARCELL—THE WASHINGTON POST

Shaken Pentagon worker Tracy Williams watches the flames.

able terror, hundreds died, and the nation's greatest symbol of security lay shattered, thick plumes of smoke camouflaging a gaping hole in its heart.

Barbara K. Olson, the former federal prosecutor who became a prominent TV commentator during the impeachment of President Bill Clinton, called her husband twice in the final minutes. Her last words to him were, "What do I tell

See FLIGHT, A11, Col. 1

U.S. Intelligence Points To Bin Laden Network

By Dan Eggen
and Vernon Loeb
Washington Post Staff Writers

The U.S. government has strong evidence from multiple sources that the suicidal terrorists who carried out yesterday's catastrophic attacks in New York and Washington were connected to Saudi fugitive Osama bin Laden, who previously was linked to the 1993 bombing of the World Trade Center, senior officials said.

One senior official said the probability that bin Laden is behind the deadly assaults is in "the high 90s," while another U.S. official said investigators gathered evidence "strongly suggesting" that bin Laden's organization, al Qaeda, was involved.

The evidence pointing to bin Laden was gathered following the attacks in a joint effort by the CIA and the FBI, with information from domestic and overseas sources, a senior official said.

"It is more than just the analytical surmise that it would take an organization with incredible com-

mand and control capability, which bin Laden's has, to stage an attack like this," one U.S. official said. "There is other information that has been obtained after the attack against the World Trade Center pointing in the direction of bin Laden."

Unprecedented in scope and sophistication, the coordinated assault on the world's financial and political capitals caught the United States completely off guard—despite a massive intelligence and law enforcement network devoted to detecting and thwarting such attacks. With efforts focused largely on guarding against bomb threats to overseas targets, U.S. authorities conceded they were ill-prepared for hijacked jetliners purposely crashed on American soil.

Sen. Orrin G. Hatch (R-Utah), a member of the Senate intelligence committee, said he was told in a briefing that electronic intercepts yesterday showed "representatives affiliated with Osama bin Laden over the airwaves reporting that

See TERRORISTS, A20, Col. 1

New York

'I Saw Bodies Falling Out— Oh, God, Jumping, Falling'

By Barton Gellman
Washington Post Staff Writer

NEW YORK, Sept. 11—Valerie Johnson stared, transfixed, at the inferno a thousand yards to her south and west. Tears streamed furrows through a film of ash on her face. Her mind tried to grasp what her eyes beheld: a blazing gash across the tower of wealth that symbolized New York for her all her life. The fire marched downward, floor by floor, windows bursting out ahead of the flames.

Then Johnson screamed a guttural, wordless wail. A sound like nothing she ever heard—low as thunder, but louder and longer—pressed in on her chest for ten seconds or more, resounding through Centre Street at Foley Square. The northern tower, the taller of the two, was gone. It was 10:29 a.m., an hour and three quarters after the first of two jetliners ripped through New York's twin emblems of global prestige.

"Oh, God, oh God, my niece works in that building," Johnson breathed. "Oh God."

Where we stood there now came a roiling cloud—smoke and ash, ten stories tall, building speed as they reached the canyons of Manhattan's southern tip. Survivors screamed, choked and gagging, behind the cloud. Among them, stumbling

BY ERNESTO MORA—ASSOCIATED PRESS

Two women hold each other as they watch the World Trade Center burn.

blindly toward the fountain at Foley Square, were Elizabeth Belleau and Melissa Morales, strangers grasping hands with all their might as they ran. Belleau plunged her head into the cooling waters and retched, coughing out ash and phlegm. The fountain enclosed a sculpture: "Triumph of the Human Spirit."

Belleau had been running for nearly two hours. Her morning commute on the BM-3 bus had stalled,

See SCENE, A17, Col. 1

ATTACK ON AMERICA

■ **Guide to coverage, A2**

■ **Latest updates,**
www.washingtonpost.com

Contents
© 2001
The
Washington
Post
Company

0   70628 21100   3

SUNSHINE HIGH 82, LOW 60 · C6

The Washington Times

FINAL

www.washingtontimes.com   WEDNESDAY, SEPTEMBER 12, 2001   ★★   SUBSCRIBER SERVICE: (202) 636-3333
Prices may vary outside metropolitan Washington area **25 cents**

INFAMY

22

Implosion: The north World Trade Center tower began its horrific collapse about 90 minutes after it was struck by a plane. The south tower, which also was hit by a plane, had fallen 20 minutes earlier.   AP

Bush promises to fight 'evil, despicable acts'

By Bill Sammon
THE WASHINGTON TIMES

President Bush, addressing the nation last night, promised to commit the full resources of intelligence and law enforcement to punish the masterminds of yesterday's "evil, despicable acts of terror."

"We will make no distinction between the terrorists who com-

mitted those attacks and those who harbor them," Mr. Bush said.

Speculation swirled in Washington that Osama bin Laden, who was believed to be in Afghanistan, was behind yesterday's terrorism. The Taliban government was quick to deny that bin Laden had a role.

"America has stood down ene-

see **BUSH,** *page A11*

INSIDE

Wednesday, September 12, 2001
Volume 20, Number 254
4 Sections, 50 Pages

SWIFT RESPONSE — U.S. military officers seek a swift and deadly response. **A10**

DAY OF INFAMY — Americans recall "day of infamy," Japan's Dec. 7, 1941, sneak attack on Pearl Harbor. **A13**

AMERICA AT WAR — For the first time in a generation, America finds itself at war — and war is the proper term. **A22**

AREA UNDER SIEGE — D.C. area copes with attack on Pentagon. **B1**

ICON OF PEACE — The World Trade Center was created as "a living symbol of man's dedication to world peace." **C1**

7 02803 87040 7

D.C. area thrown into chaos

By Stephen Dinan
THE WASHINGTON TIMES

Washington erupted into chaos and then settled into eerie calm yesterday after an airplane carrying 64 persons from Washington Dulles International Airport bound for Los Angeles crashed into the Pentagon about 9:40 a.m.

American Airlines Flight 77 was one of four flights that apparently were hijacked and crashed yesterday morning. Two other planes struck the twin towers of the World

see **SCENE,** *page A10*

Out of harm's way: Emergency workers responding to the explosion at the Pentagon fled after hearing that a second aircraft might be circling the Pentagon. The report proved false.

Photo by Gerald Herbert/The Washington Times

Hijacked planes destroy World Trade Center, ram Pentagon

By Frank J. Murray
THE WASHINGTON TIMES

Suicidal terrorists piloting airplanes hijacked from Dulles and Boston airports toppled the 110-story twin towers of the World Trade Center and demolished part of the Pentagon yesterday in the worst terrorist attack on American soil.

Police sources estimated that thousands may have been killed in the attacks, in addition to the 266 aboard the four hijacked jets and 343 New York fire and police personnel missing and presumed dead.

Reports point to bin Laden

A sensitive U.S. intelligence report indicates Saudi extremist Osama bin Laden and his associates are behind the attacks on the World Trade Center and Pentagon. **A3**

President Bush told the nation in a televised address that "thousands" lost loved ones in yesterday's attacks, and late last night New York Mayor Rudolph W. Giuliani said he "could not dispute" the president's estimate of the losses. The mayor said that the city's fire chief and deputy fire chief were among those killed.

Mr. Giuliani also said last night that people remained trapped alive under the rubble of the collapsed buildings of the World Trade Center.

Survivors were found among the ruins of the twin

see **ATTACKS,** *page A8*

South Florida Sun-Sentinel

BROWARD METRO EDITION | WEDNESDAY | SEPTEMBER 12, 2001

GET THE LATEST BREAKING NEWS @ Sun-Sentinel.com

ATTACKED

TERRORISTS DESTROY WORLD TRADE CENTER

GHASTLY SPECTACLE: A fireball erupts from one of the towers of the World Trade Center in New York City after it was struck by a hijacked plane Tuesday morning. In the background, smoke billows from the other tower, which was struck by another aircraft minutes earlier. The Brooklyn Bridge appears in the foreground. **New York Times photo/Steve Ludlum**

DEATHS

Toll could reach into the thousands at towers

MILITARY

Pentagon takes major strike in jet crash

ACT OF WAR

Angry cries for revenge arise across the country

NAVY ON ALERT

Carriers, destroyers prepare for action

THE PRESIDENT

Bush vows to identify, punish those responsible

28 PAGES OF COVERAGE INSIDE

VOL. 42, NO. 149 — 8 SECTIONS — COPYRIGHT © 2001 — ALL RIGHTS RESERVED — FOR HOME DELIVERY CALL 954-421-1771

23

24

MIAMI
el NuevoHerald
m!ami•com
Miami.com/ElNuevoHerald
EDICION EXTRAORDINARIA
MARTES 11 DE SEPTIEMBRE DEL 2001
35¢

El ZARPAZO DEL TERROR

UNA DENSA bola de fuego estalla en una de las torres del World Trade Center de Nueva York, después que un segundo avión se estrellara contra la poderosa mole a la 8:42 a.m. hora del este, como parte del enajenado ataque terrorista que sacude a la nación y al mundo.

Foto de ABC

> UN DIARIO KNIGHT RIDDER >

The Miami Herald

98th YEAR, No. 363
Copyright © 2001 The Miami Herald   BRYOG   WEDNESDAY, SEPTEMBER 12, 2001 ▶ FINAL EDITION   F   35 Cents
For home delivery, call 305 350-2000
www.miami.com

'EVIL ACTS'

Bush vows revenge for attacks

28 PAGES OF COVERAGE

CHRONOLOGY OF HORROR
Sudden terrorist attacks at the start of the workday virtually shut down the country. How Tuesday's events unfolded, **17–19A**

IN NEW YORK
▶ **Scene at St. Vincents:** Friends and families deluge hospital with inquiries for loved ones, **8A**
▶ **Leveled:** Specialists say the intense blaze from aviation fuel causes towers to collapse, **9A**

THE PENTAGON
▶ **The injuries:** Many suffer severe burns after an aircraft slams into the Pentagon, **13A**

TERRORISM
▶ **Watermark:** The magnitude of the attacks raises worries about the future of terrorism, **6A**
▶ **Security:** Swift military strikes likely, **6A**
▶ **Aviation:** Officials cite lax security, **15A**

COVERAGE: 2–31A

MOMENT OF IMPACT: With one of the World Trade Center towers already on fire after being struck by a plane, a second plane heads toward the other tower. It, too, burst into flames. Both towers later collapsed. — ASSOCIATED PRESS

Thousands killed as hijacked jets hit World Trade Center

BY MARTIN MERZER
mmerzer@herald.com

Addressing the nation after one of the most horrific days in history, President Bush vowed revenge Tuesday night for the full-scale terrorist assault that destroyed both towers of the World Trade Center, crushed a wing of the Pentagon, pulverized four hijacked jetliners and slaughtered thousands of Americans.

"The search is underway for those who are behind these evil acts . . .," Bush said on national television after spending several hours sheltered in an underground bunker in Nebraska. He returned to Washington in a plane escorted by military fighters.

"We will make no distinction between the terrorists who committed these acts and those who harbor them."

Federal investigators served search warrants Tuesday night at the homes of four Broward residents who were aboard the planes. No details were immediately available.

Bush said "thousands of lives were suddenly ended by evil," and there was no doubt that the ghastly blitz of terror inflicted massive devastation and monstrous carnage.

It utterly destroyed two 110-story symbols of the nation's financial power, and it wrecked part of a huge, five-sided building known worldwide as the seat of American military might.

More than 50,000 people might have been in the World Trade Center and no one knew how many people were buried under mountains of rubble that still smoldered in New York City — and at the Pen-

▶ PLEASE SEE ATTACK, 2A

'It was grim. It was unspeakable. You cannot imagine.'

BY ELINOR J. BRECHER
ebrecher@herald.com

NEW YORK — Millions of pieces of paper — letters, business cards, confidential files, uncashed personal checks, invoices — fluttered in clouds of dust and ash blocks from Ground Zero. Each was attached to a life that will never be the same.

But by 5 p.m., there were neither signs of life nor death. A few shoes lay about, owners apparently entombed by debris. Abandoned push carts remained filled with fresh flowers and doughnuts.

Oddly, flagpoles still stood outside World Trade Center Plaza. Banners flapped in acrid swirls of dust that turned the setting sun blood red. A huge American flag had wrapped around a traffic signal pole, flapping upside down in front of two charred stumps that had once been the twin towers.

Scores of bombed-out trucks, vans and police cars, tires melted, sat on charred rims, the fates of drivers and passengers unknown.

Even the living had the pallor of death. Tan and gray ash, stirred by a stiff breeze, coated shoe-tops, clothes and the faces of anyone near Ground Zero.

One was Dr. Gerald Ginsberg, a plastic surgeon at New York University Medical Center, who had told his staff in the morning: "Forget the face-lifts today." Hours later, he was downtown, treating a woman with burns over 90 percent of her body.

His colleague, Dr. Steven Brandeis, performed a colostomy on a woman whose entire pelvic area had been sliced off "as if she were guillotined," Ginsberg said.

Gusts of wind like desert dust devils picked up columns of debris and swirled them down the

▶ PLEASE SEE SCENE, 10A

STAN HONDA/AFP

HORRIFIC DAY: A survivor covers his mouth as he walks through debris from the World Trade Center. At left, President Bush's visit to a Sarasota school is interrupted by an urgent message from Chief of Staff Andrew Card.

PAUL J. RICHARDS/AFP

0 77785 13333 9
05255

> KNIGHT RIDDER >   INFORMATION FOR LIFE

THE TAMPA TRIBUNE

WEDNESDAY, SEPTEMBER 12, 2001 ★ FINAL EDITION ★ TBO.com

28

The shock of seeing jets fly into two of the world's tallest buildings Tuesday gave way to panic when the towers began falling, folding like accordions.

TARGET: AMERICA

FEAR, SHOCK, ANGER RESONATE ACROSS NATION

DEATH TOLL EXPECTED TO BE IN THE THOUSANDS

OSAMA BIN LADEN IDENTIFIED AS PRIME SUSPECT

Photos by The Associated Press

Twin terror engulfs the World Trade Center as a jet — United Airlines Flight 175 bound from Boston to Los Angeles — slams into the south tower about 18 minutes after a plane hit the north tower.

MOURNING U.S. LEADERS RESOLVE TO CATCH KILLERS

By GERALDINE BAUM
and MAGGIE FARLEY
Los Angeles Times

NEW YORK — Terrorists struck at the pre-eminent symbols of America's wealth and might Tuesday, flying hijacked airliners into the World Trade Center and the Pentagon, killing and injuring thousands of people.

As a horrified nation watched on television, the twin towers of the World Trade Center in lower Manhattan collapsed into flaming rubble after two Boeing 767s rammed their upper stories. A third airliner, a Boeing 757, flattened one of the Pentagon's famed five sides.

A fourth hijacked jetliner crashed in western Pennsylvania.

The assaults, which stirred fear and anxiety across the country and evoked comparisons to Pearl Harbor, were carefully planned and coordinated, occurring within 50 minutes. No one claimed responsibility, but official suspicion quickly fell on Saudi fugitive Osama bin Laden.

Addressing the nation Tuesday night, President Bush vowed to "find those responsible and bring them to justice." This country, he said, would retaliate against "those behind these evil acts" and any country that harbors them.

The stunning failure of airport security was unexplained, but in at least one instance, early information suggested that some of the hijackers were armed with knives and boxcutters.

See TARGET AMERICA, Page 22 |
More than 200 firefighters feared dead.

BAY AREA RESIDENTS SHOCKED, REVULSED BY TERROR ATTACKS

By JOE HENDERSON
jhenderson@tampatrib.com

Terrorism's tentacles reached beyond the death and chaos at the World Trade Center and the Pentagon, dragging a global catastrophe onto Tampa's doorstep Tuesday.

It obliterated the sense of security on the city's streets and left fear in its homes. The unprecedented attacks on New York and Washington, symbols of America's financial and military might, spared no one.

Its impact was felt with every busy signal a frantic caller received after dialing for news of loved ones in harm's way, or with fretful parents who rushed to take their children home early from school.

Travelers were marooned at Tampa International Airport when the nationwide air system was grounded. Security was increased at MacDill Air Force Base and the Sam Gibbons Federal Courthouse in downtown Tampa. Police SWAT teams armed with automatic rifles patrolled around city hall.

Blood drives were organized throughout the area as Tampa tried to help. Scheduled events were canceled as Tampa showed both fear and respect. Major shopping malls closed for the day, and people throughout the area stood hushed around televised images of the smoky maelstrom, each news update more jolting than the previous.

"This country was founded on heart and how people support each other in a

See TAMPA SHOCKED, Page 10 |
Events incomprehensible to young, old.

THE TAMPA TRIBUNE
200/202 S. Parker St.
Tampa FL 33606-2395

A Media General
Newspaper

Copyright © 2001
The Tribune Co.
107th Year, No. 219

To reach us from inside
Hillsborough County,
call (813) 259-7711;
outside Hillsborough,
call 1-800-282-5588.

69% of
The Tampa
Tribune is
printed on
recycled
paper.

An index to our complete coverage of the terrorist attack on America. Page 2

AMERICA UNDER ATTACK: SPECIAL 24-PAGE REPORT

The Atlanta Constitution

ajc.com

*****
WEDNESDAY, SEPT. 12, 2001

50¢

OUTRAGE

MIKE BUSCHER / Associated Press

It was a clear day Tuesday, but clouds of **foul dust** on the Manhattan skyline were markers of **death and destruction**. Terrorists had hijacked airliners and slammed them into the World Trade Center, causing the mighty twin structure to crumble. A similar scene unfolded at the **Pentagon**. For America, it was a day of monstrously coordinated carnage.

Reprinted with permission from *The Atlanta Journal* and *The Atlanta Constitution*.

29

Thousands dead, a nation staggered as terrorists strike New York, Washington

By JAY BOOKMAN
jbookman@ajc.com

We occupy a different reality than we did a day ago. Thousands lie dead, many still buried in the smoking rubble in New York and Washington. Millions grieve. Two landmarks of the Manhattan skyline have been obliterated, and an atmosphere of war pervades Washington. A nation slow to anger has been brought to justified fury.

But fury against whom? Retaliation, when it comes, will have to be as coolly calculated and well targeted as Tuesday's attack. The memory of our dead deserves no less.

In American history, only one comparable event springs obviously to mind: Pearl Harbor. Those of us who could only guess at the effect of Dec. 7, 1941, on our parents and grandparents now understand much better. They must have felt then what we feel now: an initial disbelief and stunned horror, followed by a stern resolve to see justice done.

In the wake of Pearl Harbor, we at least knew our enemies. Not this time. Not quite yet. It's frustrating to be sucker-punched in such a devastating fashion and not know for sure who threw the punch.

The terrorists chose their targets well. They hit the twin towers of U.S. power: the heart of commerce, in the World Trade Center, and the heart of our military, at the Pentagon. Any illusion of this nation as Fortress America, able to insulate itself from the troubles of the world, crumbled along with those buildings. It was humbling to see people stumbling through the debris-strewn streets of mighty Manhattan, survivors of a carnage that had long ago grown familiar, on a lesser scale, in scenes from Beirut, Sarajevo, Jerusalem and Tel Aviv.

The most sophisticated, technologically advanced nation in the world had been brought to its knees by an attack of brutal simplicity. But for a day, and only for a day.

Last night, members of Congress joined in singing "God Bless America" on the Capitol steps, and President Bush reaffirmed the nation's strength and resolve against evil. This morning the sun came up again, and with it came a new day. The rebuilding and healing begins.

And the day to settle accounts will come.

ERNESTO MORA / Associated Press

Watching the **death throes** of the World Trade Center, two women cling together in disbelief Tuesday.

➤ Log on to ajc.com for constant news updates throughout the day.

➤ Coverage of news unrelated to the attack begins today in section B.

ATTACK ON AMERICA

The Telegraph
MACON

Sun and clouds, chance of rain
High 88, low 64 / 2B

HOME EDITION
4 sections, 44 pages
175th year, No. 255, Macon, Ga.
50¢ Daily / $1.50 Sunday

Wednesday
September 12, 2001

═══ www.macontelegraph.com ═══

'DESPICABLE'

Thousands believed dead in attacks on World Trade Center, Pentagon

By David Crary and Jerry Schwartz
Associated Press

NEW YORK — In the most devastating terrorist onslaught ever waged against the United States, knife-wielding hijackers crashed two airliners into the World Trade Center on Tuesday, toppling its twin 110-story towers. The deadly calamity was witnessed on televisions across the world as another plane slammed into the Pentagon, and a fourth crashed outside Pittsburgh.

"Today, our nation saw evil," President Bush said in an address to the nation Tuesday night. He said thousands of lives were "suddenly ended by evil, despicable acts of terror."

Said Adm. Robert J. Natter, commander of the U.S. Atlantic Fleet: "We have been attacked like we haven't since Pearl Harbor."

Establishing the U.S. death toll could take weeks. The four airliners alone had 266 people aboard and there were no known survivors. At the Pentagon, about 100 people were believed dead.

In addition, a union official said he feared half of the 400 firefighters who first reached the scene had died in rescue efforts at the trade center — where 50,000 people worked — and dozens of police officers were believed missing.

"The number of casualties will be more than most of us can bear," a visibly distraught Mayor Rudolph Giuliani said.

Police sources said some people trapped in the twin

Please see **ATTACKS, 8A**

INSIDE

■ Terrorist leader Osama bin Laden emerges as the prime suspect in Tuesday's attacks. 4A

■ The attack has shut down the nation's air traffic system, affected other modes of travel. 6A, 11A

■ Macon's Brendan Smith, a graduate of Stratford Academy, tells of his escape from one of the Trade Center's towers. 10A

■ Who needs help, and how you can give it, including blood donations. 11A

■ Robins Air Force Base is among the U.S. military installations worldwide that are on high security alert. 10A

Complete coverage on Pages 3A-14A, 1C, 13C-14C

For updates, visit macontelegraph.com

VICTIMS' INFORMATION HOTLINE: (800) 331-0075

A fiery blasts rocks the World Trade Center after two hijacked airplanes crashed into the towers Tuesday in New York City.
Associated Press

Flight 77's passengers call home, say goodbye

Woman tells husband, 'Our plane is being hijacked,' as aircraft heads toward Pentagon

By Marc Fisher and Don Phillips
Washington Post

WASHINGTON — There was not even the grace of instant death. Instead, there was time to call from the sky over Virginia to loved ones, fingers pumping cell phones, voices saying quick, final good-byes.

Herded to the back of the plane by hijackers armed with knives and box-cutters, the 64 passengers and crew of American Airlines Flight 77 — including the wife of Solicitor General Theodore Olson, a Senate staffer, three

D.C. schoolchildren and three teachers on an educational field trip, and a suburban family of four headed to Australia for a two-month adventure — were ordered to call relatives to say they were about to die.

About an hour after takeoff from Dulles International Airport on Tuesday morning, Flight 77, a Boeing 757 headed for Los

Olson

Angeles, became a massive missile aimed at the White House. The target would change suddenly, but the symbolism was equally devastating.

By 9:45 a.m., when the diving plane carved out a massive chunk of the Pentagon, its passengers had experienced unspeakable terror, untold dozens died and the nation's greatest symbol of security lay shattered, thick plumes of smoke camouflaging a gaping hole in its heart.

Barbara Olson, the former federal prosecutor who became a prominent TV commentator during the

impeachment of President Clinton, called her husband twice in the final minutes. Her last words to him were "What do I tell the pilot to do?"

"She called from the plane while it was being hijacked," Theodore Olson said. "I wish it wasn't so, but it is."

The two conversations each lasted about a minute, said Tim O'Brien, a CNN reporter and friend of the Olsons who is acting as family spokesman. In the first call, Barbara Olson told her husband, "Our plane is being

Please see **FLIGHT 77, 8A**

═══ INSIDE TODAY ═══

6 46012 00001 2

> KNIGHT RIDDER >

INFORMATION FOR LIFE

NIGHT ★ FINAL

Honolulu Star-Bulletin

TUESDAY, SEPTEMBER 11, 2001 / THE PULSE OF PARADISE / STARBULLETIN.COM / 50¢ ON OAHU

DAY OF TERROR

Flames and debris explode from the south tower of the World Trade Center as the north tower billows with smoke. Two hijacked airliners crashed into the buildings where 50,000 people work.

[INSIDE]

HAWAII

- **Tight security:** Authorities shut down Honolulu Airport; emergency crews go on alert; military bases closed. A10 & A11

NEW YORK

- **Nightmare in the sky:** People jumped in terror from the towers just before they collapsed. A6
- **Financial markets close:** U.S. dollar plunged on global markets. C1

ELSEWHERE

- **Bush responds:** Promises to hunt down the terrorists. A3
- **Fourth crash:** United Airlines airliner crashes near Pittsburgh. A3
- **Global reaction:** World leaders condemn the attack. A4
- **Palestinians celebrate:** "Let America have a taste of what we've tasted," said one. A5

Two women embrace as they watch the World Trade Center burn in lower Manhattan.

Both World Trade Center towers collapse after being struck by hijacked airplanes

Another hijacked jet crashes into the Pentagon, forcing an evacuation

FAA halts all domestic flights and orders international flights diverted

Thousands feared dead and injured as rescuers struggle amid debris

— See story, A2

Classifieds	C6	Donnelly	D4	Kokua Line	A2	Obituaries	C6
Comics	D4	Editorials	C4	Local News	A13	Sports	B1
Commentary	C5	Hawaii Inc.	C1	Movies	D3	Television	D2
Crossword	D5	Horoscope	D4	Mutual funds	C3	Today	D1

Mostly sunny, with isolated windward and mauka showers. Trades 10-20 mph. Expect a high of close to 90 degrees with a low of about 75. Details, D6.

Classifieds/Call 529-4800

Volume 1 / Number 177 / 4 sections
Copyright © 2001 / Honolulu Star-Bulletin
All rights reserved

Chicago Tribune
SPECIAL EXTRA

155TH YEAR — NO. 254 © CHICAGO TRIBUNE   TUESDAY, SEPTEMBER 11, 2001   50¢

U.S. under attack
Hijacked jets destroy World Trade Center, hit Pentagon

An aircraft, at right, is seen as it is about to fly into the World Trade Center in New York in this image made from television, Tuesday.

AP photo

Officials fear thousands killed in New York City

By Charles M. Madigan
Tribune staff reporter

Terrorists in at least three hijacked airliners staged a coordinated attack on the nation's financial, military and government centers Tuesday morning, devastating the World Trade Center in New York and the Pentagon in Washington and setting off a national panic as bewildered citizens raced for safety from a determined, but as yet unknown, enemy.

Although there were no early estimates, authorities feared a heavy loss of life in the attacks. One New York police official said thousands of people may have been killed or injured in the attacks.

Both towers of the huge World Trade Center, which houses some 50,000 workers, were destroyed after they were hit by two airliners that had been hijacked earlier in the day. Smoke billowed from the burning buildings, which collapsed at midmorning. The Federal Aviation Administration ordered all commercial airliners grounded. Financial and government centers were shut down and evacuations were underway all across the country.

The FAA said at least five planes operated by American Airlines and United Airlines were reported to have crashed or were "in trouble." The American planes were hijacked from Boston and

PLEASE SEE **ATTACK**, BACK PAGE

A fireball explodes from one of the towers at the World Trade Center after a plane crashed into it.
AP photo

Terrified New Yorkers flee a massive cloud of dust and debris as the World Trade Center collapses.
AP Photo

GET UPDATES THROUGHOUT THE DAY AT CHICAGOTRIBUNE.COM

EXTRA EDITION

TUESDAY
SEPTEMBER 11, 2001 · 50¢
Special edition
www.dailysouthtown.com

Daily Southtown

Covering the Southland since 1906

ATTACK ON AMERICA

7:50 A.M. / WORLD TRADE CENTER TOWER HIT BY PLANE

8:04 A.M. / SECOND WORLD TRADE CENTER TOWER HIT BY PLANE

8:30 A.M. / AIRCRAFT CRASHES INTO PENTAGON IN WASHINGTON

8:50 AND 9:30 A.M. / WORLD TRADE CENTER TOWERS COLLAPSE

9 A.M. / PLANE CRASHES 80 MILES SOUTHEAST OF PITTSBURGH

Nation, pages 2-3

COVERAGE AND MORE PHOTOS FROM
SCENES OF TERROR IN
NEW YORK AND WASHINGTON

Local, pages 4-5

■ Area schools locked their doors and students watched TV throughout the day as word spread of the terrorist attacks in the United States. Government buildings closed, and area police stepped up efforts to maintain public calm.

■ Stranded at Midway Airport when the FAA shutdown the nation's air travel system, Ellen Menoni learned her husband was aboard the ill-fated United Flight 175.

■ Thousands of people fled Chicago, leaving the city a ghost town where streets roiled as officials tried to come to grips with terror attacks in Washington, D.C., and New York City. Security throughout Chicago has been increased.

■ The White Sox game with the New York Yankees in the Bronx today has been canceled, as have all other major league baseball games out of a concern for "security and mourning."

Expanded, pages 6-8

THE NATION AND WORLD WATCHES
IN HORROR AS ATTACKS ON THE
UNITED STATES UNFOLD.

WEDNESDAY
Look for comprehensive national, world and local coverage of today's events.

Home delivery: (708) 633-6900

The Daily Southtown is a newspaper of
Midwest Suburban Publishing,
a division of Hollinger International.

33

SPECIAL EDITION

INDIANA DAILY STUDENT

WEDNESDAY
September 12, 2001

Volume 134 • Issue 83   www.idsnews.com   4 pages • Free

DISASTER

World Trade Center gone

Hijacked airplanes crash into twin towers, the Pentagon and a rural Pennsylvania town

**David Crary
and Jerry Schwartz**
The Associated Press

NEW YORK – In the most devastating terrorist onslaught ever waged against the United States, hijackers crashed two airliners into the World Trade Center on Tuesday, toppling its twin towers. The world watched on television as another plane slammed into the Pentagon and a fourth crashed outside Pittsburgh.

"Today, our nation saw evil," President Bush said in an address to the nation Tuesday night. He said thousands of lives were "suddenly ended by evil, despicable acts of terror."

Establishing the death toll could take weeks. The four airliners alone had 266 people aboard, and there were no known survivors. Officials put the number of dead and wounded at the Pentagon at about 100 or more,

with some news reports suggesting it could rise to 800.

In addition, a union official said he feared 300 firefighters who first reached the scene had died in rescue efforts at the trade center – where 50,000 people worked – and dozens of police officers were missing.

"The number of casualties will be more than most of us can bear," a visibly distraught Mayor Rudolph Giuliani said.

Police sources said that some people trapped in the twin towers managed to call authorities or family members and that some trapped police officers made radio contact. In one of the calls, which took place in the afternoon, a businessman phoned his family to say he was trapped with policemen, whom he named, the source said.

see **DISASTER**, page 3

CHAO SOI CHEONG • THE ASSOCIATED PRESS

Smoke billows from one of the towers of the World Trade Center, and flames and debris explode from the second tower Tuesday after the New York landmark was hit by terrorist plane attacks. The destruction was one of most horrifying attacks against the United States in history. Damage from the blows caused the twin 110-story towers to crash to the ground.

GULNARA SAMOILOVA • THE ASSOCIATED PRESS

People make their way amid debris near the World Trade Center in New York Tuesday. In one of the most horrifying attacks ever against the United States, terrorists crashed two airliners into the World Trade Center in a deadly series of blows that brought down the twin 110-story towers.

A city torn apart

Helen O'Neill
The Associated Press

NEW YORK – As night fell, the city moved past the nightmarish scenes of people on fire jumping from buildings and braced itself for more pain: picking through the rubble for the dead and the injured.

Crews began heading into ground zero of the terrorist attack to search for survivors and recover bodies. The downtown area was cordoned off and a huge rescue effort was under way. Gov. George Pataki mobilized the National Guard to help, and hundreds of volunteers and medical workers converged on triage centers, offering services and blood.

One man caught under the rubble used his cell phone to reach family in Pennsylvania with a plea for help.

"She received a call from him saying he was still trapped under the World Trade Center. He gave specific directions and said he was there along with two New York City sergeants," said Brian Jones, 911 coordinator in Allgeheny County. He would not give their names, but said the message was passed to New York authorities.

Paramedics waiting to be sent into the rubble were told that "once the smoke clears, it's going to be massive bodies," according to Brian Stark, an ex-Navy paramedic who volunteered to help. He said the paramedics had been told that "hundreds of police and firefighters are missing" from the ranks of those sent in to respond to the initial crash.

"I hope we get patients," said medical student Eddie Campbell, who rushed to help at one of the centers.

"But they're not coming out. They're in there," he said, pointing down the street to where the World Trade Center once stood.

Emergency Medical Service worker Louis Garcia said initial reports indicated that bodies were buried beneath the two feet of soot on streets around the twin towers. Garcia, a 15-year veteran, said bodies "are all over the place."

Eight hours after the catastrophe began, hundreds of firefighters sat on the West Side Highway or leaned against their rigs, waiting for orders to go into the leveled skyscrapers and search for what they feared would be hundreds of bodies – including many colleagues.

KAMNEKO PAJIC • THE ASSOCIATED PRESS

Rescue workers look over damage at the Pentagon Tuesday. The Pentagon burst into flames and a portion of one side of the five-sided structure collapsed after the building was hit by an aircraft in an apparent terrorist attack.

Bush addresses a nation in chaos

Sandra Sobieraj
The Associated Press

WASHINGTON – A grim-faced President George W. Bush condemned ghastly attacks in Washington and New York on Tuesday and vowed to "find those responsible and bring them to justice."

In the second Oval Office address of his presidency, Bush said the United States would retaliate against "those behind these evil acts," and any country that harbors them.

"Today, our nation saw evil," he said.

Bush said the government offices deserted after the bombings Tuesday would open on Wednesday.

Seeking to comfort an anxious nation, he said, "These acts shattered steel, but they cannot dent the steel of American resolve."

He asked the nation to pray for the families of the victims and quoted the Book of Psalms, "And I pray they will be comforted by a power greater than any of us spoken through the ages in Pslam 23.

In his address, Bush said: "Today, our fellow citizens, our way of life, our very freedom,

DOUG MILLS • THE ASSOCIATED PRESS

President George W. Bush's Chief of Staff Andy Card whispers into the ear of the commander in chief to give him word of the plane crashes.

came under attack in a series of deliberate and deadly terrorist acts." He said thousands of lives were "suddenly ended by evil, despicable acts of terror."

ids   **CONTACT US**   ERNIE PYLE HALL 120, 940 E. 7TH STREET, BLOOMINGTON, IN 47405   NEWSROOM: 855-0760 • ADVERTISING: 855-0763 • CLASSIFIED: 855-0763 • FAX 855-8009 • E-MAIL: IDS@INDIANA.EDU • WWW.IDSNEWS.COM   Please recycle

EXTRA

AMERICA UNDER ATTACK

THE INDIANAPOLIS STAR

50¢ newsstand price

"Where the Spirit of the Lord is, there is Liberty" II Cor. 3:17

A GANNETT NEWSPAPER   TUESDAY, SEPTEMBER 11, 2001   WWW.INDYSTAR.COM

ATTACKED

Flight from horror: Panic-stricken pedestrians stream from the vicinity of the World Trade Center as the south tower collapses. Two hijacked jetliners crashed into the twin 110-story towers just minutes apart this morning, destroying the New York City landmark and leaving an unknown number of people dead and injured. Some compared the devastation to the bombing of Pearl Harbor, which catapulted the United States into World War II in 1941.

Associated Press / Amy Sancetta

NATION

Hijacked jets strike Pentagon, Trade Center

Page A3

Associated Press / Will Morris

Direct hit: Flames and smoke pour from a building at the Pentagon this morning.

RESPONSE

President Bush vows to 'hunt down' terrorists

Page A3

NEW YORK

'Everyone was screaming, crying, running'

Page A2

EDITORIAL

We must unite, then strike back at terrorists

Page A6

INDIANA

Governments, schools, offices go on alert

Pages A7, A8

Copyright 2001
The Star

YOUR LOCAL NEWS SOURCE

ILLINOIS FINAL
An edition of The Times serving Chicago's Southeast Side and the southern suburbs

WEDNESDAY SEPTEMBER 12, 2001

THE TIMES

SPECIAL REPORT

5 SECTIONS, 54 PAGES   www.thetimesonline.com   Newsstand: 50 cents

36

DAY OF TERROR
'THIS IS THE SECOND PEARL HARBOR'

UNITED STATES UNDER ATTACK | COMPLETE COVERAGE INSIDE

IN WASHINGTON

PRESIDENT SPEAKS: Bush says the United States will punish those behind the deadliest attack in U.S. history. **A3**

IN NEW YORK

THE SCENE: It was the image of a nightmare: people on fire jumping from the World Trade Center towers before the buildings collapsed. **A4**

IN CHICAGO

CITY SHUTS DOWN: An eerie silence filled the Loop as many buildings were evacuated and somber workers hurried home. **A8**

AT AIRPORTS

PLANES GROUNDED: Airports in Chicago, the south suburbs, and Lake and Porter counties are ordered closed. **A10-11**

AT WORSHIP

CLERGY REACT: Local clergy try to make sense of the tragedy, offer words of comfort to faithful in churches, synagogues. **B1**

AT SCHOOL

EXTRA PRECAUTIONS: High school students wonder if it's war, while teachers shield younger children from the news. **B2**

The Times is printed with soy color inks, exclusively on recycled paper.

INDEX

Bridge E12	Crossword (Classified) E8
Business E1	Crossword (Newsday)......D6
Classifieds ....E7, F	Horoscopes D6

Local B1	Sports C1
Movies.............................D2	Stocks...............................E2
Obituaries E4	TV Listings.......................D5

★ ★ ★ **EXTRA** ★ ★ ★

A NATIONAL TRAGEDY
12 pages of local and national coverage

Quad-City Times

TUESDAY, SEPTEMBER 11, 2001

'Hunt down the folks who committed this act.'
PRESIDENT BUSH

COPYRIGHT 2001 ■ QUAD-CITY TIMES   WWW.QCTIMES.COM ■ 50 CENTS

BEYOND BELIEF

Horrific sequence of terrorist attacks hits America; thousands feared dead

37

The World Trade Center Towers in New York burn out of control after being hit by two commercial airliners this morning. Within 40 minutes of the first collision, both towers tumbled to the street.

EXTRA EDITION

The Des Moines Register

A

The Newspaper Iowa Depends Upon ■ DesMoinesRegister.com ■ Price 50 Cents

TUESDAY
September 11, 2001

TERROR
America under attack

38

Bush: 'We will pass this test'

President Bush spoke from Barksdale Air Force Base in Louisiana on terrorist attacks this morning :

"The resolve of our great nation is being tested. But make no mistake, we will show the world that we will pass this test," Bush declared.

"Freedom itself was attacked this morning by a faceless coward and freedom will be defended,"

With the White House itself under threat of attack, the president's whereabouts were kept secret.
Page 11AA

Pentagon takes terrorist hit

The Pentagon took a direct, devastating hit from an aircraft.

The departments of Justice, State, Treasury and Defense, and the Central Intelligence Agency were evacuated — an estimated 20,000 at the Pentagon alone.

Authorities immediately began deploying troops.
Page 3AA

Air travel halted in U.S.

International airlines scrambled to divert or cancel flights to the United States today following a wave of airborne terror attacks on New York and Washington.

At least four commercial airline flights have crashed this morning. The Federal Aviation Administration has shut down all the nation's airports, for the first time in history.
Page 9AA

Iowa delegates amid chaos

Members of Iowa's congressional delegation in Washington, D.C., were amid chaos this morning as officials evacuated any building deemed to be in danger. "To be honest with you I don't feel very safe on the seventh floor of the Hart Office Building," said a staffer in Democratic Sen. Tom Harkin's office.

 Printed with SOY INK

Copyright 2001 Des Moines Register and Tribune Company
A Gannett Newspaper

September 11, 2001

AMY SANCETTA/ASSOCIATED PRESS

Attack: Pedestrians flee the area of the World Trade Center this morning as the center's south tower crashes following an attack on the New York landmark. Two airplanes crashed into the towers and thousands are feared dead.

EXTRA

GLOBE GAZETTE

www.globegazette.com

TUESDAY, SEPT. 11, 2001 – 50¢

MASON CITY/CLEAR LAKE, IOWA

ATTACKED!

AP photo

Smoke billows from one of the towers of the World Trade Center as flames and debris explode from the second tower Tuesday. In one of the most horrifying attacks ever against the United States, terrorists crashed two airliners into the World Trade Center in a deadly series of blows that brought down the twin 110-story towers.

In an apparent terrorist attack, hijacked jetliners smash into the twin towers of New York's World Trade Center and the Pentagon. Another jet crashes into the ground outside Pittsburgh. Loss of life is expected to number in the thousands.

Inside this special Extra edition of the Globe Gazette:

39

JOURNAL-WORLD

ljworld.com
LAWRENCE, KANSAS
85 PAGES
Vol.143/No.255
50 CENTS

WEDNESDAY • SEPTEMBER 12 • 2001

'Evil'

40

FIERY BLASTS ROCK the World Trade Center after being hit by two planes. Later Tuesday morning, another plane rammed into the Pentagon outside Washington, D.C.

Spencer Platt/Getty Images

www.ljworld.com

Inside: America's day of terror

A

World Trade Center, Pentagon targeted. 3A

Bin Laden emerges as top suspect. 4A

Stateless enemy confronts U.S. 6A

B

Lawrence prays for blast victims. 1B

Grief, astonishment hit Lawrence. 1B

Public schools remain open. 8B

C

Games come to standstill. 1C

D

Flights skid to halt at KCI Airport. 1D

Investors remain upbeat. 1D

Blow by blow Page B1

Fleeing Page B8

WEDNESDAY
SEPTEMBER 12, 2001
SALINA, KANSAS

the Salina Journal

Serving Kansas since 1871 ★ 50 cents

Under Attack

Inquiry focuses on bin Laden

By The Associated Press

WASHINGTON — U.S. officials began piecing together a case linking Osama bin Laden to the worst terrorist attack in U.S. history, aided by an intercept of communications between his supporters and harrowing cell phone calls from victims aboard the jetliners before they crashed Tuesday.

U.S. intelligence intercepted communications between bin Laden supporters discussing the attacks on the World Trade Center and the Pentagon, said Utah Sen. Orrin Hatch, the top Republican on the Senate Judiciary Committee.

"They have an intercept of some information that included people associated with bin Laden who acknowledged a couple of targets were hit," Hatch said. He declined to be more specific.

Hatch also said law enforcement has data possibly linking one person on one of the four-diated flights to bin Laden's organization.

Government and industry officials said at least one flight attendant and two passengers called from three of the planes as they were being forced down in New York and Washington — each describing similar circumstances.

The callers indicated hijackers armed with knives, in some cases stabbing flight attendants, took control of the plane and were forcing them down toward the ground, officials said.

One of the passengers was Barbara Olson, the wife of a top Justice Department official who called her husband as the hijacking was occurring.

Olson, the wife of Solicitor General Theodore Olson, was aboard American Airlines Flight 77 that left Dulles International Airport in Washington and was forced to crash into the Pentagon.

The officials said Olson told her husband the attackers had used knife-like instruments to take over the plane and forced passengers to the back of the jet.

Theodore Olson confirmed his wife made the calls before dying.

"She called from the plane while it was being hijacked. I wish it wasn't so, but it is," he said.

Photos by The Associated Press
Firefighters make their way through the rubble Tuesday from the collapsed World Trade Center.

Rescuers assess the damage done to the Pentagon after it was struck Tuesday by a hijacked airliner.

Emergency workers assist a woman injured in New York.

Terrorists strike at heart of America

By DAVID CRARY
and JERRY SCHWARTZ
The Associated Press

NEW YORK — In the most devastating terrorist onslaught ever waged against the United States, knife-wielding hijackers Tuesday crashed two airliners into the World Trade Center, toppling its twin 110-story towers. The deadly calamity was witnessed on televisions across the world as another plane slammed into the Pentagon, and a fourth crashed outside Pittsburgh.

"Today, our nation saw evil," President Bush said in an address to the nation Tuesday night. He said thousands of lives were "suddenly ended by evil, despicable acts of terror."

Adm. Robert Natter, commander of the U.S. Atlantic Fleet, said: "We have been attacked like we haven't since Pearl Harbor."

Establishing the U.S. death toll could take weeks. The four airliners alone had 266 people aboard and there were no known survivors. At the Pentagon, about 100 people were believed dead.

In addition, a firefighters union official said he feared an estimated 200 firefighters had died in rescue efforts at the trade center — where 50,000 people worked — and dozens of police officers were believed missing.

No one took responsibility for the attacks that rocked the seats of finance and government. But federal authorities identified Osama bin Laden, who has been given asylum by Afghanistan's Taliban rulers, as the prime suspect.

At the World Trade Center, the dead and the doomed plummeted from the skyscrapers, among them a man and woman holding hands.

Shortly after 7 p.m., crews began heading into ground zero of the attack to search for survivors and recover bodies. All that remained of the twin towers by then was a pile of rubble and twisted steel that stood barely two stories high, leaving a huge gap in the New York City skyline.

See ATTACK, Page A10

Bush assures nation he will avenge deaths

By SANDRA SOBIERAJ
The Associated Press

WASHINGTON — A grim-faced President Bush mourned the deaths of thousands of Americans in Tuesday's atrocities and vowed to avenge their killings. "Today, our nation saw evil," he said.

In his first prime-time Oval Office address, Bush said the United States would retaliate against "those behind these evil acts" and any country that harbors them.

Bush spoke from the Oval Office just hours after bouncing between Florida and air bases in Louisiana and Nebraska for security reasons. Fighter jets and decoy helicopters accompanied his evening flight to Washington and the White House.

With smoke still pouring out of rubble in Washington and New York, he said, "These acts shat-

BUSH

tered steel, but they cannot dent the steel of American resolve."

Bush spoke for less than five minutes from the desk that Bill Clinton and John F. Kennedy used before him. Beside the door, a TelePrompTer operator fed Bush the words that he and his speechwriters hastened to pen just an hour earlier.

He stumbled a couple of times even as he strove to maintain a commanding air. Aides pushed an American flag and one with the presidential seal behind him for the somber occasion.

Bush said the government offices deserted after the bombings Tuesday would open today.

He asked the nation to pray for the families of the victims and quoted the Book of Psalms, "And I pray they will be comforted by a power greater than any of us spoken through the ages in Psalm 23. Even though I walk through the valley of the shadow of death, I fear no evil for you are with me."

See BUSH, Page A10

Kansans on front line

By SHARON MONTAGUE
The Salina Journal

Margaret McGavran, Minneapolis, heard screams in the background as she talked to her son, Mark McGavran, 25, Tuesday morning as he fled from the World Trade Center's south tower.

Mark told his mother he was OK, then quickly said, "I gotta go," and the phone went dead.

At that moment, Margaret McGavran knew the north tower at the World Trade Center had been struck by a plane hijacked by terrorists, but she didn't realize while her son was talking to her using his cellular phone, the south tower — the one he was in — was struck by a second hijacked plane.

"She was at work at the Ada grain elevator," said Ray Mc-

Gavran, Mark's father. "She didn't have a television, and I don't think she had a radio on at the time. We thought he was all right. He told us they were evacuating, that it didn't hit his tower."

Minutes later, the McGavrans' daughter called from Kansas City with a report of the second explosion.

It was another 30 minutes before the McGavrans heard from their son that he was out of the building.

"I walked in circles," Ray McGavran said. "I just prayed that he'd be OK."

Mark McGavran, who got out of the building without a scratch, later told his parents that when the second plane hit, "it was just like a vibration."

See KANSANS, Page A2

Rumors send Salinans out for gas

By TIM UNRUH
The Salina Journal

Someone from Oklahoma City called someone in Salina about gasoline prices soaring, who told neighbors, co-workers and friends.

Radio stations were alerted, as were news organizations, which spread the news.

Then all hell broke loose.

Vehicles lined up Tuesday at fuel outlets around Salina. It became busy just before 3 p.m. at the Green Lantern convenience store, Ninth and Crawford. A line stretched more than a block from there south to Franklin Elementary School.

They filled the store's parking lot as folks waited 20 minutes or more for a tank of gas.

"It's five bucks (a gallon) at Great Bend already," said John Halpain, 617 Stoehlin, who works at Tony's Pizza Service in Salina. "I should've known something like this would happen."

Actually, the price in Great Bend ranged from $1.75 to $1.89 a gallon, said Lisa Whipple, a pharmacist in the Barton County seat.

Five-dollar gas, she said, "was just somebody's big story," but there were long lines.

RYAN SODERLIN / The Salina Journal
Salinans line up Tuesday at the Sinclair station, Ninth and Claflin, to fill up after rumors of skyrocketing gas prices spread.

See GAS, Page A10

WEATHER
High: 82 Low: 60
Sunny today with southeast wind 5 to 10 mph.

PAGE B3
Air traffic around the nation was halted Tuesday as stunned travelers watched televised pictures of the terrorists' attacks.

PAGE D6
The cost of mailing a letter will go up again next year, jumping 3 cents to 37 cents as the Postal Service tries to overcome a $1.65 billion deficit.

INSIDE
Classified / C3
Comics / C10
Crossword / C10
Deaths / A4

Food / C1
Lottery / A4
Money / D8
Sports / D1
Weather / C9
Viewpoints / A9

College Heights **Herald** Extra

Volume 77, Number 7   Western Kentucky University ◆ Bowling Green, Kentucky 42101   Wednesday, September 12, 2001

9.11.01

42

Getty Images

"THIS IS THE SECOND PEARL HARBOR. I DON'T THINK THAT I OVERSTATE IT."
Sen. Chuck Hagel, R-Neb.

EXTRA

"TERRORISM AGAINST OUR NATION WILL NOT STAND."
President Bush, who was in Florida at the time of the attacks and was taken immediately to a secure military base in Louisiana.

LEXINGTON
HERALD-LEADER

Tuesday, September 11, 2001   www.kentucky.com   Metro Final Edition • 50¢

Terrorists strike

2 hijacked planes destroy Trade Center; one hits Pentagon

'Horrendous number' of lives feared lost; U.S. airports closed

By Jerry Schwartz
ASSOCIATED PRESS

NEW YORK — In an apparent terrorist attack, two airliners were hijacked and crashed into the World Trade Center this morning, collapsing the twin 110-story towers. A plane also slammed into the Pentagon, raising fears that the seat of government itself was under attack.

"I have a sense it's a horrendous number of lives lost," Mayor Rudolph Giuliani said. "Right now we have to focus on saving as many lives as possible."

Authorities had been trying to evacuate those who work in the twin towers, but many were thought to have been trapped. About 50,000 people work at the Trade Center. American Airlines said its two aircraft were carrying a total of 156 people.

"This is perhaps the most audacious terrorist attack that's ever taken place in the world," said Chris Yates, an aviation expert at Jane's Transport in London. "It takes a logistics operation from the terror group involved that is second to none. Only a very small handful of terror groups is on that list. ... I would name at the top of the list Osama bin Laden."

President Bush ordered a full-scale investigation to hunt down the perpetrators.

Within the hour, the Pentagon took a direct, devastating hit from an aircraft. The fiery crash collapsed one side of the five-sided structure.

The White House, the Pentagon and the Capitol were evacuated along with other federal buildings in Washington and New York.

The Federal Aviation Administration closed all the nation's airports, for the first time in history, and ordered all U.S.-based airlines to cancel domestic and international flights until at least 6 p.m.

Airlines with flights in the air were to told land their planes at the nearest available airport.

The one exception was Pittsburgh International Airport, which the FAA said was a security threat, ac-
See **ATTACK, back page**

What happened

American Airlines Flight 11: A Boeing 767 en route from Boston to Los Angeles crashes into Tower 1 of the World Trade Center at 8:50 a.m. The plane was carrying 81 passengers, nine flight attendants and two pilots.

American Airlines Flight 77: A Boeing 757 en route from Dulles Airport near Washington to Los Angeles crashes into Tower 2 of the World Trade Center at 9:05 a.m. The plane was carrying 58 passengers, four flight attendants and two pilots. Both 110-story towers eventually collapse upon themselves.

Within the hour a passenger aircraft of undetermined size crashes into the side of the Pentagon. The attacks trigger immediate security measures in the Washington area, including evacuation of the White House, the State Department and the Capitol building.

United Airlines Flight 93: A Boeing 757 crashes southeast of Pittsburgh while en route from Newark, N.J., to San Francisco. The plane was carrying 38 passengers, two pilots and five flight attendants.

United Airlines Flight 175: A Boeing 767 bound from Boston to Los Angeles crashes at an undisclosed location. It was carrying 56 passengers, two pilots and seven flight attendants.

■ The Federal Aviation Administration closes all the nation's airports for the first time in history and orders all U.S.-based airlines to cancel domestic and international flights until at least 6 p.m.

■ The U.S. financial markets halt all trading.

■ Vice President Dick Cheney, national security adviser Condoleezza Rice and other top federal officials huddle in the wake of the terrorist attacks. The Federal Emergency Management Agency opens its operation center to respond to the attacks.

KELLY GUENTHER/ASSOCIATED PRESS
This sequence shows the approach of the second aircraft that crashed into the World Trade Center towers this morning, followed by the explosion. The two planes hit the towers with 18 minutes.

SUZANNE PLUNKETTE/ ASSOCIATED PRESS
People ran from the collapse of one of the 110-story World Trade Center towers in Manhattan this morning. Both towers collapsed after they were hit by hijacked airplanes.

43

7 01540 10891 0

>KNIGHTRIDDER>   INFORMATION FOR LIFE

The Times-Picayune

50 CENTS 165th year No. 232 | **WEDNESDAY, SEPTEMBER 12, 2001** | **METRO EDITION**

TERROR HITS HOME

DARKEST DAY

44

It's the beginning of a horrible end as the towers of the World Trade Center, packed with thousands of New Yorkers just beginning their work day, erupt in flame and smoke Tuesday morning after being hit by two airplanes. Both towers later collapsed, spewing ash, glass, steel and smoke through the streets of Manhattan. 'The number of casualties will be more than most of us can bear,' said a distraught Mayor Rudolph Giuliani.

NEW YORK TIMES PHOTO

NEW YORK
HIJACKED JETS BLAST TOWERS INTO FIERY RUBBLE

WASHINGTON
Third plane slices into Pentagon

PENNSYLVANIA
Fourth airliner crashes outside Pittsburgh

By Serge Schmemann
©2001, The New York Times

NEW YORK — Hijackers rammed jetliners into each of New York's World Trade Center towers Tuesday morning, toppling both in a hellish storm of ash, glass, smoke and leaping victims, while a third jetliner crashed into the Pentagon in Virginia.

There was no official count, but President Bush said thousands had perished, and in the immediate aftermath the calamity was already being ranked as the worst and most audacious terror attack in American history.

The attacks seemed carefully coordinated. The hijacked planes were all en route to California, and therefore gorged with fuel, and their departures were spaced within an hour and 40 minutes. The first, American Airlines Flight 11, a Boeing 767 out of Boston for Los Angeles, crashed into the north tower at 8:48 a.m. Eighteen minutes later, United Airlines Flight 175, also headed from Boston to Los Angeles, plowed into the south tower.

Then an American Airlines Boeing 757 left Washington's Dulles International Airport bound for Los Angeles but instead hit the western part of the Pentagon, the military headquarters where 24,000 people work, at 9:40 a.m. Finally, United Airlines Flight 93, a Boeing 757 flying from Newark, N.J., to San Francisco, crashed near Pittsburgh.

See **TERROR,** *A-5*

METRO: A STUNNED COMMUNITY MOURNS AND PRAYS
MONEY: THE AILING ECONOMY SUFFERS ANOTHER BLOW
SPORTS: THE SPORTING WORLD IS PUT ON HOLD, TOO

Bangor Daily News

It's what you need. To know.

Our 113th Year • Issue 75　　　Wednesday, September 12, 2001　　　34 Pages • 60 Cents

AP PHOTOS/ABC

Terror Hits Home

Machias native flees burning skyscraper

By Mary Anne Clancy
Of the NEWS Staff

Moments after the first plane crashed Tuesday, 22-year-old Lisle Leonard called her mom in Machias from her 34th-floor office in New York City's World Trade Center.

"She said it happened two minutes ago and she could see the shrapnel and glass flying by her window," said her mother, Sissy Leonard. Her daughter thought a bomb had exploded. "I told her to get out of there."

But Lisle, a 2000 graduate of Bowdoin College, said the stock market hadn't opened and that she and her co-workers with a Japanese securities firm were going to stay put. So the mother and daughter hung up, and Sissy turned on the TV set in Machias. She also called her other daughter, Sarah, who lives in Brooklyn Heights, just one subway stop away from the World Trade Center.

> "MUMMY, I JUST HEARD ANOTHER EXPLOSION."
>
> — Sarah Leonard, Brooklyn Heights, on phone to her mother in Machias

As Sissy was telling 25-year-old Sarah that she'd spoken to Lisle and she was all right, her daughter interrupted: "Mummy, I just heard another explosion."

Michael and Sissy Leonard were counting their blessings Tuesday after learning later in the day that Lisle had escaped from the World Trade Center just moments before the building collapsed.

The couple spent a harrowing half-hour Tuesday morning after seeing television video of a plane crashing into the tower where their daughter worked as a bond analyst for the securities firm Nomura.

Michael Leonard, who is a lawyer, was just returning to the family home from the Washington County Courthouse, where he had heard about the World Trade Center attack.

"I called Lisle's cell phone, but there
See Sisters, Page A12

AP PHOTO BY ERNESTO MORA

Two women (above) hold each other as they watch the World Trade Center burn after a terrorist attack on the twin skyscrapers in New York City on Tuesday. In a series of television images (top, from left), a second hijacked aircraft approaches and strikes the other tower.

Hijackers use passenger jets as weapons against U.S.

By David Crary And Jerry Schwartz
The Associated Press

NEW YORK — In the most devastating terrorist onslaught ever waged against the United States, knife-wielding hijackers crashed two airliners into the World Trade Center on Tuesday, toppling its twin 110-story towers. The deadly calamity was witnessed on television across the world as another plane slammed into the Pentagon, and a fourth crashed outside Pittsburgh.

"Today, our nation saw evil," President Bush said in an address to the nation Tuesday night. He said thousands of lives were "suddenly ended by evil, despicable acts of terror."

Said Adm. Robert J. Natter, commander of the U.S. Atlantic Fleet: "We have been attacked like we haven't since Pearl Harbor."

Establishing the U.S. death toll could take weeks. The four airliners alone had 266 people aboard and there were no known survivors. Sources said that about 100 people were believed dead at the Pentagon, but NBC News, quoting other Pentagon sources, listed the casualties there at more than 800.

In addition, a firefighters union official said he feared 300 firefighters who first reached the scene had died in rescue efforts at the World Trade Center — where 55,000 people worked — and dozens of police officers were believed missing.

"The number of casualties will be more than most of us can bear," a visibly distraught Mayor Rudolph Giuliani said.

"We have entire companies that are just missing."
See Terror, Page A2

Twin towers fall

Within an hour and a half of a terrorist attack, both towers of the World Trade Center in lower Manhattan collapsed.

AP

Edition
City/Penobscot

13781 12345

© 2001 Bangor Publishing Co.
Periodicals postage paid at
Bangor, Maine 04401
Publication number
USPS 041000

Gov. King shuts down government as precaution

By A.J. Higgins
Of the NEWS Staff

AUGUSTA — As sentries stood watch outside Maine National Guard headquarters in Augusta, a stony-faced Gov. Angus S. King arrived Tuesday morning to brief reporters on how a terrorist attack hundreds of miles away had shut down state government.

"I'd like to take a moment to reflect on the families of those who were the unfortunate and unwitting targets of this cowardly attack," King said before a brief prayer and a moment of silence.

A little more than a half-hour after the Federal Aviation Administration's 9:50 a.m. decision to shut down the Portland International Jetport and Bangor International Airport, the governor and legislative leaders closed the State House and Cross State Office Building.

More than 5,000 state workers streamed out of the two office complexes toward their cars in the nearby parking lots, quickly choking the capital's major arteries with home-bound traffic.

From the basement of the National Guard headquarters, which also houses the control center for the Maine Emergency Management Agency, King downplayed a possible terrorist threat here, at the same time he was assembling his emergency response team.

"We have heard from the FBI that there is no intelligence whatsoever that there is any threat to Maine," King said. "Of course there were
See Maine, Page A8

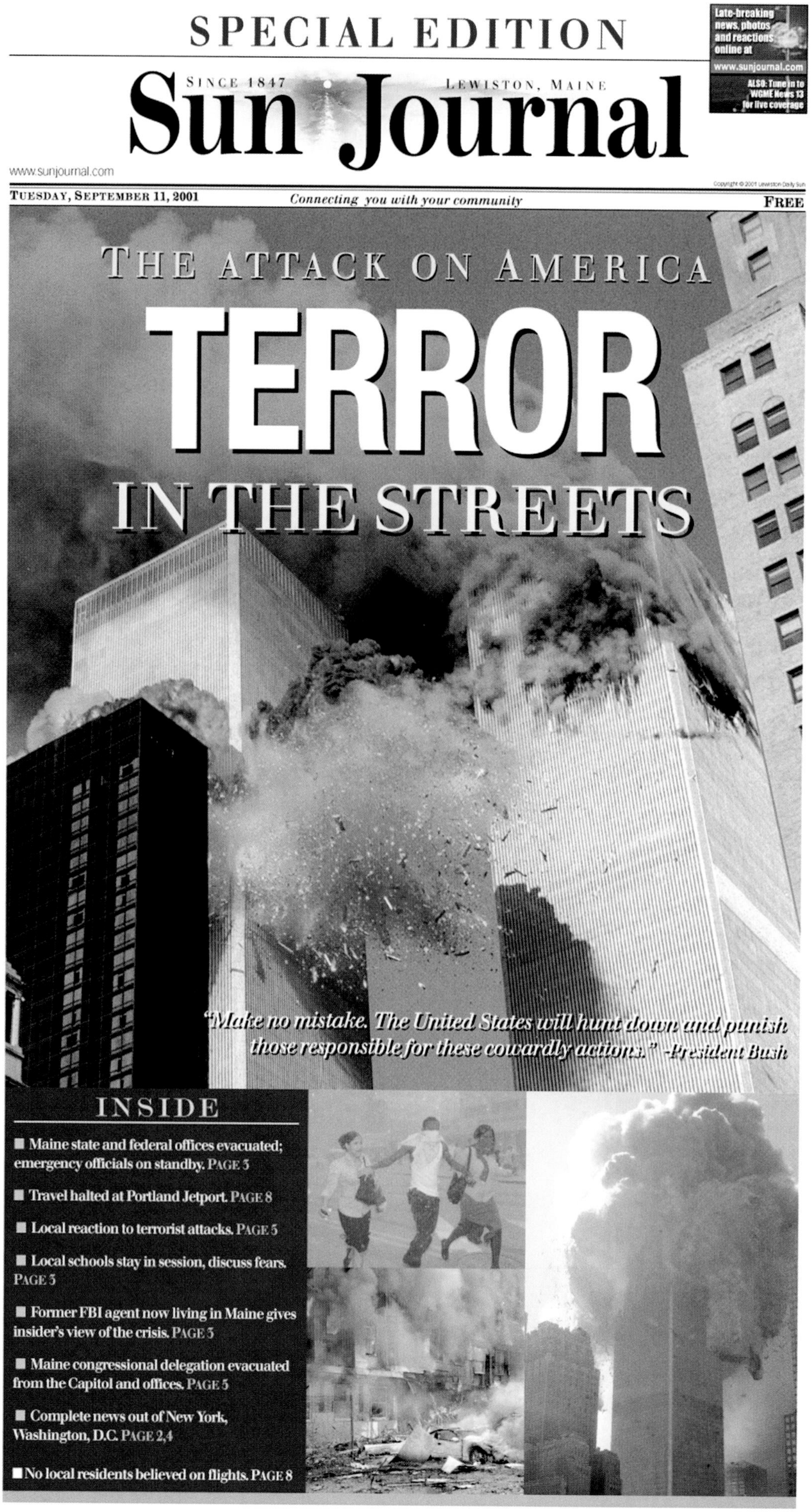

SPECIAL EDITION

Late-breaking news, photos and reactions online at www.sunjournal.com

ALSO: Tune in to WGME News 13 for live coverage

Sun Journal

SINCE 1847 · LEWISTON, MAINE

www.sunjournal.com

Copyright © 2001 Lewiston Daily Sun

TUESDAY, SEPTEMBER 11, 2001   *Connecting you with your community*   **FREE**

46

THE ATTACK ON AMERICA

TERROR
IN THE STREETS

"Make no mistake. The United States will hunt down and punish those responsible for these cowardly actions." -President Bush

INSIDE

■ Maine state and federal offices evacuated; emergency officials on standby. PAGE 3

■ Travel halted at Portland Jetport. PAGE 8

■ Local reaction to terrorist attacks. PAGE 5

■ Local schools stay in session, discuss fears. PAGE 3

■ Former FBI agent now living in Maine gives insider's view of the crisis. PAGE 3

■ Maine congressional delegation evacuated from the Capitol and offices. PAGE 5

■ Complete news out of New York, Washington, D.C. PAGE 2,4

■ No local residents believed on flights. PAGE 8

FINAL
★★★★★

THE ☼ SUN

Wednesday, September 12, 2001 — Baltimore, Maryland — 50 cents

DEVASTATION

Destruction: *Smoke billows from the World Trade Center towers after hijacked airliners struck them. Within two hours of the attack, both had collapsed.*

SPENCER PLATT : GETTY IMAGES

Hijacked planes destroy World Trade Center towers

Third jetliner slams into Pentagon

Thousands feared dead in worst U.S. terror attacks

By Dan Fesperman
and Cheryl Lu-Lien Tan
SUN NATIONAL STAFF

NEW YORK — Terrorists carried out the most destructive attack on the United States in history yesterday, a horrifying rain of four hijacked airliners that toppled both towers of the World Trade Center in New York and destroyed a section of the Pentagon.

Although the death toll won't be known for days, thousands were believed dead, including 266 aboard the planes, hundreds of firefighters and police missing in the rubble in New York and scores of people in the 1,300-foot-plus-high towers, where about 50,000 worked.

At the Pentagon, a source said, "the services believe they have fewer than 500 unaccounted for," including military, civilian and contract personnel.

Buildings in Manhattan's financial district were still burning late last night, as was a part of the Pentagon.

The fiery assault on prominent symbols of the nation's financial and martial strength jolted the nation. Airports, schools, government buildings and virtually every place a large crowd might gather were closed, and comparisons were made to the bombing of Pearl Harbor in 1941.

This time the enemy is unknown and the response uncertain, although President Bush signaled last night in a nationwide address that he hasn't ruled out a broad retaliation, saying, "We will make no distinction between the terrorists who committed these acts, and those who harbor them."

As Bush   [See Terror, 8A]

AGENCE FRANCE-PRESSE
President Bush *speaks to the nation from the Oval Office. (Text of address, Page 6A)*

Jet flies headlong into the Pentagon

Plane carrying 64 shears freeway lights before crashing

'Still taking bodies out'

By Paul West
SUN NATIONAL STAFF

WASHINGTON — The nation's capital came under deadly terrorist assault yesterday morning when a hijacked jetliner flew full-throttle into the Pentagon, the storied seat of U.S. military power. Scores were killed and dozens injured.

The crash, part of a coordinated terrorist attack on the United States, took place less than an hour after two other hijacked commercial jets tore into the World Trade Center towers in New York City, with devastating results. A fourth jet, which also may have been targeted at Washington, crashed in southwestern Pennsylvania as it headed toward the capital.

President Bush was out of town at the time of the attack. He learned of the initial strikes, on New York, while visiting an elementary school in Sarasota, Fla.

After delivering a brief statement condemning the assault, Bush was flown to air force bases in Louisiana and Nebraska as a security precaution.

He arrived back at the White House last night and addressed the nation from the   [See Washington, 12A]

---

17 pages inside

Chaos: From Manhattan to BWI to the Capitol, life's routines yield to nightmare. [*Pages 4-20A*]

Weather

Mostly sunny. High, 78; low, 59. Yesterday's city high, 83; low, 66. [*Page 24B*]

SunSpot

The Sun on the Internet:
http://www.sunspot.net

The Sun's 165th Year:
Number 255

On warm Md. day, chill of fear spreads

Heightened alert empties schools, offices across state

Frantic calls to D.C., N.Y.

By Michael James
SUN STAFF

The ripples of terror spread throughout Maryland yesterday as the unbelievable sank in, a realization that sent horrified parents flocking to get their children from schools, state officials scrambling to move government out of Annapolis, and police with submachine guns patrolling around downtown Baltimore's World Trade Center.

For millions of Marylanders, the unprecedented terrorist attacks in New York and outside Washington left apocalyptic images of burning buildings in their minds, and left many wondering what today will bring.

"This is turning the world upside down as we know it," said Donald R. Howell of Howard County, who heads a nonprofit agency that works with rescue workers and others in the wake of disasters. "This will traumatize the nation like no other event has in our recent history. We're seeing it as it happens."

Maryland Gov. Parris N. Glendening took the extraordinary step of evacuating government offices in Annapolis, including the State House, and the World Trade Center at the Inner Harbor because of fears that they could be terrorist targets.

In Baltimore, Mayor Martin O'Malley said city officials were on the highest state of alert   [See Maryland, 15A]

Aftermath

Everything changed yesterday

■ **Vulnerable:** *By midmorning, we were already a country wistful for its sense of security.*

By Michael Ollove
SUN STAFF

Yesterday, September 11th, 2001, will be remembered as the day America stopped feeling like America.

No longer can we tell ourselves that we are safe simply because we live in the United States. No more can we cling to the faith that our military and economic might are sufficient to protect us from our enemies. Never again can we derive comfort from our geographic remoteness.

Everything changed yesterday. Lying in the rubble that was the World Trade Center is the American sense of well-being.

"This will be a transforming event," said Steven Da-

vid, a professor of international relations at the Johns Hopkins University, as much in disbelief as people across the nation.

We are vulnerable, and vulnerability has rarely squared

with America's self-image.

"The notion that Americans as a people are in jeopardy flits poorly with the national sense of self and its sense of destiny," said Todd Git-   [See Vulnerable, 14A]

ASSOCIATED PRESS
In horror: *Two women console each other on a New York street as they watch the World Trade Center burn.*

0 08345 00003 7
1 2 3 4 L

SPECIAL EDITION

WEDNESDAY
SEPTEMBER 12, 2001

The Diamondback

92ND YEAR
ISSUE NO. 10

A t about 8:45 a.m. yesterday, Americans were shocked as a hijacked passenger jet plowed through the north tower of the World Trade Center in New York. Eighteen minutes later, as flames swarmed up the pillar of capitalism, a second jet pulverized the other tower; both collapsed within an hour. Millions stared in disbelief as they discovered a third plane had plunged into the epicenter of national defense and a fourth had crashed away from the national icons the world suddenly no longer took for granted. All had been sent on a kamikaze mission for an unknown cause. The images, sounds and stories of the second Tuesday in September of 2001 will be seared forever in the nation's memory.

AMERICAN TRAGEDY

Terror strikes home in an unprecedented attack on U.S. soil as thousands perish at the whim of a faceless faction. Sadness and anger sweep across the country as our culture and way of life are threatened. Complete coverage inside.

EXTRA EDITION

VOLUME 260
NUMBER 73
50 cents
* *

The Boston Globe

TUESDAY, SEPTEMBER 11, 2001

THE WEATHER
TODAY: *Mix of sun and clouds,* high 74-79
TOMORROW: *Mostly sunny,* high 75-80
HIGH TIDE: 5:54 a.m., 6:10 p.m.
FULL REPORT: PAGE B12

Reign of terror

Concerted attacks destroy World Trade Center; plane hits Pentagon; thousands are feared dead

AP PHOTOS

A plane approaching the World Trade Center and then crashing in a ball of fire.

Southeast of Pittsburgh
10 a.m.: United Flight 93 from Newark crashes

Boston
8 a.m.: American Airlines Flight 11 and United Flight 175 hijacked.

New York
8:45 a.m. Plane hits North tower and at about **9:00 a.m.** South tower hit by another plane. Both towers collapse by **10:28 a.m.**

Virginia
8:10 a.m.: American Flight 77 hijacked from Dulles; **9:40 a.m.** Pentagon hit by an aircraft

GLOBE STAFF GRAPHIC / JIM KARAMN

Bin Laden at top of suspects list

By Charles M. Sennott
GLOBE STAFF

LONDON — Who was behind the most devastating terror attack ever carried out against the United States?

The highest security officials in the United States — some operating out of institutions that were targeted, including the Pentagon and State Department — worked against time today to pinpoint the perpetrators. There has so far been no confirmed claim of responsibility.

But experts on terrorism were cautiously making assessments as to who had the capability of coordinating an attack on such a scale, and most agreed it would more than likely be a constellation of terrorist groups opposed to American foreign policy in the Middle East.

Several said an attack of such sophistication and coordination would require massive funding and years of planning. The attack included two airplanes crashing into New York's World Trade Center, a plane crashing into the Pentagon, and another plane crash outside of Pittsburgh.

The immediate timing and message behind the attacks was uncertain, but most experts linked them to surging anger across the Muslim world at US foreign policy in the Middle East and specifically over its failure, as many militant organizations see it, to restrain Israel in its military effort to quell a Palestinian uprising that began one year ago this month.

TERROR, Page A3

For breaking news, updated Globe stories, and more, visit:

Boston.com

0 947725 4 37222

REUTERS PHOTO

Firefighters working amid the rubble of the World Trade Center this afternoon after both towers collapsed.

By Anne Barnard,
Liz Kowalczyk,
and Elizabeth Neuffer
GLOBE STAFF

NEW YORK — The twin towers of the World Trade Center were destroyed this morning after two airplanes crashed into them, in what seems to have been the largest terrorist attack in history. The raid, followed by a plane that crashed into the Pentagon and another plane crash outside Pittsburgh, prompted comparisons to the Japanese attack on Pearl Harbor in 1941.

Police estimated that casualties in New York alone were in the thousands, and airlines said that four crashed planes had carried a total of 266 passengers and crew.

New York's mayor, Rudolph W. Giuliani, said there had been no threat or warning of the attack. He asked people in other parts of the city to go about their business.

Less than an hour after two passenger airplanes — at least one hijacked from Boston — crashed into the World Trade Center, another hit the Pentagon, the nerve center of the US military, in northern Virginia.

A bit later, a United Airlines flight bound from Newark to San Francisco crashed southeast of Pittsburgh.

Initially, American said both planes that hit the World Trade Center were theirs, Flight 11 from Boston to Los Angeles and Flight 77 from Washington to Los Angeles. But the United pilots' union said that United Flight 175 had also struck the tower, leaving some confusion as to where the planes had crashed.

In Washington, officials denied a report of a car bomb explosion

CRASH, Page A2

Two flights from Logan are hijacked

By Stephen Kurkjian
and Raphael Lewis
GLOBE STAFF

Two jets that left Boston's Logan International Airport this morning — American Airlines Flight 11, with 92 people aboard, and United Airlines Flight 175, carrying 65 people — were hijacked, and airline officials said both planes had crashed.

United officials have yet to disclose where Flight 175, a Boeing 767 that departed at 7:45 a.m., went down.

The American Airlines flight was one of two aircraft that slammed into New York's World Trade Center towers, both of which later collapsed into rubble.

On board American's Flight 11 were 81 passengers, nine flight attendants, and two pilots, said Laura Mayo, a spokeswoman for American Airlines. All are believed to be dead. Mayo said that because of this morning's events — the flight was one of two American jets that crashed today — the airline has been advised by the federal government not to release details yet.

However, Donald J. Carty, American's chief executive, issued a statement that said: "We are horrified by the tragic events. Our thoughts and prayers go out to the families of all involved."

American Airlines Flight 11 left at 7:59 a.m., on time for a nonstop flight to Los Angeles, according to a Massport official.

LOGAN, Page A2

Inside

Boston shutdowns
Logan International Airport is closed and workers and residents of some high-rise buildings are evacuated. **A3.**

Suspects sought
Authorities in Boston began searching for a terrorist cell that carried out the most crucial part of the attack. **A6.**

Capital chaos
In Washington, desperate questions punctuate the shock — questions about how and why — along with sirens, screams of fear, and rumors. **A6.**

Election is on
The 9th Congressional District special primary proceeds as scheduled despite Secretary of State William F. Galvin's attempt to suspend voting. **A7.**

Full coverage, A2-9.

AP PHOTO

Crowds fleeing the collapse of the World Trade Center this morning.

The Harvard Crimson

The University Daily Since 1873
CAMBRIDGE, MASSACHUSETTS

WEDNESDAY, SEPTEMBER 12, 2001

www.thecrimson.com
THIRTY CENTS

50

TERRORISTS ATTACK AMERICA, THOUSANDS FEARED DEAD

World Trade Center destroyed; Pentagon severely damaged

Despite Attack, University Stays Open

By GARRETT M. GRAFF
and KATE L. RAKOCZY
CRIMSON STAFF WRITERS

As students and administrators grapple with the scope of the largest terrorist attack ever on U.S. soil, University officials are responding to the unprecedented events.

Immediately after yesterday's attacks, University officials set up a command post in Holyoke Center and beefed up staffing at the Operations Center that oversees facilities. The Harvard University Police Department (HUPD) also added patrols and briefed President Lawrence H. Summers on security threats and concerns around the campus.

"The University is, of course, very concerned about the safety of the campus," HUPD spokesperson Steven G. Catalano said.

Many HUPD officers were called in early or asked to stay late last night to

Please see **UNIVERSITY**, *page* **5**

University Plans Blood Donations

By JULIET J. CHUNG
CRIMSON STAFF WRITER

University Health Services (UHS) is planning a University-wide blood drive in coordination with the American Red Cross in response to yesterday's events. Initial plans are for buses to take donors to Massachusetts General Hospital (MGH), Brigham and Women's Hospital and other donation sites during the next several days.

Buses will pick people up from Cambridge and the Business School, Times and locations are still to be determined.

The blood drive is an alternative to what many have been hoping to do—give blood independently at the Red Cross or at hospitals. Indeed, interest in giving blood has been so overwhelming that the Red Cross has asked potential donors to wait

Please see **BLOOD**, *page* **6** **TERROR:** *Rescue workers search through the debris of one of the collapsed World Trade Center towers in New York City yesterday.*

Two Hijacked Planes Took Off From Logan

By IMTIYAZ H. DELAWALA and DANIELA J. LAMAS
SPECIAL TO THE CRIMSON

BOSTON—In the most deadly and horrific attack on the United States in its 225-year history, terrorists crashed two hijacked passenger jets into the World Trade Center towers in New York City, toppling the 110-story structures in a cloud of smoke and ash yesterday morning. Less than an hour later, another passenger jet crashed into the Pentagon in Washington, D.C. in an unprecedented attack upon the U.S. government.

221 passengers aboard the jets used in the attacks were killed, with an unknown number—most likely ranging in the thousands—killed in the three targeted buildings. A fourth hijacked jet crashed near Pittsburgh, Penn., killing an additional 45 people.

"Today we've had a national tragedy," President George W. Bush said from Sarasota, Fla. yesterday morning as reports of the attacks began filtering in.

At 8 a.m. EST, American Airlines Flight 11, carrying 92 people from Boston's Logan Airport, crashed into the north tower of the World Trade Center, igniting the top stories of the building in a ball of fire.

Eighteen minutes later, United Airlines Flight 175, carrying 65 people bound for Los Angeles, crashed into the south tower of the center.

The two crashes covered the New York City skyline in billowing smoke and flames, as hundreds of New Yorkers began streaming out of the twin steel and glass structures.

But before all of the nearly 50,000 World Trade Center employees could evacuate, the two towers collapsed to the ground in a scene similar to a staged building implosion, covering the downtown business district in ash and debris less than 90 minutes after the initial plane impacts.

Ten minutes before the south tower collapsed, an apparently coordinated strike occurred in the nation's capital, as American Airlines Flight 77 crashed into a wall of the Pentagon, the

Please see **HIJACKINGS**, *page* **6**

EMERGENCY CONTACTS

Families looking for information about victims and about services for survivors can call the phone line set up by the Justice Department's Office of Victims of Crime, at (800) 331-0075.

Families of passengers on American Airlines flights can call (800) 245-0999 for information. Family of passengers on United Airlines can call (800) 932-8555.

For mental health counseling, call University Health Services at (617) 495-2042 from 8 a.m. to 6 p.m. and (617) 495-5711 from 6 p.m. to 8 a.m.

Those wishing to donate blood or other goods should e-mail donations@uhs.harvard.edu with contact information and donation type. If blood, specify blood type. For updated information on the University-wide blood drive, check out www.uhs.harvard.edu.

Those wishing to donate blood are advised by the American Red Cross to call (800) GIVE-LIFE after Thursday. To donate cash or other goods, call (800) HELP-NOW.

To donate to The September Eleventh Fund, set up by the United Way of New York and the New York Community Trust to help victims and their families, call (212) 251-4035.

Students who missed Harvard Registration yesterday are advised to contact their Allston Burr Senior Tutor. They will likely not incur any penalties or late fees.

BREAKING NEWS:

The Boston Herald reported this morning that Massachusetts authorities have identified five Arab men as suspects in yesterday's terrorist hijackings and attacks. The five men include two brothers with passports traced to the United Arab Emirates, and two who flew to Logan International Airport yesterday from Portland, Maine. An FBI spokesperson would neither confirm nor deny the Herald's report.

GETTING BY

TODAY: Sunny, high in the low 70s.
TOMORROW: Mostly sunny, high of 75.

For breaking news and updated stories, visit HTTP://WWW.THECRIMSON.COM
Newsroom (617) 576-6565 | Business (617) 576-6600
Copyright ©2001 The Harvard Crimson Inc.

Terrorist Acts Stun, Sadden Harvard Students

By EUGENIA V. LEVENSON
and EUGENIA B. SCHRAA
CRIMSON STAFF WRITERS

After a tense and difficult day trying to get in touch with family and friends, many Harvard students affected by yesterday's attacks on the World Trade Center and the Pentagon gathered for a University-wide vigil on the steps of Memorial Church last night which attracted more than 3000 members of the Harvard community.

Many had spent the day trying to reach family members and friends, while others stayed glued to television, radios, and the Internet to learn about the latest developments.

Across campus, early phone calls from parents roused many students from their beds.

"My mom called and forced my roommate to wake me up," said Eugene Chislenko '04. "I believed her barely enough to go watch it on television."

"At first, I just laughed. I thought it was another stupid little crash like that parachute over the Statue of Liberty," said Mark J. Stanisz '05. "But then the [New York Times] website started crashing, and I saw that something was very wrong."

Some students were registering for classes in Sever Hall or en route to meetings and rehearsals in preparation for the first day of

Please see **REACTION**, *page* **6**

MOURNING: *Harvard students attend yesterday's Harvard prayer vigil.*

WEDNESDAY, SEPTEMBER 12, 2001

Detroit Free Press

METRO FINAL ✦✦✦   ON GUARD FOR 170 YEARS   50 cents outside 6-county metropolitan area 35 cents

WWW.FREEP.COM

AMERICA'S DARKEST DAY

SHOCK WAVES
Tuesday's attack caused many Detroit area schools, workplaces, courts and shopping malls to close. Some will reopen today.
PAGES 4A-5A

A RUSH ON GAS
Worried motorists line up for gasoline, and some stations charge up to $5.
PAGE 13A

MITCH ALBOM
We've all been hijacked, he writes. Rochelle Riley, Desiree Cooper and Brian Dickerson also comment. **PAGE 12A**

SURVIVOR'S TALE
Michigan native was on 30th floor of World Trade Center but escaped to safety.
PAGE 8A

THE ECONOMY
Consumers and markets are likely to recoil, Susan Tompor writes. Plus other fallout for banking, trading and for brokerages. **PAGE 7A**

FLIGHTS HALTED
Metro Airport and the nation's air traffic system are shut down until at least noon today. Airports may soon turn into armed camps. **PAGE 6A**

EDITORIAL
Free Press readers and Mike Thompson react to the tragedy.
PAGES 14A-15A

MATTHEW McDERMOTT/Corbis Sygma

IN RUINS: With the skeleton of the World Trade Center looming behind them, firefighters search through the rubble left by the terrorist attack.

Terrorists will be hunted down, Bush tells the nation

FREE PRESS NEWS SERVICES

Photo from ABC-TV

MOMENT OF IMPACT: As one of the World Trade Center towers burns after being hit by a hijacked jet, another jet approaches the second tower, obscured behind the first. A split second later, the second tower erupted into a fire ball. Many people jumped to their deaths before the towers collapsed.

In the worst attack ever on the United States, terrorists struck Tuesday at the symbols of American financial and military might, using hijacked jetliners as suicide missiles to level the twin towers of the World Trade Center in New York City and blast into the Pentagon outside Washington, D.C.

Not since Pearl Harbor has a day suggested such infamy. A red-eyed President George W. Bush went before the nation Tuesday night to mourn the victims and promise justice.

The day was filled with horror from the moment television broke into morning programs to tell viewers that an airplane had struck a tower at the World Trade Center. Then, with a stunned nation watching, a second plane struck the second tower. An hour later, with cameras focused on the burning buildings, one of the towers collapsed; 30 minutes later, the second one followed.

At no time in the nation's history had such a calamity been so instantly shared with the entire country, which watched riveted.

Cities came to virtual standstills as office workers and schoolchildren saw the disasters unfold on television.

Reports began to course through news circuits that the Pentagon had been at-

tacked, that the State Department and White House were being evacuated, and that the U.S. Capitol may be a target.

In an unprecedented move, the government ordered all commercial flights grounded.

By 2:15 p.m., only military aircraft and Air Force One were in the air.

When Bush's plane landed at a military base in Nebraska, he told the National Security Council: "We will find these people and they will suffer the consequences of taking on this nation. We will do what it takes. No one is going to diminish the spirit of this country."

The stunning attacks led to an evacuation of key government buildings

Please see TERROR, Page 13A

15 PAGES OF COVERAGE IN SECTION A   **PLUS** WHAT YOU CAN DO. 1C
NO TIME FOR GAMES. 1D

7 8 9 10 11 12 13 14 15 A B C D E F

>KNIGHT RIDDER>   *INFORMATION FOR LIFE*

The Detroit News

29 PAGES OF TERROR COVERAGE INSIDE

Wednesday, September 12, 2001   www.detnews.com   7 8 9 10 11 12 13 14 15   **Metro Edition**

"These acts shattered steel, but they cannot dent the steel of American resolve."
PRESIDENT GEORGE W. BUSH

Terror Sweeps U.S.

"It's shocking to think human life is so cheap to these people."
ANDREW GRAY, *rescue worker in New York City*

Stuart Ramson / Associated Press
The Statue of Liberty is backshadowed by smoke billowing from the World Trade Center.

Ernesto Mora / Associated Press
Shock and grief swept New York after the attack.

Tom Horan / Associated Press
The Pentagon in Washington, D.C., burns after another hijacked jetliner plowed into it.

AMERICA SAVAGED, FOREVER CHANGED

| Hijacked airliners devastate World Trade Center, Pentagon | Bush praises America's resolve, vows retaliation against 'evil acts' | Americans face uncertainty as terrorism changes landscape |

Essay

Nation reels in new face of war

By Ron French
The Detroit News

More than the New York skyline changed Tuesday.

When hijacked airliners crashed into our national psyche, the American landscape changed forever.

In one cruel morning, any notion of America being invincible was buried in the rubble. And the morning after, we awaken to an America with a shattered sense of security, a people bound together by grief, anger and resolve.

In the smoke and the flames, we saw a future less certain, less safe, than any this generation has known.

It was made-for-TV terror, death brought live into the kitchens and offices of a stunned nation. Thousands may have lost their lives, and millions may have lost their way.

"I don't know how to cope with this," said Vincent Sciarrino, manager of Westborn Market in Berkley.

Please see ESSAY, Page 17A

Shawn Baldwin / Associated Press
New York firefighters wade through the rubble of the World Trade Center after two airliners crashed into the twin towers Tuesday morning, bringing down the landmark buildings and killing yet-unreported numbers of people.

Detroit News wire services

NEW YORK

The most devastating terrorist attack ever waged against the United States struck at the heart of government and financial capitals Tuesday as hijacked commercial jets plowed into the twin World Trade Center towers in New York and the Pentagon outside Washington.

"We have been attacked like we haven't since Pearl Harbor," said Adm. Robert J. Natter, commander of the U.S. Atlantic Fleet.

Establishing the death toll could take weeks, but it is expected that casualties will be in the thousands. There were reports that six people had been rescued overnight.

President Bush condemned the attacks in an Oval Office address to the nation Tuesday night, vowing to "find those responsible and bring them to justice." Bush said the United States would retaliate against "those behind these evil acts," and any country that harbors them.

Seeking to comfort an anxious nation, he said, "These acts shattered steel, but they cannot dent the steel of American resolve."

U.S. officials began piecing together a case linking Islamic fundamentalist Osama bin Laden to the attack. They were helped by an intercept of communications between his supporters and harrowing cell phone calls from victims aboard the jetliners before they crashed.

Today, bin Laden congratulated

the people who carried out the attacks, but denied any involvement. Utah Sen. Orrin Hatch, the top Republican on the Senate Judiciary Committee, said U.S. intelligence has intercepted communications between bin Laden supporters discussing the attacks on the World Trade Center and Pentagon.

And at least one flight attendant and two passengers called from three of the planes as they were being forced down in New York and Washington — each describing similar circumstances.

The callers, including Barbara Olson, the wife of U.S. Solicitor General Theodore Olson, indicated hijackers armed with knive-like weapons, in some cases stabbing flight attendants, took control of the planes and were forcing them down toward the ground.

More than nine hours after the U.S. attacks began, explosions could be heard north of the Afghan capital of Kabul, but American officials said the United States was not responsible. Bin Laden has been granted asylum in Afghanistan.

Please see TERROR, Page 17A

138th year, No. 2
© The Detroit News
Printed in the USA

GANNETT

35¢ 35¢ daily for home delivery. 50¢ outside 6-county metro area.
For home delivery call (800) 395-3300

WEDNESDAY'S WEATHER

High 69
Low 48
See Page 28A

INSIDE •••

Recycled newsprint is used to print The Detroit News.

Gulnara Samoilova / Associated Press
A woman gets help after the attack on New York.

WHAT'S INSIDE THE DETROIT NEWS

N.Y. in chaos
Stunned New Yorkers try to contact loved ones. **Page 2A**

Day of tragedy
Hijacking of four jets sets tone for day of terror. **Page 3A**

Pentagon attack
Terrorists destroy America's sense of security. **Page 4A**

Bush faces test
Acts of terrorism to test, define Bush presidency. **Page 7A**

World horrified
Governments around the world offer condolences. **Page 9A**

Terrorism warnings
State Department unaware of any domestic threats. **Page 11A**

Shock waves
Metro Detroiters concerned for safety. **Page 13A**

Safety fears
Local Arabs worry about possible backlash. **Page 16A**

News hurts turnout
Turnout for primary elections down. Metro, **Page 21A**

Economic impact
Attacks add to economic woes. **Business, Section B**

Sports stands still
Games postponed as nation mourns. **Sports, Section D**

Coping with terror
Metro Detroiters can learn from Europeans. **Features, Section E**

U.S. attacked: Continuing reports at
www.detnews.com

▶ Read late-breaking news.
▶ Join the News Talk discussion.
▶ Browse photos and videos.
▶ Link out to worldwide coverage and opinion.

detnews.com
The Detroit News

The Flint **JOURNAL**

Special Edition

U.S. attacked

**Terrorists destroy trade center;
plane slams into Pentagon
in 'second Pearl Harbor'**

Special coverage: A2, A6 and A7.

MORNING EXTRA

AMERICA UNDER SIEGE

Kalamazoo Gazette

Wednesday, September 12, 2001   Kalamazoo, Michigan   50¢

54

'Our nation saw evil'

How you can help

Numbers to call to offer assistance to victims of Tuesday's terrorist attacks:

• American Red Cross, blood donations: (800) 448-3543
• American Red Cross, cash donations: (800) HELP-NOW
• Salvation Army, cash donations: (800) SAL-ARMY
• Medical personnel who wish to donate their services should contact their local American Red Cross office. The Federal Emergency Management Agency does not accept donations, but coordinates volunteer agencies at disaster sites.

ERNESTO MORA/ASSOCIATED PRESS

Two women hold each other as they watch the World Trade Center burn following a terrorist attack on the twin skyscrapers in New York City Tuesday. Terrorists crashed two planes into the World Trade Center and the twin 110-story towers collapsed Tuesday morning.

Suspect search focuses on bin Laden

BY DAVID CRARY
and JERRY SCHWARTZ
THE ASSOCIATED PRESS

NEW YORK — In the most devastating terrorist onslaught ever waged against the United States, knife-wielding hijackers crashed two airliners into the World Trade Center on Tuesday, toppling its twin 110-story towers. The deadly calamity was witnessed on televisions across the world as another plane slammed into the Pentagon, and a fourth crashed outside Pittsburgh.

"Today, our nation saw evil," President Bush said in an address to the nation Tuesday night. He said thousands of lives were "suddenly ended by evil, despicable acts of terror."

Said Adm. Robert J. Natter, commander of the U.S. Atlantic Fleet: "We have been attacked like we haven't since Pearl Harbor."

Establishing the death toll could take weeks. The four airliners alone had 266 people aboard and there were no known survivors. Officials put the number of dead and wounded at the Pentagon at about 100 or more, with some news reports suggesting it could rise to 800.

In addition, a union official said he feared 300 firefighters who first reached the scene had died in rescue efforts at the trade center — where 50,000 people worked — and dozens of police officers were missing.

"The number of casualties will be more than most of us can bear," a visibly distraught Mayor Rudolph Giuliani said.

Police sources said some people trapped in the twin towers managed to call authorities or family members and that some trapped police officers made radio contact. In one of the calls, which took place in the afternoon, a businessman phoned his family to say he was trapped with policemen, whom he named, the source said.

Because of fires and unstable debris, no rescue attempts were going on Tuesday night at the site of the towers, however.

No one took responsibility for the attacks that rocked the seats of finance and government. But federal authorities identified Osama bin Laden, who has been given asylum by Afghanistan's Taliban rulers, as the prime suspect.

More than nine hours after the U.S. attacks began, explosions could be heard north of the Afghan capital of Kabul, but American officials said the United States was not responsible. "It isn't us. I don't know who's doing it," Pentagon spokesman Craig Quigley said.

Kalamazoo comes together to pray for country

Hundreds listen to calls for healing and forgiveness.

BY BARBARA WALTERS
KALAMAZOO GAZETTE

Near dusk Tuesday they gathered in Bronson Park to pray and sing, because what they felt was beyond words.

"There are no words" to describe the resounding impact of the terrorist attacks on Washington, D.C. and New York that began earlier in the day, Kalamazoo Mayor Robert Jones told about 800 people who came with lawn chairs and baby strollers, small candles and American flags.

"We've come together now to pray for the victims, for our country, for each other that we can find peace amidst the terrible tragedy that has befallen us."

Just how closely that tragedy touched Kalamazoo came in the announcement from The Rev. David Van Arsdale that a member of his downtown Presbyterian congregation had lost a daughter, a stewardess in one of the planes that hit the World Trade Center.

The crowd gasped.

The pain is just beginning, said Van Arsdale and the more than a dozen other ministers, priests and rabbis who spoke. The healing and forgiveness must begin, they said, turning to song and biblical psalms to say what words could not. In modern Hebrew, Rabbi Stephen Forstein of Temple B'nai Israel sang Psalm 118, "God is my strength and my song. He is salvation for me."

The Rev. Lee Krahenbuhl, co-pastor of Skyridge Church of the Brethren played his guitar and soon the crowd joined in. "Come rain, come down heaven's tears of mercy. Wash away this awful stain."

The stain was as much in their own minds and hearts as in the act itself, especially if it turned into general rage toward ethnic Arabs, the speakers said.

"We confess we're enraged at man's inhumanity to man," the Rev.

Please see **VIGIL**, A2

SPECIAL EDITION

THE OAKLAND PRESS
Tuesday September 11 2001

AMERICA UNDER ATTACK

Trade Center, Pentagon bombings strike fear across U.S., world

World Trade terror

One of two planes that crashed into the upper floors of both World Trade Center towers was hijacked after takeoff from Boston in an apparent terrorist attack Tuesday, according to U.S. officials.

An aircraft is seen as it is about to fly into the south tower as the north tower burns following the earlier strike.

Seconds later, a ball of fire explodes from the south tower as the plane crashes into it.

The south tower collapses following the second strike.

Sources: ABC, The Associated Press   AP-Oakland Press graphic

INSIDE: COMPLETE COVERAGE

50 cents

Special report

Wednesday
SEPTEMBER 12, 2001
50¢

StarTribune

NEWSPAPER OF THE TWIN CITIES

Metro Edition

R W B G Y ••

www.startribune.com

56

Terrorized

➤ Hijacked jets hit World Trade Center, Pentagon
➤ Anguish turns to anger as death toll climbs

Photo by Kristen Brochmann, New York Times

The World Trade Center's south tower erupted as a jetliner struck it Tuesday morning. The north tower took a nearly identical blow 18 minutes earlier. Both towers later collapsed.

➤ Twin towers of the World Trade Center collapse after attack by two hijacked jets.

➤ Airliner plunges into the Pentagon; White House, Capitol, federal buildings evacuated.

➤ Death toll so far: 266 on four jets; 100 to 800 reported at Pentagon. About 300 firefighters missing in NYC.

➤ Air travel suspended for the first time in U.S. history.

➤ The country and the world watch, aghast.

Attackers from the air create a sense of vulnerability, fear

From News Services

In the most devastating terrorist onslaught ever waged against the United States, knife-wielding hijackers crashed two airliners into the World Trade Center on Tuesday, collapsing both towers into flaming rubble, and crashed another aircraft into the Pentagon, shutting down the government and financial markets and spreading fear throughout America.

The toll of dead and injured was expected to climb into the thousands.

The calamity was witnessed on televisions across the world as a fourth airliner went down in western Pennsylvania. The crash came minutes after a passenger reportedly called an emergency dispatcher from his cell phone and said that the plane had been hijacked.

"Today, our nation saw evil," Presi-

dent Bush said in an address to the nation Tuesday night. He said thousands of lives were "suddenly ended by evil, despicable acts of terror."

Said Adm. Robert Natter, commander of the U.S. Atlantic Fleet: "We have been attacked like we haven't since Pearl Harbor."

For the first time, the nation's aviation system was completely shut down as officials considered the frightening flaws that had been exposed in security. Financial markets were closed.

Establishing the death toll could take weeks. The four airliners alone had 266 people aboard, and there were no known survivors. Officials said 100 or more were dead and wounded at the Pentagon, with some reports suggesting it could reach 800.

TERROR continues on S2

Walking and breathing were arduous tasks anywhere in Manhattan near where the World Trade Center had stood before terrorists felled the mighty twin towers.

Photo by Stan Honda, Agence France-Presse

25 pages of coverage inside; continuing updates at www.startribune.com

Rybak, Sayles Belton advance in Minneapolis; Benanav, Kelly will square off in St. Paul: Pages A1, B1

Please read and recycle

Information   612-673-4000
Classifieds   612-673-7000
Circulation   612-673-4343
............or 1-800-775-4344

Wednesday,
September 12, 2001
Copyright 2001
Star Tribune
Volume XX/No. 161
7 sections

28 PAGES OF SPECIAL COVERAGE ON TRADE CENTER ATTACK

ST. PAUL **PIONEER PRESS**

WWW.TWINCITIES.COM WEDNESDAY, SEPTEMBER 12, 2001 MINNESOTA/WISCONSIN EDITION

BEYOND BELIEF

- Hijackers crash two airliners into World Trade Center, one into Pentagon.

- Air traffic halted. ▪ U.S. borders restricted.

- No immediate claim of responsibility made.

- Government, businesses, schools disrupted.

Minutes after the north tower of the World Trade Center in New York was struck by a hijacked airliner, a second plane plunged into the side of the south tower.

CARMEN TAYLOR, ASSOCIATED PRESS

SHAWN BALDWIN, ASSOCIATED PRESS

Firefighters make their way through the rubble of the World Trade Center in New York after two airliners crashed into the landmark's twin towers Tuesday morning, causing their collapse.

MORE INSIDE

A TIMELINE and maps of attack sites. **PAGE 5**

THE SCALE of the attacks points to a rogue state, experts say. **PAGE 6**

PRESIDENT BUSH vows to defend freedom. **PAGE 9**

HOW IS IT POSSIBLE that terrorists could attack the Pentagon? **PAGE 10**

ALL BETS ARE OFF on the U.S. economy for the rest of this year. **PAGE 12**

A day's horror captured in photographs. **PAGE 14**

LOCAL REACTION, NEXT SECTION

KNIGHT RIDDER INFORMATION FOR LIFE

★ **TUESDAY SPECIAL EDITION INSIDE** ★

WEDNESDAY

THE SUN HERALD

www.sunherald.com

SEPTEMBER 12, 2001 ■ 50¢   COVERING THE MISSISSIPPI COAST   VOL. 117, NO. 341

SPECIAL EDITION

With thousands dead, friends and families grieve
and a nation struggles with a devastating attack on native soil.

WHAT NOW?

Prayer soothes hurting nation

Coast residents join a weeping nation in turning to prayer for solace. At offices, homes, schools and churches, people are gathering to pray, **A-3**

Gas stations are gouging

Gov. Ronnie Musgrove declares a state of emergency in response to stations hiking gas prices. The state is investigating price gouging and anti-trust violations, **A-6**

Gun owners grab ammo

"Some people think this could be the beginning of the end, and others think we might be getting ready to go to war," gun-shop owner says as customers flood store to stock up on ammunition, **A-3**

Donors line up

Hundreds of Coast residents turn out to give blood for victims of Tuesday's attacks. Collection hours have been expanded for today, **A-4**

Games halted

For the first time since 1945, the entire day's baseball schedule is canceled, World Cup soccer matches are postponed, racetracks are dark, and the NCAA and NFL are considering whether to go ahead with weekend games, **D-1**

SOUND OFF OF THE DAY

"As I watch the billowing clouds of smoke and debris issuing from the World Trade Center and the Pentagon, one image keeps coming to mind: Pearl Harbor. These attacks are cowardly acts equal to a declaration of war against the United States. Only this time, we are not certain who is the enemy. May God bless and protect this nation, the people of this nation, and bring comfort to those whose lives have been affected by this tragedy."

More Sound Offs, **A-2**

THE ASSOCIATED PRESS

Firefighters make their way through rubble Tuesday after terrorists crashed two hijacked airliners into the World Trade Center in New York City, bringing the twin 110-story towers crumbling to the ground. The audacious attack on U.S. soil, coupled with an attack on the Pentagon, claimed the lives of thousands of people.

Tragedy reaches to Coast

An agonizing day waiting for word

By GEOFF PENDER
THE SUN HERALD

Coast families went through the depths of agony after Tuesday's terrorist attacks, waiting to hear from loved ones living in or visiting Manhattan or Washington, D.C.

For many, relief came in the form of a telephone call or an e-mail message that their family or friends were OK.

But for some the agony continued late Tuesday, and phone service into or out of each city remained hit-and-miss.

"We still haven't heard anything," Ronald Brown, a Gulfport physician, said of his son-in-law Stephen Poulos, who works for an insurance company on the 105th floor of the World Trade Center in Manhattan.

Please see **Coast,** *A-6*

DAVID PURDY/THE SUN HERALD

Biloxi firefighter Mike Watts puts up an American flag at the city's historical flag display next to the Biloxi Lighthouse on U.S. 90 Tuesday afternoon. Mayor A.J. Holloway ordered the display changed to eight U.S. flags; American flags at municipal buildings are being flown at half-staff. 'This is a time of national tragedy,' Holloway said. 'We must show unified support for our country. I encourage all citizens to show their support by flying the American flag, and praying for the victims and their families.'

Terror from air kills thousands

Intercepted calls point to bin Laden

By DAVID CRARY
and JERRY SCHWARTZ
THE ASSOCIATED PRESS

Emergency contact numbers, **A-6**

WASHINGTON — In the most devastating terrorist onslaught ever waged against the United States, knife-wielding hijackers crashed two airliners into the World Trade Center on Tuesday, toppling its twin 110-story towers. The deadly calamity was witnessed on televisions across the world as another plane slammed into the Pentagon, and a fourth crashed outside Pittsburgh.

U.S. officials began piecing together a case linking terrorist mastermind Osama bin Laden to the attack, aided by an intercept of communications between his supporters and harrowing cell phone calls from victims aboard the jetliners before they crashed on Tuesday.

U.S. intelligence intercepted communications between bin Laden supporters discussing the attacks on the World Trade Center and Pentagon,

according to Utah Sen. Orrin Hatch, the top Republican on the Senate Judiciary Committee.

"They have an intercept of some information that included people associated with bin Laden who acknowledged a couple of targets were hit," Hatch said in an interview with The Associated Press. He declined to be more specific.

Hatch also said law enforcement has data possibly linking one person on one of the four ill-fated flights to bin Laden's organization.

Government and industry officials said at least one flight attendant and two passengers called from three of the planes as they were being forced down in New York and Washington.

The callers indicated hijackers

Please see **Terror,** *A-6*

© 2001 The Sun Herald

Printed in part on recycled paper; please recycle your newspapers.

INDEX

TODAY'S WEATHER

Mostly sunshine
High: **88°**
Low: **72°**

Winds from NE at 10-20 knots
Relative humidity: 70%;
Weather, C-6

Storm in Gulf

A large slow-moving storm system in the Gulf of Mexico off southwest Florida could become a tropical depression today, **A-9**

Hot college prospect

Harrison Central quarterback Jeremy Lee is making a name for himself with college recruiters. Lee is being courted by schools such as Stanford, Colorado, Jackson State and Southern, **D-4**

▷KNIGHT RIDDER▷ *INFORMATION FOR LIFE*   FOR HOME DELIVERY, CALL 1-800-346-2472

7 98256 00006 5

WEDNESDAY

ASB ELECTION RESULTS
• Page 7

Sunny
High: 86 Low: 64

The Daily Mississippian

The University of Mississippi   September 12, 2001 • Vol. 94, No. 85   www.thedmonline.com

One Nation ...
INDIVISIBLE

Nation suffers worst tragedy in its history

JULIE FINLEY &
LAURA HOUSTON

DM SENIOR STAFF WRITERS

The nation's worst terrorist attack ever kept the eyes and ears of Americans glued to the TV Tuesday.

Hijackers crashed two airliners into the World Trade Center, destroying both towers, a third into the Pentagon and a fourth outside of Pittsburgh. The World Trade Center towers, each 110 stories, were composed of seven office buildings, a shopping concourse, restaurants and observation decks. Over 50,000 people were employed there and many more visited each day.

A final death toll could take weeks, according to authorities. The four airplanes used in the attacks were carrying a total of 266 people, none of whom survived. About 100 people are expected to be dead from the crash at the Pentagon and an estimated 200 firefighters and rescue workers are dead.

Eleanor Twitford, a 2001 Ole Miss graduate, was in New York during the explosion.

"This is devastating," Twitford said. "There are ambulances everywhere. I can see what was left of the World Trade Center from the roof of my building."

About 30 minutes after the World Trade Center crashes, the Pentagon was hit.

Matthew Nicholas, a 2000 Ole Miss graduate, was in Washington D.C. working as assistant to the director of the Republican National Committee, when the crash occurred.

"I was driving by the Pentagon when the plane hit it," Nicholas said. "I heard the report and turned around and saw all the smoke and the plane exploding. I tried to get to the RNC headquarters but all the streets were closed down. When I tried to head back home to Virginia, all the roads were closed so I had to go to some friends' house and now I'm stuck there."

The Boeing 757, en route from Washington-Dulles to Los Angeles, crashed into the Pentagon, the nation's military headquarters at 9:30 a.m.

Former Associated Student Body President Nic Lott is working in Washington D.C.

See **Tragedy**, page 6

Nathan Latil/The Daily Mississippian

A TIME FOR HEALING – Kirsten Butler, a junior from Pontotoc, comforts friend Erin Rahaim, a junior from Jackson, after Tuesday night's vigil held at the Union Plaza in honor of the victims of earlier terrorist attacks.

Ole Miss mourns victims of attacks

ELIZABETH YOSTE
DM NEWS EDITOR

Over 400 students came together at the Union Plaza last night to remember the victims and their families after several terrorist attacks claimed thousands of lives Tuesday.

Many were silent and reflective, while others physically showed their grief at the loss of life hundreds of miles away in New York City and Washington D.C.

Students gathered in the Union and watched in shock as news unfolded throughout the day. Many began watching as the first of four hijacked planes flew into the first tower of the World Trade Center before 8 a.m. classes. Before the disbelief faded, a second hijacked plane flew into the second tower. News of The Pentagon being attacked soon followed.

"I feel for the people in New York and Washington D.C.," said junior Chelsey Magee, a biochemistry major from Jackson. "I hope these attacks are over (and) now the country will come together and focus on healing."

In response to the students' reactions to what is being considered the worst terrorist attack ever in the world, the university scheduled a vigil for students Tuesday night.

Clarence Webster, ASB president, solemnly addressed the gathering.

"I know Sept. 11 is a day we'll never forget," Webster said.

Chancellor Robert Khayat acknowledged that many students had connections with people affected by the attacks.

"We may seem removed from New York or Washington or Camp David, but we are citizens of the world," Khayat said. "I think it affects all of us and probably without exaggerating that we will forever be changed by this."

International programs acting director, Michael Johansson, has been receiving phone calls of parents of international students who have expressed concern for their safety and welfare.

"Now, more than ever, is a time for the university community to stand united and together," Johansson said. "Certainly,

international students are no different than other U.S. students on this campus whose reactions have been those of fear, shock and disbelief."

Brad Skinner, a graduate assistant with Office of Orientation, said freshmen may not be handling the terrorist attacks as well as upperclassmen.

"I don't know how they're handling it. They're already dealing with thoughts of homesickness," Skinner said. "(They) must be feeling scared, confused ... I can't imagine them being three weeks into school ..."

Skinner thinks the vigil might give new students insight on how Ole Miss comes together in times of crisis.

"Ole Miss is a family and we take care of that family," Skinner said.

"This is a time to take special care of ourselves and of each other," Khayat said.

"United driven by love, respect, thoughtfulness and kindness: we will as, Mr. Faulkner has said, not only endure, but prevail."

Members of the Blue Ten

See **Students**, page 6

59

THE KANSAS CITY STAR.

www.kansascity.com

50¢   METROPOLITAN EDITION

Wednesday, September 12, 2001

Thousands feared killed as hijacked jets destroy World Trade Center

Pentagon also damaged; U.S. forces around world put on high alert

Air traffic grounded, gas stations mobbed and Wall Street shut down

ATTACK ON AMERICA

As a stunned world watched, a ball of fire erupted from the South Tower of the World Trade Center on Tuesday morning after the complex was hit by a second hijacked plane.

KRISTEN BROCHMANN/The New York Times

In a few hours, U.S. sense of security is shattered

By SCOTT CANON
The Kansas City Star

Today your stock market is on hold, your gasoline is a question mark, even your mall may be closed. Disney World is shuttered, baseball is suspended and this morning even those travelers who would fly cannot.

So much of what America takes for granted, at least for a time, vanished.

Even in the Kansas City area — where security at everything from government offices to prisons to day-care centers has shot upward — the world is different.

Now it is just you, news reports and a world dreadfully different from the one to which you woke Tuesday — the place you knew before terrorists plowed airliners into America's sense of security.

"We can't pretend any longer that it won't happen," said psychiatrist Walter Menninger, chief executive officer of the Menninger Foundation and Clinic in Topeka.

"We're all injured."

Not when truck bombs struck the Murrah Federal Building in Oklahoma City or the World Trade Center in the 1990s. Not with the Persian Gulf War, the Vietnam War or the Korean War.

Not even, perhaps, with the attack on the military mother lode of Pearl Harbor has civilian America felt so in the cross hairs of hate.

So the country went to bed uneasily Tuesday night with the embers of a violent new history still smoldering in Manhattan and at the Pentagon.

"I'm a little surprised the Statue of Liberty is still standing," said Jason Pate, a terrorism expert at the Monterey Institute of International Studies. "I'm not sure how long I'll be able to count it being there. I'm not sure we can count anything

See MOOD, A-24

Anguished witnesses could do nothing but watch as the inferno destroyed the 110-story towers where at least 50,000 people worked.

ERNESTO MORA/The Associated Press

'Nation saw evil' ...and vows justice

By RICK MONTGOMERY
The Kansas City Star

The unthinkable came true Tuesday: a catastrophic, full-scale terrorist attack on the world's strongest nation that left thousands dead and America's most recognizable symbols of power burning.

Ominous, twisted columns of smoke rose Tuesday night from the collapsed ruins of New York City's World Trade Center — a gleaming monument to commerce — and from the nation's military nerve center, the Pentagon in Washington.

U.S. leaders promised justice in the wake of the most devastating terrorist onslaught ever waged against the United States.

A grim-faced President Bush appeared on national television Tuesday night to mourn the victims, and he vowed to avenge their killings. "Today," he said, "our nation saw evil."

The unknown terrorists, mounting an audacious morning assault as Americans headed off to work, crashed two hijacked airliners into the trade center's twin 110-story towers where at least 50,000 people worked.

With terrified workers jumping from the top floors of the towers to escape spreading flames, one tower after the other crumbled in giant mushrooms of dust. A horrified country watched it all.

At roughly the same time in

See TERROR, A-24

MORE COVERAGE INSIDE

Terror's horrifying hold

In an instant, a bustling American city's daily routine is strangled by chaos, and suddenly, it seems, "New York is crying." A-2

Comfort in prayer

Searching for solace, Kansas City area residents of all faiths turn to their churches and religious leaders amid a day of emotional anguish. B-1

Frantic drivers

Motorists overrun Kansas City area service stations as fears of a huge gasoline price boost cause panic. C-1

Sports in perspective

Flags fly at half-staff at empty stadiums as the world of sports, from high school golf to professional baseball, comes to a halt. D-1

Emotional fallout

Say a prayer. Write a letter. Work for peace. People can cope with disaster best by taking action, grief counselors say. F-1

U.S. must show courage

The United States must resolve to meet this catastrophe with compassion toward victims and determination to protect the nation's people. Forum, B-8

Vol. 121, No. 360   9 sections

KNIGHT RIDDER

INFORMATION FOR LIFE

ST. LOUIS POST-DISPATCH

Vol. 123, No. 255 9/2001   WEDNESDAY, SEPTEMBER 12, 2001   1 2 3 4 5 6 ★★★★★ ●●●●   50¢

STUART RAMSON / THE ASSOCIATED PRESS

Smoke billows behind the Statue of Liberty on Tuesday after terrorists crashed two jetliners into the towers of the World Trade Center, bringing down both 110-story buildings.

"NONE OF US WILL EVER FORGET THIS DAY"

Terrorists turn passenger jets into missiles

Smoke pours from the north tower of the World Trade Center while an explosion rocks the south building from the crash of a second airliner into the complex. In all, 266 people on four hijacked airliners were killed Tuesday.

CHAO SOI CHEONG / THE ASSOCIATED PRESS

Thousands are feared dead; Bush vows retaliation against attackers and their protectors

By HARRY LEVINS
Post-Dispatch Senior Writer

Terrorism hit home with apocalyptic force on Tuesday, as hijackers punched airliners into the twin towers of New York's World Trade Center and then into the Pentagon.

The towers collapsed as a shocked nation watched — and wondered whether more attacks loomed.

Nobody knows yet how many Americans perished. But on a typical day, the Trade Center alone is filled with 50,000 workers.

"Today, our nation saw evil," President George W. Bush said in a four-minute speech to the nation Tuesday evening.

He did not identify suspects and made no specific mention of retaliation, except to say that those responsible would be found and brought to justice, as would those who harbored them.

"Our military is powerful — and it's prepared," he said.

Bush said, "None of us will ever forget this day" — a reminder that Sept. 11, 2001, would forever be a date with the evocative power of Dec. 7, 1941, the attack on Pearl Harbor, or Nov. 22, 1963, the assassination of President John F. Kennedy.

Despite the shattering impact of Tuesday's events, Bush cited "a quiet, unyielding anger"

across America.

Word of the attacks reached Bush on Tuesday morning in Sarasota, Fla., where he was visiting an elementary school. Bush quickly flew out, landing first at Barksdale Air Force Base, La. Then he flew on to Offutt Air Force Base, Neb. — the headquarters of the U.S. Strategic Command, America's nuclear strike arm.

Finally, Bush flew to Washington to address the nation. En route, he said in a phone call to aides: "We will find these people. They will suffer the consequences of taking on this nation. We will do what it takes."

But so far, nobody in authority has pinpointed the identity of the terrorists. Speculation centered on Osama bin Laden, the exiled Saudi with a grudge against the United States.

Among the other unanswered questions:
■ How did the hijackers slip past airport security nets?
■ Why did America's intelligence agencies fail to sniff out what was coming?
■ What were the terrorists trying to accomplish?
■ How does the United States respond?

Altogether, Tuesday's hijackers commandeered four planes carrying 266 people, all of whom perished.

See Attack, A20

HOW COULD THIS HAPPEN?

No one was openly taking credit or firmly fixing blame, but the scope of Tuesday's attacks suggested that massive, precision coordination lay behind the hijackers. Some critics wondered how the U.S. could have remained oblivious to the elaborate scheme and said that intelligence gathering leans too heavily on technology, not enough on people. Others said that airport security needs to be tougher, even if that makes it more intrusive.

WHAT HAPPENED HERE?

At Lambert, marooned and diverted passengers sought information. At churches, mosques and temples, worshippers sought solace. At area schools, teachers and students sought ways to understand the magnitude and meaning of the events. At work and at home, St. Louisans sought out each other, recounting — and knowing they'd remember — where they were when they heard the horrible news.

WHAT'S NEXT?

President George W. Bush and other officials vow not to let terrorism undermine American life, but Tuesday's attacks will surely alter it. Expect airport waits to be longer and stock prices to fluctuate. Gasoline prices may rise. Other changes may be less concrete, more fundamental as Americans come to grips with a new sense of vulnerability. "The open society is going to be less open," historian David McCullough predicted.

TO OUR READERS

Coverage of Tuesday's terrorist attacks in the United States has resulted in changes in where some things appear in today's paper. The first two sections are devoted to stories of the terrorism and its impact on our lives, including its business implications. An index to the report appears on A2. The third section contains sports, other national and world news, local news, obituaries and the weather report.

WEATHER ON C10

POST-DISPATCH WEATHERBIRD ®

For Post-Dispatch news updates throughout the day, look on STLtoday.com.

0 09189 21100 9

30 PAGES OF COVERAGE INSIDE — SUMMARY ON A2

Billings Gazette

AMERICA UNDER ATTACK
EXPANDED COVERAGE
For latest updates, log on to www.billingsgazette.com

WEDNESDAY, SEPTEMBER 12, 2001   *The Source*   STATE EDITION

- Second airliner crashes into World Trade Center exploding into a fireball, right. Photo sequence, **9A**
- Pearl Harbor vets see parallels, **5A**
- Billings travelers find airport shut down, reopening uncertain, **7A**

- A grim President Bush condemned the "evil" acts; nation looks to him for answers, **11A**
- Survivors recount tales of terror on streets of Manhattan, **10A**
- Attack on Pentagon shocks Washington, **11A**

'EVIL ACTS'

All eyes look to rich Arab terrorist

By JOHN WOLCOTT and WARREN P. STROBEL
Knight Ridder News

WASHINGTON — Before the smoke cleared from the Pentagon and the World Trade Center, the fugitive Saudi Arabian terrorist leader Osama bin Laden emerged as the prime suspect in Tuesday's carnage.

"Bin Laden is the leading candidate," said a senior intelligence official who requested anonymity. "There's nothing hard, but he's one of a very few people who would want to do this and who also has access to the tools and the kind of people you need to do this."

While the attack took the CIA and its sister spy agencies by surprise, a second senior U.S. intelligence official said investigators were rapidly building a case against bin Laden.

Analysis of the terrorists' methods and intelligence data gathered after the attacks points to individuals associated with bin Laden, said the official, who also spoke on condition of anonymity.

The official compared the clues all pointing in a single direction to the aftermath of the August 1998 bombings of American embassies in Kenya and Tanzania, when bin Laden quickly became the focus. President Clinton responded with cruise missile attacks on Afghanistan and Sudan shortly afterward.

Bin Laden is on the FBI's Ten Most Wanted list and is also believed to have sponsored the suicide bombing of the destroyer USS Cole. That he might try to stage such an ambitious attack isn't surprising. What's surprising is that the chain of hijackings and suicide bombings took America by surprise — especially if bin Laden was behind it.

If it was bin Laden, Michael Swetnam, a former U.S. intelligence official, said President

Please see Bin Laden, 16A

Index

©2001 The Billings Gazette, a Lee Newspaper, 116th year, No. 133

A shell of what was once part of the facade of one of the twin towers of the World Trade Center rests on the rubble of the collapse of the buildings Tuesday.
Associated Press

Terror attacks horrify nation

NEW YORK (AP) — In the most devastating terrorist onslaught ever waged against the United States, knife-wielding hijackers crashed two airliners into the World Trade Center on Tuesday, toppling its twin 110-story towers. The deadly calamity was witnessed on televisions across the world as another plane slammed into the Pentagon, and a fourth crashed outside Pittsburgh.

"Today, our nation saw evil," President Bush said in an address to the nation Tuesday night. He said thousands of lives were "suddenly ended by evil, despicable acts of terror."

Said Adm. Robert J. Natter, commander of the U.S. Atlantic Fleet: "We have been attacked like we haven't since Pearl Harbor."

Establishing the U.S. death toll could take weeks. The four airliners alone had 266 people aboard, and there were no known survivors. At the Pentagon, about 100 people were believed dead.

In addition, a firefighters union official said he feared that an estimated 200 firefighters had died in rescue efforts at the trade center — where 50,000 people worked — and dozens of police officers were believed missing.

"The number of casualties will be more than most of us can bear," a visibly distraught Mayor Rudolph Giuliani said.

No one took responsibility for the attacks that rocked the seats of finance and government. But federal authorities identified Osama bin Laden, who has been given asylum by Afghanistan's Taliban rulers, as the prime suspect.

Aided by an intercept of communications between his supporters and harrowing cell phone calls from at least one flight attendant and two passengers aboard the jetliners before they crashed, U.S. officials began assembling a case linking bin Laden to the devastation.

U.S. intelligence intercepted

Please see Attacks, 16A

 Voice your thoughts about yesterday's terrorist attacks on our message boards. Also take a look at our growing gallery of photos.

billingsgazette.com

For the faithful, Tuesday was day of prayer, mourning

Gazette Staff

On a sunny day that seemed too beautiful to confront tragedy, people gathered at several Billings churches and public spaces to mourn the nation's loss.

People came together for lunch-hour prayer services in many places, among them Rocky Mountain College, the lawn of the Yellowstone County Courthouse, at St. Patrick's Co-Cathedral and at the First United Methodist Church.

"God, what prayer, or cry, or curse, do we speak this day?" asked Rocky's chaplain, Deb Bergeson-Graham. "Do we pray, 'Thou art our refuge and strength in times of trouble?' Or do we shout 'All is vanity?' Do we cry, 'God, why hast Thou forsaken us?' Or do we pray, 'Father, forgive them for they know not what they do?'"

Some of the more than 50 students and faculty gathered in front of the student center.

Please see Prayer, 16A

Emilie Morgenstern, a freshman at Rocky Mountain College, joins a lunch-hour prayer service in front of Rocky's student center. She learned Tuesday that a family friend worked at a law office in the World Trade Center.

JAMES WOODCOCK/
Gazette Photo

TO SUBSCRIBE TO THE GAZETTE, CALL 657-1298 OR 1-800-762-NEWS

WEDNESDAY
Missoulian

SEPTEMBER 12, 2001 · www.missoulian.com · 50 CENTS

ATTACK ON THE U.S.

Four planes hijacked ■ World Trade Center, Pentagon hit

TERROR STRIKES

ABOVE: A fiery blast rocks the World Trade Center in New York after it is hit by two planes Tuesday. **BELOW:** Debris from the World Trade Center's twin towers lies below after their collapse.

SPENCER PLATT/Getty Images

INSIDE

■ UM terrorism
expert comments
– Page A5

■ World reacts
to attacks
– Pages A6-7

■ Americans pull
together
– Page A11

■ New Yorkers
recount escapes
– Page A12

■ Bush says U.S.
will respond
– Page A13

■ Local election
goes on
– Page B1

■ Area gas stations
feel crunch
– Page B1

■ Local
churchgoers seek
solace
– Page C1

Thousands believed dead in series of attacks

By RALPH VIGODA
Philadelphia Inquirer

PHILADELPHIA – A series of near-precision assaults shattered two symbols of America's military and financial power Tuesday, killing untold numbers of people, halting Americans' daily routine and forever destroying a nation's feeling that it can't happen here.

Within minutes at the start of the workday, unidentified terrorists hijacked two commercial jets and plunged them into the twin towers of New York's World Trade Center – reducing the 110-story landmarks to rubble and sending some workers leaping out windows – then crashed a third jet into the Pentagon outside Washington. A fourth hijacked plane, possibly also diverted toward the Washington area, crashed in Somerset County in western Pennsylvania.

The terrorists' audacity was matched by the stunning coordination of their operation – all four commandeered planes left three airports within 12 minutes of one another – and experts scrambled to

ALEX FUCHS/Associated Press

start investigating how they bypassed security and pulled it off. U.S. officials said they had had no reports the attacks were imminent and can expect questions about the breakdown in intelligence.

The carnage seemed destined to

stand as the worst attack on civilians in U.S. history. The death toll – which could take days, even weeks, to emerge – was likely to be far more catastrophic than the 2,400 killed nearly 60 years ago in the surprise bombing at Pearl Harbor.

Emergency workers at the trade center site in lower Manhattan faced a gruesome, blazing scene.

"There were bodies everywhere, body parts everywhere," said Angelo Otchy, a National Guardsman from New Jersey. "We're just trying to pull people out. We used shovels, anything. We heard people saying, 'Help! Help! Help!' "

Some people were still alive in the debris, New York Mayor Rudolph Giuliani said last night, but workers, hampered by continuing fire from the wrecked buildings, could not reach them. The hospitalized numbered in the four figures.

Between 40,000 and 50,000 people worked at the World Trade Center complex, 20,000 of them in the towers; an additional 90,000 visited on an average day. Pentagon officials told one congressman the building appeared to have sustained about 100 casualties. The four hijacked flights – two from American Airlines, two from United – carried 266 people in all.

President Bush, preceded by a

See **TERROR,** *Page A14*

Index

Mild

High 78° / Low 50°
Page C14

To subscribe, call
(406) 523-5280

Omaha World-Herald

SUNRISE EDITION
WEDNESDAY, SEPTEMBER 12, 2001

AN INDEPENDENT NEWSPAPER OWNED BY EMPLOYEES

64

'Our nation saw evil'

Smoke billows Tuesday across the New York skyline after the collapse of the World Trade Center towers. Before the towers fell, people on fire leapt from windows to certain death, including a man and a woman holding hands.

THE ASSOCIATED PRESS

Terrorist 'act of war' rains death on U.S.

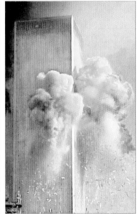

A jet flies toward the World Trade Center and explodes as it hits the south tower shortly after 9 a.m. At right, an emergency worker helps a woman injured in the attack. An estimated 300 firefighters died in rescue efforts, and dozens of police officers were reported missing.

THE ASSOCIATED PRESS

NEW YORK (AP) — In a staggering attack on the United States, terrorists struck Tuesday at the symbols of American financial and military might, using two hijacked jetliners as suicide missiles to level the twin towers of the World Trade Center in New York City and a third to blast into the Pentagon outside Washington, D.C.

A fourth jetliner, also apparently hijacked, crashed near Pittsburgh.

"Today, our nation saw evil," President Bush said in an address to the nation Tuesday night. He said thousands of lives were "suddenly ended by evil, despicable acts of terror."

"This is the second Pearl Harbor. I don't think that I overstate it," said Sen. Chuck Hagel, R-Neb., referring to the attack 60 years ago that surprised the nation's intelligence apparatus and propelled the country into World War II.

Sen. John McCain, R-Ariz., said: "These attacks clearly constitute an act of war."

Establishing the death toll could take weeks. The four airliners alone had 266 people aboard, and there were no known survivors. Officials put the number of dead and wounded at the Pentagon at about 100 or more, with some news reports suggesting it could rise to 800.

In addition, Fire Commissioner Thomas Von Essen said more than 300 firefighters were missing after rescue efforts at the Trade Center — where 50,000 people worked — and dozens of police officers were believed missing.

"The number of casualties will be more than most of us can bear," a visibly distraught Mayor Rudolph Giuliani said.

A police source said some people trapped in the twin towers managed to call authorities or family members, but it was not clear how many people or when all the calls were made. In one of the calls, which took place in the afternoon, a businessman called his family to say he was trapped with police officers, whom he named, the source said.

No one took responsibility for the attacks — which took place minutes apart around 9 a.m. EDT — that rocked the seats of finance and government. But federal authorities identified Osama bin Laden, who has been given asylum by Afghanistan's Taliban rulers, as the prime suspect.

Aided by an intercept of communications between his supporters and harrowing cell-phone calls from at least one flight attendant and two passengers

Please see Terror: Page 2

Intercepted messages link bin Laden to attacks; Bush pledges retaliation

■ Cell-phone calls from passengers described hijackers stabbing flight attendants, taking control of the planes and forcing the flights down.

WASHINGTON (AP) — U.S. officials began piecing together a case linking Osama bin Laden to the worst terrorist attack in U.S. history. They were aided by an intercept of communications between bin Laden's supporters and harrowing cell-phone calls from passengers aboard the jetliners before they crashed Tues-

day.

At the White House, a grim-faced President Bush mourned the deaths of thousands of Americans in Tuesday's atrocities and vowed to avenge their killings. "Today, our nation saw evil," he said.

bin Laden

The president said the United States would retaliate against "those behind these evil acts," and any country that harbors them.

U.S. intelligence also intercepted communications between bin Laden supporters discussing the attacks on the World Trade Center and Pentagon, according to Utah Sen. Orrin Hatch, the

ranking Republican on the Senate Judiciary Committee.

"They have an intercept of some information that included people associated with bin Laden who acknowledged a couple of targets were hit," Hatch told the Associated Press.

Hatch also said authorities have information possibly linking a person on one of the four flights to bin Laden's organization.

Authorities were focusing some of their efforts on possible bin Laden supporters in Florida, law enforcement officials said.

The officials said the FBI was preparing to search locations in Broward County in south Florida and Daytona Beach in central Florida. The locations had links to the suspected bin Laden supporter on the manifest of one of the jets that crashed, the officials said.

Please see Bin Laden: Page 2

Mutual of Omaha employee Earl Cushman watches the World Trade Center fall. Mutual projected TV coverage onto two large screens Tuesday.

LAURA INNS/THE WORLD-HERALD

In Midlands, stunned silence as all eyes turn to East Coast

BY DAVID HENDEE
AND CHRISTOPHER BURBACH
WORLD-HERALD STAFF WRITERS

As they watched and listened in numbed disbelief and horror, time stopped Tuesday for Nebraskans — and Americans everywhere — as they huddled around TVs and radios.

Malls and offices closed. Some college professors canceled classes. Office phones stopped

ringing. People stopped working. Government buildings closed. Flags were lowered to half-staff. Planes were grounded.

The series of terrorist attacks in New York City and Washington, D.C., stunned the nation and evoked images of sneak attacks, national honor and war.

"It's Pearl Harbor all over again," said Sandy Wolfe over lunch at the food court in

Please see Midlands: Page 2

Today's Weather

Partly sunny. Highs 70s and 80s. Lows tonight low to mid-50s.

On the Web

omaha.com
The World-Herald on the Web

Despite being hit by a hijacked airliner, "the Pentagon is functioning. It will be in business tomorrow," Defense Secretary Donald Rumsfeld said. **Page 5A.**

The economic impact of the terrorist attacks could cause a recession that could last for years.

The financial markets did not open Tuesday and will remain closed today. **Business, Page 1D.**

Worried drivers lined up for gas. Most Nebraska and Iowa stations maintained normal prices, but a few Midwest cities saw prices balloon to $3 to $4. **Page 6A.**

America under attack

Ten pages of terrorism news inside, Pages 2A through 11A.

Index

52 PAGES

50 cents

EXTRA

Sept. 11, 2001   *50 Cents*

ASBURY PARK PRESS

A GANNETT NEWSPAPER

TERROR

9:03 A.M. EDT
SECOND HIJACKED
PASSENGER JET STRIKES
SOUTH TOWER OF
WORLD TRADE CENTER,
NEW YORK CITY

U.S. UNDER ATTACK

TERROR EXTRA

The Star-Ledger

| SPECIAL EDITION | Dramatic new photos inside | WEDNESDAY, SEPTEMBER 12, 2001 **35** CENTS |

THE NEWSPAPER FOR NEW JERSEY

SURVIVORS

A BREATH OF LIFE FROM THE RUBBLE
BUSH TODAY CALLS ATTACKS 'WAR'
ABANDONED CARS OFFER CLUES

66

GEORGE McNISH/THE STAR-LEDGER

Emergency workers pull out an injured colleague during the overnight search for survivors in the wreckage of the south tower of the World Trade Center in the aftermath of the terrorist attack.

Paralyzed

Manhattan tunnels and bridges still blocked to inbound traffic as commuters search for alternatives. **Page 3**

D.C. daze

Civilian, military leaders turn to finding attackers. **Page 11**

How to help

Numbers to call, services to use. Complete listings on **Pages 2 and 28**

Families grasp for hope amid devastation

BY TOM FEENEY AND MARY JO PATTERSON
STAR-LEDGER STAFF

Rescue workers toiling in the rubble of lower Manhattan were heartened early this morning by muffled voices coming from the mountain of concrete and steel, but sobered by the gruesome, inescapable reality that awaited them.

As the United States government officials scrambled to affix blame for the most audacious act of terrorism they had ever seen, rescue crews set about the grim task of digging through the toppled towers of the World Trade Center for the thousands who had been buried in yesterday's attack.

Among the sparks of life amid the devastation was Port Authority Police Sgt. Jay McLaughlin. Rescuers pulled him free at about 7:35 a.m. today and took him by ambulance to a hospital. At least six others — all firefighters — were also pulled from the rubble alive today, said Bill Doody, a Brooklyn

firefighter. Rescuers are certain of at least one other survivor is in there, too, New York Mayor Rudolph Guiliani said at a news conference this morning.

The coordinated attacks on the World Trade Center and the Pentagon yesterday morning left the nation crippled for a second day. The financial markets remained closed. Domestic air travel remained suspended, at least until noon. And the American military remained on the highest level of alert.

Federal authorities believe they have identified five of the terrorists who boarded planes at Logan International Airport in Boston, including two who used New Jersey drivers' licenses to rent a car they ditched in Maine.

Searches of another rental car left in Boston and luggage believed to belong to the suspects revealed a flight training manual and Arabic religious materials, according to a report

[See **TERROR**, Page 4]

Heroes

Going into the rubble of the World Trade Center with the rescue workers. **Page 9**

Floor by floor

A graphic look at the Twin Towers and where offices were located. **Page 26**

ATTACK ON THE U.S.: SPECIAL COVERAGE

ALBUQUERQUE JOURNAL

HOME-OWNED AND HOME-OPERATED ■ MADE IN THE U.S.A.
121ST YEAR, NO. 255 ■ 48 PAGES IN 5 SECTIONS

WEDNESDAY MORNING, SEPTEMBER 12, 2001

STATE ★★★
Copyright © 2001, Journal Publishing Co. ■ Daily 50 cents

Infamy!

> **"** *Today, our nation saw evil.* **"**
>
> **PRESIDENT BUSH**

CARMEN TAYLOR/THE ASSOCIATED PRESS

MOMENTS BEFORE: United Flight 175 from Boston lines up with the World Trade Center's south tower in New York minutes after 9 a.m. Tuesday.

Stunned Americans grieved for the thousands killed Tuesday in the deadliest terrorist attack in history and drew a collective breath as they evoked memories of Pearl Harbor. Much of the government closed and air travel was shut down, along with the financial markets. Americans sought news of missing loved ones, gathered in prayer, donated blood and worried about the safety of our cities and our skies. And there were so many questions. Who did this, and why? How could it have happened? How will America respond?

MOMENTS AFTER: A fireball explodes from the south tower after the United jet airliner crashes into the building. The tower collapsed around 10 a.m.

Inside

Search begins

Bush vows to "hunt down and pursue those responsible"; U.S. security experts try to figure out who's to blame — and how officials missed any warning signs.

A3, A5

N.M. reacts

Security tightens across state; New Mexicans visiting D.C. "heard the noise, felt the shudder."

A9, A10

What went wrong

Anatomy of the attack: a time line of Tuesday's terror, from the hijackings to the explosions.

A8

TIMES UNION

THE INFORMATION SOURCE FOR THE CAPITAL REGION · SINCE 1856

50 CENTS ★★★★★   ALBANY, NEW YORK ■ WEDNESDAY, SEPTEMBER 12, 2001

FREEDOM UNDER SIEGE

SPECIAL REPORT

World Trade Center collapses, Pentagon hit

Bush vows retaliation for 'cowardly actions'

Thousands feared dead beneath the rubble

America under Attack

18 pages of disaster coverage

▶ **DAY OF TERROR:** U.S. must respond firmly, responsibly — and with all the resolve so frequently absent in the past. **Editorial on AA6**

▶ **READY TO HELP:** From the National Guard to area hospitals to police and firefighters, the Capital Region reaches out to help. **Coverage on B1**

▶ **TRYING TO COPE:** In the face of unimaginable tragedy, Americans called their loved ones, visited churches and looked for answers to give their children. **Coverage on D1**

CARMEN TAYLOR/ASSOCIATED PRESS

By DAVID CRARY and JERRY SCHWARTZ
Associated Press

NEW YORK — In the most devastating terrorist onslaught ever waged against the United States, knife-wielding hijackers crashed two airliners into the World Trade Center on Tuesday, toppling its twin 110-story towers. The deadly calamity was witnessed on televisions across the world as another plane slammed into the Pentagon and a fourth crashed outside Pittsburgh.

"Today, our nation saw evil," President Bush said in an address to the nation Tuesday night. He said thousands of lives were "suddenly ended by evil, despicable acts of terror."

Said Adm. Robert J. Natter, commander of the U.S. Atlantic Fleet: "We have been attacked like we haven't since Pearl Harbor."

Establishing the U.S. death toll could take weeks. The four airliners alone had 266 people aboard and there were no known survivors.

While The Associated Press reported that the death toll at the Pentagon was estimated at 100, ABC and NBC, quoting fire officials, said as many as 800 people were feared dead in that attack.

In addition, it was feared 300 firefighters who first reached the scene had died in rescue efforts at the Trade Center — where 50,000 people worked — and dozens of police officers were believed missing.

"The number of casualties will be more than most of us can bear," a visibly distraught Mayor Rudolph Giuliani said.

Police sources said some people trapped in the twin towers managed to call authorities or family

Please see **ATTACK A8** ▶

SourceLine 446-4000
SourceLine is the *Times Union's* free, 24-hour telephone news and information service. Details, page A2

timesunion.com
Check our news, weather, sports and classifieds at: **http://timesunion.com** Details, page A2

6 54806 00004 9

Today's weather
Clouds crowd in, likely bringing rain on Thursday.
High 74° Low 52° Details, see **page B3**

EXTRA!

Newsday

www.newsday.com   TUESDAY, SEPT. 11, 2001   50¢

AMERICA ATTACKED

24-PAGE EXTRA EDITION

With Tower One of the World Trade Center already in flames after it was hit by a plane, a second plane flies collision course toward Tower Two.

ABC Video Image via APTN

COPYRIGHT 2001, NEWSDAY INC., VOL. 62, NO. 9

SPORTS ★ ★ ★ ★ FINAL

DAY OF TERROR • SPECIAL EDITION

DAILY  NEWS

50¢ www.nydailynews.com **NEW YORK'S HOMETOWN NEWSPAPER** September 12, 2001

70

IT'S WAR

Just an instant before the second jetliner hit the south tower of the World Trade Center

ABC VIA AP

"All the News That's Fit to Print"

The New York Times

Late Edition

New York: **Today,** sunny, a few afternoon clouds. High 77. **Tonight,** slightly more humid. Low 65. **Tomorrow,** sun then clouds. High 81. **Yesterday,** high 81, low 63. Weather map, Page C19.

VOL. CL .. No. 51,874 · Copyright © 2001 The New York Times · NEW YORK, WEDNESDAY, SEPTEMBER 12, 2001 · $1 beyond the greater New York metropolitan area. · 75 CENTS

U.S. ATTACKED

HIJACKED JETS DESTROY TWIN TOWERS AND HIT PENTAGON IN DAY OF TERROR

A CREEPING HORROR

Buildings Burn and Fall as Onlookers Search for Elusive Safety

By N. R. KLEINFIELD

It kept getting worse.

The horror arrived in episodic bursts of chilling disbelief, signified first by trembling floors, sharp eruptions, cracked windows. There was the actual unfathomable realization of a gaping, flaming hole in first one of the tall towers, and then the same thing all over again in its twin. There was the merciless sight of bodies helplessly tumbling out, some of them in flames.

Finally, the mighty towers themselves were reduced to nothing. Dense plumes of smoke raced through the downtown avenues, coursing between the buildings, shaped like tornadoes on their sides.

Every sound was cause for alarm. A plane appeared overhead. Was another one coming? No, it was a fighter jet. But was it friend or enemy? People scrambled for their lives, but they didn't know where to go. Should they go north, south, east, west? Stay outside, go indoors? People hid beneath cars and each other. Some contemplated jumping into the river.

For those trying to flee the very epicenter of the collapsing World Trade Center towers, the most horrid thought of all finally dawned on them: nowhere was safe.

For several panic-stricken hours yesterday morning, people in Lower Manhattan witnessed the inexpressible, the incomprehensible, the unthinkable. "I don't know what the gates of hell look like, but it's got to be like this," said John Maloney, a security director for an Internet firm in the trade center. "I'm a combat veteran, Vietnam, and I never saw anything like this."

The first warnings were small ones. Blocks away, Jim Farmer, a film composer, was having breakfast at a small restaurant on West Broadway. He heard the sound of a jet. An odd sound — too loud, it seemed, to be

Continued on Page A7

A Somber Bush Says Terrorism Cannot Prevail

By ELISABETH BUMILLER with DAVID E. SANGER

WASHINGTON, Sept. 11 — President Bush vowed tonight to retaliate against those responsible for today's attacks on New York and Washington, declaring that he would "make no distinction between the terrorists who committed these acts and those who harbor them."

"These acts of mass murder were intended to frighten our nation into chaos and retreat, but they have failed," the president said in his first speech to the nation from the Oval Office. "Our country is strong. Terrorist acts can shake the foundation of our biggest buildings, but they cannot touch the foundation of America."

His speech came after a day of trauma that seems destined to define his presidency. Seeking to at once calm the nation and declare his determination to exact retribution, he told a country numbed by repeated scenes of carnage that "these acts shattered steel, but they cannot dent the steel of American resolve."

Mr. Bush spoke only hours after returning from a zigzag course across the country, as his Secret Service and military security teams moved him from Florida, where he woke up this morning expecting to press for his education bill, to command posts in Louisiana and Nebraska before it was determined the attacks had probably ended and he could safely return to the capital.

It was a sign of the catastrophic

Continued on Page A4

Steve Ludlum

Justin Lane for The New York Times

Paul Hosefros/The New York Times

Ruth Fremson/The New York Times

AMERICAN TARGETS A ball of fire exploded outward after the second of two jetliners slammed into the World Trade Center; less than two hours later, both of the 110-story towers were gone. Hijackers crashed a third airliner into the Pentagon, setting off a huge explosion and fire.

President Vows to Exact Punishment for 'Evil'

By SERGE SCHMEMANN

Hijackers rammed jetliners into each of New York's World Trade Center towers yesterday, toppling both in a hellish storm of ash, glass, smoke and leaping victims, while a third jetliner crashed into the Pentagon in Virginia. There was no official count, but President Bush said thousands had perished, and in the immediate aftermath the calamity was already being ranked the worst and most audacious terror attack in American history.

The attacks seemed carefully coordinated. The hijacked planes were all en route to California, and therefore gorged with fuel, and their departures were spaced within an hour and 40 minutes. The first, American Airlines Flight 11, a Boeing 767 out of Boston for Los Angeles, crashed into the north tower at 8:48 a.m. Eighteen minutes later, United Airlines Flight 175, also headed from Boston to Los Angeles, plowed into the south tower.

Then an American Airlines Boeing 757, Flight 77, left Washington's Dulles International Airport bound for Los Angeles, but instead hit the western part of the Pentagon, the military headquarters where 24,000 people work, at 9:40 a.m. Finally, United Airlines Flight 93, a Boeing 757 flying from Newark to San Francisco, crashed near Pittsburgh, raising the possibility that its hijackers had failed in whatever their mission was.

Kelly Guenther for The New York Times

SECOND PLANE United Airlines Flight 175 nearing the trade center's south tower.

There were indications that the hijackers on at least two of the planes were armed with knives. Attorney General John Ashcroft told reporters in the evening that the suspects on Flight 11 were armed that way. And Barbara Olson, a television commentator who was traveling on American Flight 77, managed to reach her husband, Solicitor General Theodore Olson, by cell phone and to tell him that the hijackers were armed with knives and a box cutter.

In all, 266 people perished in the four planes and several score more were known dead elsewhere. Numerous firefighters, police officers and other rescue workers who responded to the initial disaster in Lower Manhattan were killed or injured when the buildings collapsed. Hundreds were treated for cuts, broken bones, burns and smoke inhalation.

But the real carnage was concealed for now by the twisted, smoking, ash-choked carcasses of the twin towers, in which thousands of people used to work on a weekday. The collapse of the towers caused another World Trade Center building to fall 7 hours later, and several

Continued on Page A14

Awaiting the Aftershocks

Washington and Nation Plunge Into Fight With Enemy Hard to Identify and Punish

By R. W. APPLE Jr.

WASHINGTON, Sept. 11 — Today's devastating and astonishingly well-coordinated attacks on the World Trade Center towers in New York and on the Pentagon outside of Washington plunged the nation into a warlike struggle against an enemy that will be hard to identify with certainty and hard to punish with precision.

News Analysis

The whole nation — to a degree the whole world — was shaken as hijacked airliners plunged into buildings that symbolize the financial and military might of the United States. The sense of security and self-confidence that Americans take as their birthright suffered a grievous blow, from which recovery will be slow. The aftershocks will be nearly as bad, as hundreds and possibly thousands of people discover that friends or relatives died awful, fiery deaths.

Scenes of chaos and destruction evocative of the nightmare world of Hieronymus Bosch, with smoke and debris blotting out the sun, were carried by television into homes and workplaces across the nation. Echoing Franklin D. Roosevelt's description of the attack on Pearl Harbor as an event "which will live in infamy," Gov. George E. Pataki of New York, a Republican, spoke of "an incredible outrage" and Senator Charles E. Schumer of New York, a Democrat, spoke of "a dastardly attack."

But mere words were inadequate vessels to contain the sense of shock and horror that people felt.

As Washington struggled to regain a sense of equilibrium, with warplanes and heavily armed helicopters crossing overhead, past and present national security officials earnestly debated the possibility of a Congressional declaration of war — but against precisely whom, and in what exact circumstances? Warships were maneuvering to protect New York and Washington. The North American Air Defense Command, which had seemed to many a relic of the cold war, adopted a pos-

Continued on Page A24

MORE ON THE ATTACKS

RESCUERS BECOME VICTIMS Firefighters who rushed to the trade center were killed. **PAGE A2**

SEARCH FOR SURVIVORS Some people trapped in the rubble for hours were rescued. **PAGE A2**

OFFICIALS SUSPECT BIN LADEN Eavesdropping intercepts after the attacks were cited. **PAGE A21**

TERRORISTS EXPLOIT WEAKNESS Investigators had criticized precautions against hijacking. **PAGE A17**

CASUALTIES IN WASHINGTON An unknown number of people were killed at the Pentagon. **PAGE A5**

FOR HOME DELIVERY CALL 1-800-NYTIMES

Copyright © 2001 The New York Times. Courtesy of The New York Times.

71

EXTRA EDITION

ROCHESTER

Democrat and Chronicle

TUESDAY, SEPTEMBER 11, 2001 · DEMOCRATANDCHRONICLE.COM · 50 CENTS NEWSSTAND

Chaos

- 2 planes hit Trade Center.
- Both towers collapse.
- Explosion rocks Pentagon.
- Bush blames terrorists.

72

The Associated Press

One of the towers of the World Trade Center in New York collapses in this image, made from television. Airplanes crashed into the upper floors of each tower minutes apart this morning. A third aircraft crashed near the Pentagon.

'It's the Pearl Harbor of the new millennium.'

— Lori Marra, 39, of Brighton

U.S. under attack

Inside

- Rochester on alert.
- Eyewitness accounts.
- Monroe County cancels primary elections.
- Mark Hare commentary.
- Nation, world react.
- Two-page photo report.

For the most up-to-date news on the attacks and how they're affecting the Rochester area, go online to: **DemocratandChronicle.com**

News tips Call the Metro desk at 258-2252 or 258-2214.

For home delivery call: (716) 232-5550

Copyright 2001 Gannett Rochester Newspapers Five Sections

EXTRA
A B C

President Bush calls for a moment of silence after learning of the tragedy during a visit to Sarasota, Fla.

THE ASSOCIATED PRESS

In parallel attacks in New York City and Washington, planes crashed into each of the twin towers of the World Trade Center around 9 a.m. today, and an aircraft later crashed into the outer ring of the Pentagon building, causing smoke, fire and a sense of panic across the nation.

It was not clear how many people were killed in the twin towers, which later collapsed.

President Bush ordered a full-scale investigation to "hunt down the folks who committed this act."

Authorities went on alert from coast to coast, halting all air traffic, evacuating high-profile buildings and tightening security at strategic installations.

"Everyone was screaming, crying, running — cops, people, firefighters, everyone," said Mike Smith, a fire marshal in New York City. "It's like a war zone."

As of noon today, other flights were linked to the attack:

- An aircraft crashed on a helicopter landing pad near the Pentagon. The White House, the Pentagon and the Capitol were evacuated.
- United Airlines confirmed that a flight from Newark, N.J., to San Francisco crashed near Pittsburgh. It was believed to be a Boeing 747. The fate of those aboard was not immediately known.
- In Fort Worth, Texas, American Airlines says it "lost" two aircraft carrying 156 people. ❑

NEW YORKERS AWAKE TO **WEDNESDAY** A DIFFERENT CITY — A 5

Staten Island Advance

WEST SHORE   SEPTEMBER 12, 2001   50 CENTS

SPORTS

Some day, America will smile again and be in the mood to play, but all around the nation, sporting events were canceled yesterday after the deadly terrorist attacks in New York and Washington. ■ PAGE C 1

EDITORIAL

"I want them all dead. I even want their relatives to die. Whoever is responsible for attacking this country in such a brutal way should die the death of cowards — a thousand times." ■ STEVIE LACY-PENDLETON, PAGE A 24

BUSINESS

With the attacks leaving the financial district in chaos, the nation's securities markets will remain shut down at least through today. Analysts are divided on the effect the attacks would have when trading resumes. ■ PAGE A 34

The longest day

AMERICA TREMBLES AND SEETHES AFTER TERROR ATTACKS IN NEW YORK AND D.C.

There could be thousands dead. Hundreds could be Staten Islanders. Today, a day after the most egregious terror attack on the United States, no one knows.

We do know that the incomprehensible devastation has deeply touched our community.

The Staten Island Fire Department's elite Rescue 5 unit raced into the firestorm yesterday morn-

ing. The 11-member team has not yet returned. Staten Island fire Battalion Chief Charles Kasper is listed officially as missing.

Families from St. George to Tottenville were wracked with pain, and then overjoyed, as they received telephone calls from loved ones with a simple message, "I'm OK." Others were not as fortunate and still wait. The stories that will un-

fold will forever change our lives and the world in which we live.

Today, the Advance begins its attempt to tell those stories. What you will read and see today will make your heart ache. It is the first day that Staten Island and America try to overcome the numbness that engulfed us yesterday while trying to understand how it all happened. And why.

73

ASSOCIATED PRESS

People covered in soot and dust make their way through debris caused by the catastrophic attack on the World Trade Center. The photographer chose to capture this moment in black and white.

Eyewitnesses

An ordinary morning commute turned into a spectacle of horrific proportions as Staten Island ferry riders watched the Twin Towers explode in balls of fire and smoke. **Page A 12**

Living in fear

"We're Americans, too," says Kazem Farag of Huguenot, one of the Island's many Arab Muslims afraid of being objects of reprisals for what has happened. **Page A 11**

'They came running'

By early afternoon, the halls of St. Vincent's Medical Center in West Brighton were jammed with Staten Islanders who heeded the call for blood donors and were more than willing to do their part. **Page A 14**

Facing death

"I saw myself dead." For the first time in his life, Advance City Hall reporter Reginald Patrick confronts his own mortality as he and others race for their lives in Lower Manhattan. **Page A 6**

Hunting bin Laden

Although government officials cautioned it was too early to definitively assign blame, all evidence is pointing to Osama bin Laden as the chief architect of the attacks on the U.S. Believed to be in hiding in Afghanistan, the wealthy Arab terrorist congratulated those who carried out the mass destruction, but denied he was involved. **Page A 20**

Safe havens

For hundreds of youngsters, Staten Island became their special refuge as they were transported to Curtis High School to escape the panic that gripped Lower Manhattan. **Page A 10**

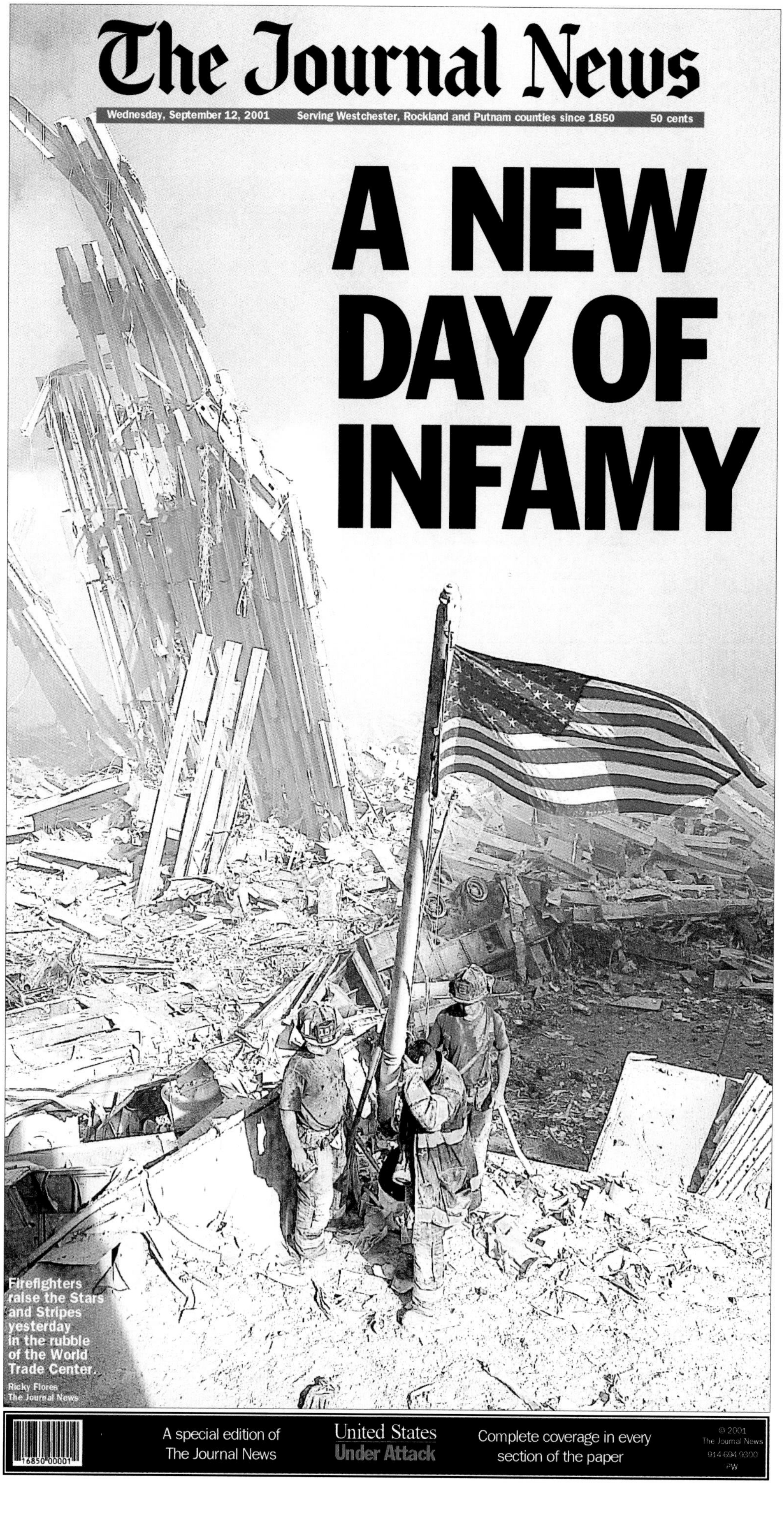

74

The Journal News

Wednesday, September 12, 2001   Serving Westchester, Rockland and Putnam counties since 1850   50 cents

A NEW DAY OF INFAMY

Firefighters raise the Stars and Stripes yesterday in the rubble of the World Trade Center.

Ricky Flores
The Journal News

A special edition of
The Journal News

United States
Under Attack

Complete coverage in every
section of the paper

© 2001
The Journal News
914 694 9300
PW

5 PAGES OF COVERAGE

EXTRA

The Charlotte Observer

www.charlotte.com +   TUESDAY, SEPTEMBER 11, 2001 | 75¢ in coastal areas | **50¢**

Terror

U.S. reels from attacks on World Trade Center, Pentagon

75

Smoke billows from the World Trade Center in New York after two planes blasted fiery, gaping holes in its towers, which later collapsed. Explosions at the Pentagon and the State Department in Washington indicated concerted attacks, authorities said. Planes were grounded nationwide and government centers in Washington were evacuated.

ASSOCIATED PRESS PHOTO

NEW YORK
World Trade Centers collapse after planes crash into towers.

WASHINGTON
Pentagon hit; State Dept. reportedly attacked.

PITTSBURGH
Airliner crashes near Pittsburgh; tie unclear.

NATION
All air traffic halted. Trading suspended on Wall Street.

CHARLOTTE
Mayor calls emergency meeting. Churches open.

EXTRA EDITION

NEWS & RECORD

Greensboro, North Carolina

Tuesday, September 11, 2001   www.news-record.com   50 CENTS

DAY OF TERROR

▶ Planes crash into World Trade Center towers in apparent terrorist attack

▶ Pentagon struck by aircraft; car bomb explodes outside State Department

▶ The FAA orders the entire nationwide air traffic system shut down

The Associated Press

A ball of fire explodes from one of the towers of the World Trade Center in New York after two planes hit, minutes apart. The number of deaths in the apparent terrorist attack was not immediately known.

World Trade Center towers destroyed; Pentagon hit in attacks

BY JERRY SCHWARTZ
The Associated Press

NEW YORK – In a horrific sequence of destruction, terrorists hijacked two airliners and crashed them into the World Trade Center in a coordinated series of attacks this morning that brought down the twin 110-story towers. A plane also slammed into the Pentagon, raising fears that the seat of government itself was under attack.

"I have a sense it's a horrendous number of lives lost," Mayor Rudolph Giuliani said. "Right now we have to focus on saving as many lives as possible."

Authorities had been trying to evacuate those who work in the twin towers, but many were thought to have been trapped. About 50,000 people work at the Trade Center. American Airlines said its two aircraft were carrying a total

of 156 people.

"This is perhaps the most audacious terrorist attack that's ever taken place in the world,' said Chris Yates, an aviation expert at Jane's Transport in London. "It takes a logistics operation from the terror group involved that is second to none. Only a very small handful of terror groups is on that list. ... I would name at the top of the list Osama bin Laden."

President Bush ordered a

full-scale investigation to "hunt down the folks who committed this act."

Afghanistan's hardline Taliban rulers condemned the attacks and rejected suggestions that bin Laden was behind them, saying he does not have the means to carry out such well-orchestrated attacks. Bin Laden has been given asylum in Afghanistan.

Within the hour, the Pentagon took a direct, devastating

hit from an aircraft. The fiery crash collapsed one side of the five-sided structure.

The White House, the Pentagon and the Capitol were evacuated along with other federal buildings in Washington and New York.

Authorities in Washington immediately began deploying troops, including an infantry regiment. The Situation Room at the White House was in full operation. And authorities

went on alert from coast to coast, halting all air traffic and tightening security at strategic installations.

"This is the second Pearl Harbor. I don't think that I overstate it," said Sen. Chuck Hagel, R-Neb.

American Airlines identified the planes that crashed into the Trade Center as Flight 11, a Los Angeles-bound jet hijacked

See **Terror**, Page **Page 2**

IN NEW YORK

About an hour after the crashes, the southern tower of the World Trade Center collapses with a roar and a huge cloud of smoke; the other tower falls about a half-hour later, covering lower Manhattan in heaps of rubble and broken glass. **Page 3**

IN WASHINGTON

An airplane crashes on a helicopter landing pad near the Pentagon, a car bomb explodes outside the State Department and the White House and the Justice, Treasury and Defense departments are evacuated amid terrorist threats. **Page 2**

IN GREENSBORO

Flights are grounded at Piedmont Triad International Airport, security is stepped up at the nearby "tank farms," and some downtown buildings close early. Meanwhile, area residents reel in shock and fear. **Page 6**

ELSEWHERE

Two United Airlines flights crash: a Boeing 757 southeast of Pittsburgh, en route from Newark, N.J., to San Francisco, and a Boeing 767 at a site not identified. The flights carried a total of 110 people. **Page 5**

IN WEDNESDAY'S NEWS & RECORD

Wednesday's edition of the News & Record takes a closer look at the events that left thousands of people dead, according to police officials, and the nation in mourning.

ADDITIONAL COVERAGE ONLINE

Regular updates on the terrorist attacks in Washington and New York, local residents' reactions, President Bush's reaction and local schools and business closings are all available at www.news-record.com

THE NEWS&OBSERVER

RALEIGH,
NORTH CAROLINA

TUESDAY, SEPTEMBER 11, 2001

LATE EDITION
50 CENTS

www.newsobserver.com

SPECIAL LATE EDITION

UNDER ATTACK

8:42 A.M.
NEW YORK

GETTY IMAGES PHOTO BY SPENCER PLATT

Two hijacked American Airlines jets crash 18 minutes apart into the World Trade Center twin towers. The 110-story buildings collapse shortly afterward. Page 3A.

9:40 A.M.
WASHINGTON

AP PHOTO BY WILL MORRIS

The Pentagon is struck and heavily damaged by an aircraft. The White House, Capitol and all federal offices are evacuated and closed.

THE LATEST
AROUND THE U.S.

● **A fourth plane crash:** A United 757 jet bound from Newark, N.J., to San Francisco crashes near Pittsburgh. Page 6A.

● **President Bush's reaction:** "Terrorism against our nation will not stand." He returns to Washington from Florida.

● **Security:** All U.S. flights are grounded; borders have been closed.

● **Casualties:** They are expected to be catastrophic; 50,000 people worked in the Trade Center, and more than 250 were aboard the four planes.

UPDATES ONLINE AT NEWSOBSERVER.COM

REACTION
THE TRIANGLE

STAFF PHOTO BY SUSANA VERA

RDU shuts down, businesses close, parents pick up students and after-school activities are canceled as the Triangle reels in disbelief. Page 7A.

A second aircraft approaches the World Trade Center moments before crashing into the skyscraper. Within 18 minutes, two planes hit the towers in what President Bush called 'an apparent act of terrorism.'

NEW YORK TIMES PHOTO BY KELLY GUENTHER

Trade Center, Pentagon devastated in 'audacious' event

BY JERRY SCHWARTZ
THE ASSOCIATED PRESS

NEW YORK — In one of the most audacious attacks ever against the United States, terrorists hijacked two airliners and crashed them into the World Trade Center in a coordinated series of blows today that brought down the twin 110-story towers. A plane also slammed into the Pentagon, bringing the seat of government itself under attack.

Thousands could be dead or injured, a high-ranking city police official said, speaking on condition they not be identified.

Authorities had been trying to evacuate those who work in the twin towers, but many were thought to have been trapped. About 50,000 people work at the Trade Center and tens of thousands of others visit each day.

American Airlines said its two hijacked planes were carrying 156 people. Two United airliners carrying a total of 110 passengers also crashed — one outside Pittsburgh, the other in a location not immediately identified.

"This is perhaps the most audacious terrorist attack that's ever taken place in the world," said Chris Yates, an aviation expert at Jane's Transport in London. "It takes a logistics operation from the terror group involved that is second to none. Only a very small handful of terror groups is on that list. ... I would name at the top of the list Osama bin Laden."

President Bush ordered a full-scale investigation to "hunt down the folks who committed this act."

Within the hour, the Pentagon took a direct, devastating hit from an aircraft. The fiery crash collapsed one side of the five-sided structure.

The White House, the Pentagon and the Capitol were evacuated along with other federal buildings in Washington and New York.

Authorities in Washington immediately began deploying troops, including an infantry regiment. The Situation Room at the White House was in full operation. And authorities went on alert from

SEE **TERROR**, PAGE 7A

78

EXTRA!

5 pages of Special Coverage

© Copyright 2001 Beacon Journal Publishing Co.

AKRON BEACON JOURNAL

TUESDAY, September 11, 2001   A B C •   News Online www.ohio.com   25¢

'OH, MY GOD!'

In an image from television, smoke and fire surround the upper floors after a second plane crashed into the World Trade Center in New York today. The two 110-story buildings later collapsed.

Associated Press/NBC

Unprecedented attack strikes U.S.

By Bob Dyer
Beacon Journal staff writer

The United States of America came under attack and was brought to a dead stop this morning:

• Terrorists flew two airplanes into the World Trade Center, destroying both towers.

• Terrorists flew another plane into the Pentagon.

• A car bomb exploded outside the State Department.

• A passenger jet went down near Pittsburgh.

• Another passenger jet went down in an undisclosed location.

Military jets were scrambled amid reports that additional hijacked planes were in the air - one of which may have been headed to Cleveland.

Another jetliner believed to contain a bomb was on the ground and isolated at Cleveland Hopkins International Airport.

American Airlines said it "lost" two aircraft carrying 156 people.

The damage in New York was massive. No reliable death toll was immediately available, but both of the Twin Towers actually collapsed. As many as 100,000 people worked in the complex.

For the first time in history, every airport in the United States was ordered closed - essentially shutting down the entire country.

"Oh, my God!" exclaimed students and employees at the University of Akron as they gathered around a television and saw another explosion rock the Pentagon. The university was closed soon after.

Trading was stopped on the stock market. Businesses across the country ground to a halt.

Please see **Terror, AE4**

Red Cross sends emergency response team

The Summit County Red Cross has sent an emergency response vehicle to Akron-Canton Regional Airport with food supplies for passengers and crew members whose planes were turned back to the airport shortly after takeoff.

All of the nation's airports have been closed.

The Summit chapter is also opening two shelters at the airport for stranded passengers.

Nationally, the Red Cross is immediately concerned with feeding the emergency workers descending on New York City. Mental health professionals will also be brought in to comfort the emergency workers.

Because the World Trade Center is a commercial building, there was no immediate plan to set up housing tents, a local spokesperson said.

"There will be no shelters or tents set up," she said. "It's mostly business people."

Special Attack Coverage: Page AE 1, 2, 3, 4   Eyewitness Account Page AE 10

EXTRA

THE CINCINNATI ENQUIRER

COPYRIGHT, 2001, THE CINCINNATI ENQUIRER · WEDNESDAY, SEPTEMBER 12, 2001 · 50 cents

ATTACKED

Getty Images/SPENCER PLATT

79

Thousands feared dead as terrorists smash planes into New York, D.C.

Inside

■ Nation stranded as airports shut down. **A2**
■ Terrorist Osama bin Laden is the primary suspect. **A3**
■ Trade Center destroyed; New York in chaos. **A4-A5**
■ Pentagon takes a hit. **A6**
■ Reaction across the nation and around the world. **A7**
■ Attacks stun the Tristate. **A8**
■ Cincinnati's mood a somber one Tuesday. **A9**
■ Millions turn to the Internet Tuesday for news. **A12**
■ How vulnerable are we? **A13**
■ Trade Center in detail. **A15**
■ Students watch in disbelief as history unfolds. **B1**
■ Clergy offers comfort. **B1**
■ Parents advised to reassure children. **B2**
■ List of today's closings. **B2**
■ We are about to find out what Americans are made of. **B6**
■ Attacks could tip economies into recession, some say **C1**
■ Fed pledges to keep banks supplied with money. **C1**
■ Reds game canceled. **D1**

Online

Get the latest news during the day at Cincinnati.Com.
Keyword: Enquirer

Portion of today's Enquirer were printed on recycled paper.

By Steven Thomma
Knight Ridder News Service

WASHINGTON — In a staggering attack on the United States, terrorists struck Tuesday at the symbols of American financial and military might, using hijacked jetliners as suicide missiles to level the twin towers of the World Trade Center in New York City and blast into the Pentagon near Washington D.C.

President Bush vowed "to hunt down and punish those responsible for these cowardly acts."

In an address to the nation he said, "We will make no distinction between the terrorists who committed these acts and those who harbor them."

Hours later, explosions rocked Kabul, the capital of Afghanistan, and host country for the prime suspect behind Tuesday's attacks. It was unclear who was behind the Kabul explosions.

Intelligence officials said initial information pointed at Osama bin Laden as the chief suspect in the attacks on Washington and New York.

Mr. bin Laden is a Saudi exile who heads the Al-Qaida, a global terrorist network that has targeted the United States repeatedly. He is blamed for masterminding the bombings of U.S. embassies in Kenya and Tanzania in 1998, and is suspected in the bombing of the USS Cole in Yemen last October. His is believed to be based in Afghanistan.

The loss of life from Tuesday's attacks is likely to be horrendous — as many as 50,000 people could have been in the two 110-story

The Associated Press/DOUG MILLS

THE PRESIDENT

President Bush addresses the nation from the Oval Office Tuesday night about the terrorist attacks at the World Trade Center and the Pentagon. **Text of speech, A2**

The Associated Press/KEVORK DJANSEZIAN

THE FEAR

A woman who feared she had lost an aunt in the attack on the World Trade Center is comforted outside a downtown Los Angeles high-rise after it was evacuated Tuesday morning.

Getty Images/JOSE JIMENEZ

THE RESPONSE

Rescue workers covered in ash rely on gulps of oxygen in between their extended efforts assisting with the massive emergency response in Lower Manhattan.

skyscrapers, and thousands in the Pentagon. Several hundred people aboard the four airliners perished as well.

The grim toll was almost certain to surpass the 2,403 who were killed in the surprise Japanese attack on the U.S. naval base at Pearl Harbor, Hawaii, on Dec. 7, 1941.

The attack was likely to have a similarly jarring effect on a stunned nation, as Americans hunkered down, suddenly unsure of the safety of their skies. Talk turned quickly to retaliation and even war.

"If you can do this to the U.S>A. and get at two symbols of the strength of America," said Sen. Chuck Hagel, R-Neb., "that tells you essentially we are at war."

Standing in a park near the evacuated Capitol, Sen. John Warner, R-Va., the senior Republican on the Senate Armed Services Committee, said: "This is our second Pearl Harbor, right here in our nation's capital."

As the U.S. military was ordered on highest alert worldwide, a sense of siege spread quickly across the land. All U.S. air traffic

See **ATTACK**, PAGE A14

METROPOLITAN EDITION | 35¢

THE PLAIN DEALER

WEDNESDAY, SEPTEMBER 12, 2001

LK GA LN SP ME LG ☆☆☆☆☆

TERROR HITS HOME

Hijackers ram 2 airliners into World Trade Center, 3rd plane slams into Pentagon, 4th crashes near Pittsburgh; thousands die

SPENCER PLATT | GETTY IMAGES

Fiery blasts rock the World Trade Center after it was hit by two hijacked airplanes. Both of the 110-story towers were toppled in the deadly terrorist attack.

Call loved ones, say you will die, passengers told

MARC FISHER AND DON PHILLIPS
Washington Post

WASHINGTON — There was not even the grace of instant death. Instead, there was time to call from the sky over Virginia to loved ones, fingers pumping cell phones, voices saying quick goodbyes.

Herded to the back of the plane by hijackers armed with knives and box-cutters, the 64 passengers and crew of American Airlines Flight 77 — including the wife of Solicitor General Theodore Olson, a Senate staffer, three D.C. schoolchildren and three teachers on an educational field trip, and a suburban family of four headed to Australia for a two-month adventure — were ordered to call relatives to say they were about to die.

SEE CALL | A6

GULNARA SAMIOLAVA | ASSOCIATED PRESS
An emergency worker helps a woman injured in the attack on the World Trade Center.

Bush vows swift revenge

JOE FROLIK
Plain Dealer Reporter

EVIL COMES ASHORE: It's time to master our fears, defeat our enemies. An editorial. **B10**

Terrorists unleashed a highly coordinated and deadly attack on America's political and financial capitals yesterday, altering the New York skyline, piercing the Pentagon and killing thousands in the worst attack on U.S. soil since Pearl Harbor.

By late evening, there were few answers as to how the assault had been plotted and carried out, who was responsible for it, even exactly how many had died. President Bush assured Americans that their government would be up and running again today, but it will take much longer before the shock of yesterday subsides.

Four commercial airliners, apparently hijacked within minutes of one another along the East Coast, were turned into killing machines. Two of the planes crashed into the twin towers of the World Trade Center in New York City, a third barreled into the Pentagon, and the last crashed 80 miles southeast of Pittsburgh on a trajectory that officials believe might have been carrying it toward the presidential retreat at Camp David, Md.

By 10:29 a.m., both World Trade Center towers had collapsed. The sun over Manhattan was hidden by dust and smoke;

screams and sobs echoed through its concrete canyons. Ash coated survivors as they fled the grisly scene, mangled bodies lay in doorways and streets, and explosions forced rescuers to retreat. Police fired gunshots into the air to drive stunned onlookers from the scene.

At the Pentagon, the massive symbol and command center of American might, military personnel and civilians pulled the dead and injured from debris. Already the White House and the Capitol had been evacuated, airplanes had been grounded across the country and Americans, long complacent behind the barriers of two oceans, had learned just how vulnerable even they can be.

SEE ATTACK | A2

Classifieds.................. H1
Deaths....................... B8
Editorials.................. B10
Weather.................... B12
Plain Speaking
and lottery on A18.

16 PAGES OF COVERAGE

INSIDE

THE HORROR: Americans are shocked to see how vulnerable the nation has become. **A5**

THE REGION: Northeast Ohio shuts down. Some stop to pray and others donate blood. **A11**

THE REACTION: World condemns attacks. **A7** Sam Fulwood and other columnists. **A16, B11**

THE GREED: There's no gasoline shortage, but some Ohio stations are jacking up prices. **A13**

CLEVELAND.COM

For news coverage and interactive forums

6 74776 18011 4

DAILY KENT STATER

Contact us at stater@kent.edu or (330) 672-2584   WEDNESDAY, SEPTEMBER 12, 2001   Visit us online at www.stater.kent.edu

America Under Attack

MORNING OF TERROR

At 8:45 a.m. yesterday, the worst terrorist attack ever put America in a state of turmoil, toppling the World Trade Center and damaging the Pentagon

David Crary and Jerry Schwartz
Associated Press

NEW YORK — In the most devastating terrorist onslaught ever waged against the United States, knife-wielding hijackers crashed two airliners into the World Trade Center on Tuesday, toppling its twin 110-story towers. The deadly calamity was witnessed on televisions across the world as another plane slammed into the Pentagon and a fourth crashed outside Pittsburgh.

"Today, our nation saw evil," President Bush said in an address to the nation Tuesday night. He said thousands of lives were "suddenly ended by evil, despicable acts of terror."

Said Adm. Robert J. Natter, commander of the U.S. Atlantic Fleet: "We have been attacked like we haven't since Pearl Harbor."

Establishing the U.S. death toll could take weeks. The four airliners alone had 266 people aboard, and there were no known survivors. In addition, a firefighters union official said he feared an estimated 200 firefighters had died in rescue efforts. Dozens of police officers were believed missing.

No one took responsibility for the attacks that rocked the seats of finance and government, but federal authorities identified Osama bin Laden — who has been given asylum by Afghanistan's Taliban rulers — as the prime suspect.

Aided by an intercept of communications between his supporters and harrowing cell phone calls from at least one flight attendant and two passengers aboard the jetliners before they crashed, U.S. officials began assembling a case

Glass and aluminum shower like confetti as a second airliner slams into the World Trade Center yesterday in New York City. The terrorist attack felled both buildings, sending the city and the nation into confusion and sorrow.
SPENCER PLATT | GETTY IMAGES

See TERROR | Page 2

AN UNEASY SILENCE

Students awoke yesterday morning to a national crisis amidst anger and uncertainty. **PAGE 5**

AT THE EPICENTER

Kent State staff and alumni in New York City gave eye-witness accounts of the tragedy. **PAGE 6**

A CALL FOR PEACE

Religious groups around campus held a vigil to mourn yesterday's tragedy and promote healing. **PAGE 10**

82

EXTRA

THE BLADE

One Of America's Great Newspapers

50 CENTS ■ SPECIAL EDITION   TOLEDO, OHIO, **TUESDAY**, SEPTEMBER 11, 2001   FINAL

DAY OF HELL

ASSOCIATED PRESS

Shortly before 9 a.m. today a plane slammed into one of the 110-story twin towers of the World Trade Center in New York. A few minutes later another plane, reported to be a hijacked American Airlines jumbo jet, was seen flying toward the second twin tower. A witness said "The plane was coming in low ... and it looked like it hit at a slight angle."

ASSOCIATED PRESS

Smoke billows from both massive World Trade Center towers in Lower Manhattan after they were attacked by terrorists, according to President Bush. The Pentagon in Washington was attacked by another plane within minutes. Federal buildings in New York, Washington, and across the nation were evacuated.

REUTERS

The upper section of the World Trade Center's Tower Two falls to the ground about an hour after being struck in a terrorist.

■ TRADE CENTER SHATTERED
■ PENTAGON ATTACKED
■ PLANE DOWN IN PA.

ASSOCIATED PRESS

NEW YORK — In a horrific sequence of destruction, terrorists crashed two planes into the World Trade Center about 9 a.m. this morning, and the twin 110-story towers collapsed. An aircraft also crashed at the Pentagon in an apparent coordinated series of attacks that spread fear across the nation.

"I have a sense it's a horrendous number of lives lost," New York Mayor Rudolph Giuliani said. "I don't know yet. Right now we have to focus on saving as many lives as possible."

Authorities have been trying to evacuate those who work in the twin towers, but many were thought to have been trapped. About 50,000 people work at the Trade Center.

"This is perhaps the most audacious terrorist attack that's ever taken place in the world," said Chris Yates, an aviation expert at Jane's Transport in London. "It takes a logistics operation from the terror group involved that is

INSIDE: MORE ON THE ATTACK

■ President Bush speaks, Page 2

■ What it was like in the streets , Page 4

■ Panic hits D.C., Page 6

■ World reaction, Page 8

■ City reaction, Page 8

second to none. Only a very small handful of terror groups is on that list. ... I would name at the top of the list Osama bin Laden."

According to Reuters at 10:15 a.m. EST, the Democratic Front for the Liberation of Palestine claimed responsibility for the world trade center attack. Later, a senior DFLP official in the Palestinian territories denied any involvement.

"I emphasise that the story released on Abu Dhabi TV by an anonymous person is totally incorrect," Taysecr Khaled, a senior official of the DFLP politburo in

the Palestinian territories, told Reuters.

President Bush ordered a full-scale investigation to "hunt down the folks who committed this act."

Within the hour, an aircraft crashed on a helicopter landing pad near the Pentagon, and the White House, the Pentagon and the Capitol were evacuated.

One of the planes that crashed into the Trade Center was American Airlines Flight 11, hijacked after takeoff from Boston en route to Los Angeles, the airline said. American Airlines issued a statement saying it had "lost" two air-

craft — Flight 11, with 92 people aboard, and Flight 77 from Washington to Los Angeles, carrying 64 people.

In Pennsylvania, United Airlines Flight 93, a Boeing 757 en route from Newark, N.J., to San Francisco, crashed about 80 miles southeast of Pittsburgh. The fate of those aboard was not immediately known and it was not clear if the crash was related to the disasters elsewhere. In a statement, the airline also said it was deeply concerned about another plane, Flight 175, a Boeing 767 bound from Boston to Los Angeles.

Authorities went on alert from coast to coast, halting all air traffic across America, evacuating high-profile buildings, and tightening security at strategic installations. The Situation Room at the White House was in full operation.

At the World Trade Center, "everyone was screaming, crying, running, cops, people, firefighters, everyone," said Mike Smith, a fire

See TERROR, Page 6 ■+

LATEST DEVELOPMENTS

COMPLETE FINAL

The Vindicator

THE TERRORIST ATTACKS IN DEPTH.

Wednesday, September 12, 2001   www.vindy.com   35 cents

EVIDENCE SO FAR POINTS STRONGLY TO BIN LADEN; CREWS HUNT SURVIVORS

For N.Y. and D.C., a grim mission

Pentagon recovery switches to dead

COMBINED DISPATCHES

NEW YORK — Hospitals began the grim accounting of the dead and injured today, as barges ferried bodies across the Hudson River to a makeshift morgue and rescuers waded through the World Trade Center's smoking rubble.

The financial capital remained closed after the attack on the twin towers and the Pentagon. The federal government said the ban on air travel would not be lifted before noon, and that it would take a while for schedules to return to normal.

Victims: Thousands were feared dead. This morning, Mayor Rudolph Giuliani said there were 41 known deaths — clearly, a tiny fraction of the dead — and 1,700 known injuries. He said 235 uniformed officers, including police and firefighters, remained unaccounted for.

The mayor said rescuers were still in contact with one person buried in the rubble.

Defense: Tuesday's assault on American government and finance led President Bush to place the military on its highest state of alert.

Smoke still drifted from the ravaged Pentagon, and authorities said they did not expect to find more survivors.

But the government went back to work today, its political leaders, diplomats and soldiers leaving no doubt the terrorist assault will be answered. "We will go after them," Secretary of State Colin Powell vowed.

The Navy said the aircraft carrier USS George Washington was in position today off the coast of New York.

Americans across the country remained on alert. For a second day, baseball's major leagues canceled all games. And Lou Dorr, an FAA spokesman, said passengers could expect tough security measures at reopened airports, suggesting that they arrive two hours early for flights.

Chronology: A day earlier, as workers poured into Wall Street, a hijacked jet tore through one of the 110-story twin towers. Another followed, striking the other tower in a fireball 18 minutes later.

A third jet struck the Pentagon at 9:40 a.m. A fourth hijacked airliner fell to earth about 80 miles southeast of Pittsburgh.

The twin towers collapsed by 10:30 a.m.

See Recovery on Page A3

The Vindicator/Jean Neice

DEPLETED: At Valley View gas station at Belle Vista and Mahoning, Wayne Mercer of C&K Petroleum recaps his truck after pumping 8,500 gallons of fuel into storage tanks depleted Tuesday after people swarmed area gas stations.

Tempers flare as drivers wait to fill their gas tanks

As some stations ran out of gas, officials asked area residents not to engage in panic-buying.

VINDICATOR STAFF REPORT

Fistfights broke out at gas pumps Tuesday night as people flocked to area gas stations out of fear of increased prices.

"People have been very hostile," said a worker who didn't want to be named at Sheetz on Salt Springs Road in Weathersfield Township.

That was one of several stations where workers reported that drivers fought with one another as they jockeyed for places at the pumps.

Many stations throughout the Mahoning and Shenango valleys had lines of cars 100 yards or more Tuesday evening. Police were directing traffic at some stations. Long lines were gone this morning, but many stations were still busy.

Violence breaks out: In Austintown, a Fitzgerald Avenue man told police he was punched in the face while waiting in line for gas Tuesday night at the Shell gas station on state Route 46 near Interstate 80.

The man said another motorist approached his driver's side window and asked, "Do you know who I am?" When the Fitzgerald Avenue man said no, he was punched in the face.

The Fitzgerald Avenue man said his girl-friend began arguing with the assailant, who then kicked the passenger side door of the car. The assailant then ran into the woods behind the gas station.

At a nearby Sunoco station, two drivers fought over their place at the pump Tuesday evening, said Gary Planton, manager at the station, which is run by Certified Oil.

He said he wasn't supposed to work but he came in to direct traffic because traffic had backed up well onto Route 46. No one was at the pumps this morning after Planton was told by corporate officials to raise the price from $1.39 a gallon to $1.88 for regular.

Prices at some stations remained at $1.39 this morning, while others were 30 cents to 50 cents more.

Some stations have been so busy that they were out of gas this morning. A worker at Sheetz on Mahoning Avenue in Austintown said the station ran out of gas around 7:30 a.m. and was waiting for its daily delivery, which was running late.

At Dairy Mart on Mahoning Avenue in Youngstown, tanks ran empty this morning, but store workers were waiting for a delivery.

What's behind this: Drivers interviewed at area stations this morning said they came out because they had heard from friends or on the radio that gas prices at some stations were $4 a gallon or more.

See Gasoline on Page A12

Four FBI divisions pursuing 700 leads

President calls it an 'act of war'

COMBINED DISPATCHES

Osama bin Laden

WASHINGTON — President Bush condemned terrorist attacks in New York and Washington as "acts of war" today and said he would ask Congress for money for recovery and to protect the nation's security.

"This will be a monumental struggle of good vs. evil. But good will prevail," the president said. He said the nation was prepared to spend "whatever it takes."

Bush spoke as administration officials said evidence in Tuesday's fearsome attacks pointed to suspected terrorist Osama bin Laden.

Today Congress returned to the Capitol and federal agencies reopened their doors for the first time since Tuesday's parallel attacks on the World Trade Center in New York and the Pentagon across the Potomac River from the nation's capital.

FBI leads: Meanwhile, the FBI has received 700 leads in the investigation of Tuesday's twin terrorist attacks, but so far no arrests have been made, a Justice Department official said.

Based on information gathered from frantic phone calls made by passengers on doomed jets just minutes before they crashed, the government believes that the hijackers were trained pilots and that three to five hijackers were aboard each of four airliners that crashed Tuesday in the worst terrorist attack on U.S. soil, said Mindy Tucker, Justice Department spokeswoman.

"It appears from what we know that the hijackers were skilled pilots," Tucker said.

Won't comment on evidence: Tucker declined to comment on evidence linking the attacks to Saudi exile Osama bin Laden or whether authorities have executed search warrants.

See bin Laden on Page A3

Valley man fled Trade Center

The conference he was attending was canceled shortly after it started.

VINDICATOR STAFF REPORT

Michael Tringhese was full of anticipation when the company that just hired him sent him to the Big Apple for training. On his third day in the city, the 22-year-old Austintown man was thankful to be alive.

Tringhese

He and 280 other trainees from around the country were at Morgan Stanley Dean Witter's offices in the World Trade Center when the landmark towers were hit by two airliners hijacked by suicide terrorists.

"We were on a break on the 61st floor in Tower 2 when the first plane hit Tower 1," Tringhese said. "I saw fire and paper and wreckage falling. Nobody waited to find out

See Tower on Page A3

Weather

Tonight, partly cloudy. Chance of showers near morning. Lows in the upper 50s. Chance of rain 30 percent. Thursday, chance of showers early. A2B

TODAY'S SPECIAL COVERAGE

Front seat to tragedy
A2 A glimpse into the confusion and horror in New York City

Two hours of terror
A4 Shortly before 8 a.m. Tuesday, American Airlines Flight 11 left Boston for Los Angeles. It and three other California-bound morning flights from the East Coast never reached their destinations.

Details of attack
A6, 7 A graphic representation illustrates how the attacks on the World Trade Center and the Pentagon were carried out Tuesday.

Terrorism and war
A4 Where do acts of terrorism end and war begin?

Remembering Pearl Harbor
A10 Area veterans recall the response of the citizenry when Pearl Harbor was attacked in World War II.

Lending a hand
A11 Local residents are answering the call to donate blood.

Gathering for prayer
A13 Mahoning Valley residents gathered in places of worship Tuesday night in response to the terrorist attacks.

Action is needed
A16 In the wake of tragedy, a strong nation must act. An editorial.

Reaction in the area
A16 Readers react to Tuesday's terrorist attack in How You See It.

Recession fears?
B1 The Fed is likely to respond to the attack by cutting interest rates, an economist said. Business.

Area stores closed
B1 Many Mahoning Valley businesses reported little activity or closed their doors early Tuesday as news of the attack filtered in.

84

EUGENE, OREGON • WEDNESDAY, SEPTEMBER 12, 2001

www.registerguard.com

The Register-Guard

Unthinkable

Countless Americans die as terrorists strike U.S.

The New York Times

A fireball erupts from the upper floors of the south tower of the World Trade Center after a hijacked United Airlines Boeing 767 hit the complex at 9:03 a.m. Eastern Time on Tuesday in New York.

More coverage inside

■ THE ATTACK: The worst terrorist attack in U.S. history spreads fear through nation / **2A**

■ THE SCENE: Survivors liken the tragedy to a bombing, a hurricane, hell / **4A**

■ THE IMAGES: Photographers capture scenes of horror, panic and devastation / **5A ►**

■ THE MARKETS: U.S. stock trading is suspended and may not resume for several days / **9A**

Associated Press
Onlookers react to the towers' destruction.

■ THE VIGIL: Lane County residents gather to express their pain, grief and sympathy / **1D**

■ THE IMPACT: Listing of changes in local services, transportation and public events / **1D**

■ THE NIGHTMARE: Columnist Karen McCowan describes waking up to a national tragedy / **3D**

■ THE SCHEDULES: Many national and local area sporting events are postponed / **1E**

E S EP SW P N W

COMPLETE COVERAGE INSIDE THIS SECTION AND METRO, BUSINESS, EDITORIAL, LIVING

WEDNESDAY
September 12, 2001

The Oregonian

SUNRISE EDITION

PORTLAND, OREGON   2001 PULITZER PRIZE WINNER FOR PUBLIC SERVICE   35¢

"We will make no distinction between the terrorists who committed these acts and those who harbor them."

PRESIDENT BUSH

LEFT: As flames from one crashed plane burn the north tower of the World Trade Center, a hijacked United Airlines jet carrying at least 65 people hurtles toward the Manhattan landmark's south tower.

RIGHT: The plane hits the 110-story south tower at 9:03 a.m. EDT and explodes. Within 90 minutes, both towers collapsed, killing office workers and their would-be rescuers.

ABC TELEVISION

Day of terror

IN NEW YORK JETS HIT WORLD TRADE CENTER; TOWERS COLLAPSE

IN WASHINGTON ANOTHER PLANE CRASHES INTO THE PENTAGON

PRESIDENT BUSH OFFERS REASSURANCE TO A SHAKEN NATION

The base of the World Trade Center in New York is an eerie, smoking ruin Tuesday after hijacked jetliners slammed into both towers, leaving thousands of victims and a shocked and grieving nation.

JUSTIN LANE/THE NEW YORK TIMES

U.S. authorities say Osama bin Laden is main suspect

By DAVID CRARY and JERRY SCHWARTZ
THE ASSOCIATED PRESS

NEW YORK — In the most devastating terrorist onslaught ever waged against the United States, hijackers crashed two airliners into the World Trade Center on Tuesday, toppling its twin 110-story towers. The calamity was witnessed on televisions across the world as another plane slammed into the Pentagon and a fourth crashed outside Pittsburgh.

"Today our nation saw evil," President Bush said in an address to the nation Tuesday night. He said thousands of lives were "suddenly ended by evil, despicable acts of terror."

Adm. Robert J. Natter, commander of the U.S. Atlantic Fleet, said: "We have been attacked like we haven't since Pearl Harbor."

Establishing the death toll could take weeks. The four airliners alone had 266 people aboard, and there were no known survivors.

Officials put the number of dead and wounded at the Pentagon at about 100 or more, with some news reports suggesting it could rise to 800.

Please see **ATTACKS,** Page A23

President quotes Scripture in offering comfort to nation

By SANDRA SOBIERAJ
THE ASSOCIATED PRESS

WASHINGTON — A grim-faced President Bush asked the nation to find comfort in Scripture as he mourned the deaths of thousands of Americans in Tuesday's atrocities and vowed to avenge their killings.

"Today, our nation saw evil," he said.

In his first prime-time Oval Office address, Bush said the United States would find and punish "those behind these evil acts," and any country that harbors them.

Bush spoke just hours after bouncing from Florida to air bases in Louisiana and Nebraska for security reasons.

Fighter jets and decoy helicopters accompanied his evening flight to Washington and the White House, where his Marine One helicopter briefly stood ready on the South Lawn in the event of another evacuation.

With smoke still pouring out of rubble in Washington and New York, Bush declared: "These acts shattered steel, but they cannot dent the steel of

Please see **PRESIDENT,** Page A24

INSIDE

Copyright © 2001
Oregonian Publishing Co.
Vol. 150, No. 50,632
80 pages

Circulation hot line 221-8240
Classified ads 221-8000

The Oregonian is printed on recycled-content newsprint

WEATHER
Clouds, then partly sunny
High: 80 Low: 56
For complete weather, see C24

THE MORNING CALL

mcall.com
The Morning Call's online source.
http://www.mcall.com

TUESDAY
SEPTEMBER 11, 2001 •

©2001 The Morning Call Inc.
All Rights Reserved

Complimentary
Special Edition

'Freedom itself was attacked this morning'

President George W. Bush

86

A fireball erupts from one of the World Trade Center towers as it is struck by an airplane in New York City today. Terrorists hijacked two airliners and crashed them into the World Trade Center in a coordinated series of attacks that brought down the twin 110-story towers.
TODD HOLLIS
Associated Press

A 16-page special report: AMERICA UNDER ATTACK

The Patriot-News

WEDNESDAY
September 12, 2001

50¢
per copy newsstand,
store & vending machines

Volume 160 — No. 216 Copyright © 2001, The Patriot-News Co.

Mostly sunny. High in low 80s. / Back Page

HARRISBURG, PA. ◇ FINAL EDITION ◇

$2.70 per week home delivered

SEPTEMBER 11, 2001:

UNTHINKABLE

In a day of mind-numbing horror, America watched as the World Trade Center was destroyed, the Pentagon was attacked, planes crashed and thousands were killed as terrorists shook our nation to its core.

DIANE BONDAREFF / OF THE ASSOCIATED PRESS

NEW YORK: People flee near the World Trade Center after terrorists crashed two planes into the towers.

HILLERY SMITH GARRISON / OF THE ASSOCIATED PRESS

WASHINGTON: The Pentagon, shortly after taking a direct, devastating hit by a hijacked plane.

DAVID LLOYD / OF THE JOHNSTOWN TRIBUNE-DEMOCRAT

SOMERSET COUNTY: Emergency personnel examine the scene of a fatal crash involving a United Airlines Boeing 757 believed to have been hijacked.

87

KRISTEN BROCHMANN / OF THE NEW YORK TIMES

A fireball erupts from the upper floors of the south tower of the World Trade Center after a second plane hit the complex yesterday. Both towers later plummeted to the ground.

Special Edition   *Special Edition*+

Eight pages of coverage inside

BUCKS COUNTY

Courier Times

TUESDAY, SEPTEMBER 11, 2001   WWW.PHILLYBURBS.COM

25¢

UNTHINKABLE

Nation stunned as terrorists attack America
World Trade Center falls, Pentagon hit; airways shut down

88

ASSOCIATED PRESS

+

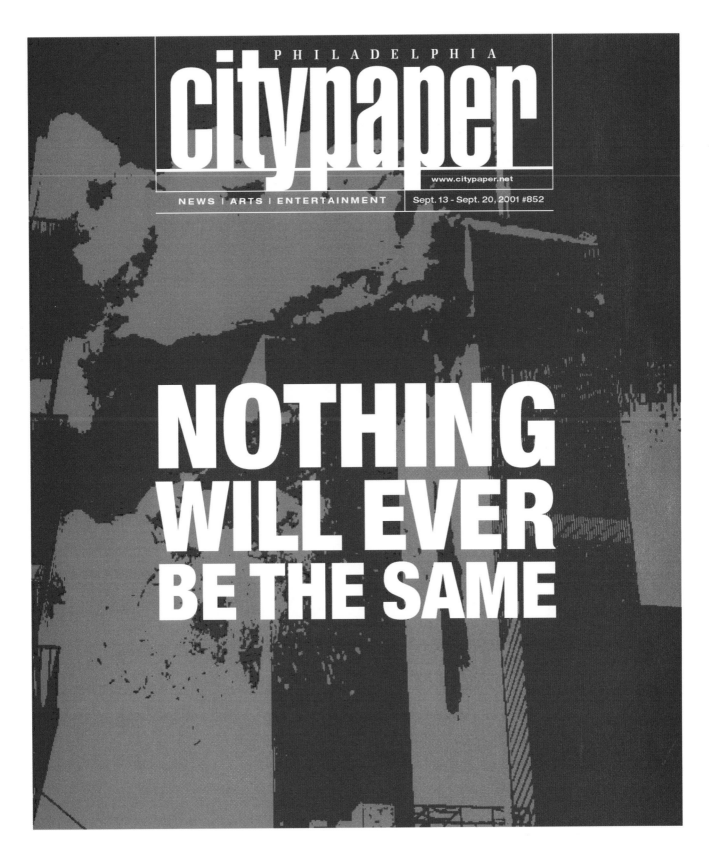

90

SPECIAL REPORT 60¢ · TUESDAY, SEPTEMBER 11, 2001

EXTRA

PHILADELPHIA

DAILY NEWS

THE PEOPLE PAPER

- ■ PLANES HIT WORLD TRADE CENTER
- ■ 110-STORY TOWERS COLLAPSE, BODIES TUMBLE OUT
- ■ EXPLOSIONS ROCK PENTAGON, STATE DEPT.
- ■ FLIGHTS GROUNDED NATIONWIDE
- ■ BUSH ORDERS FULL-SCALE PROBE
- ■ COMMERCIAL PLANE HIJACKED

ATTACK!

PAGES 2-4

EXTRA EDITION

The Philadelphia Inquirer

173d year, Number 103   EXTRA   TUESDAY, SEPTEMBER 11, 2001   www.philly.com   75 cents in some locations outside the metropolitan area   50 CENTS

ATTACKS LEVEL TRADE CENTER

Associated Press

An aircraft is shown seconds before it slammed into the World Trade Center in Manhattan, the second airplane to crash into the towers. The landmark towers later collapsed, killing people inside. Others leaped from the windows as the structure fell.

Pentagon, State Dept. Also Hit

By Jerry Schwartz
ASSOCIATED PRESS

NEW YORK — In a horrific sequence of destruction, terrorists crashed two planes into the World Trade Center and knocked down the 110-story towers this morning. Explosions also rocked the Pentagon and the State Department and spread fear across the nation.

A witness said he saw bodies falling from the twin towers and people jumping out.

President Bush ordered a full-scale investigation to "hunt down the folks who committed this act."

One of the planes that crashed into the Trade Center was American Airlines Flight 11, hijacked after takeoff from Boston en route to Los Angeles, American Airlines said.

The planes blasted fiery, gaping holes in the upper floors of the twin towers. Both towers later collapsed.

"This is perhaps the most audacious terrorist attack that's ever taken place in the world," said Chris Yates, an aviation expert at Jane's Transport in London. "It takes a logistics operation from the terror group involved that is second to none. Only a very small handful of terror groups is on that list. ... I would name at the top of the list Osama bin Laden."

All planes were grounded across the country by the Federal Aviation Administration. All bridges and tunnels into Manhattan were closed down.

See **ATTACKS** on A2

NYC's World Trade Center   MANHATTAN

Site of collisions   City Hall

World
Trade
Center   FULTON ST.

North tower
1,368 feet
110 stories
Struck at
8:42 a.m

South tower
1,362 feet
110 stories
Struck at
approx.
9 a.m.

New York
Stock Exchange

Battery
Park

East
River

BROOKLYN BRIDGE

BROADWAY

MAIDEN LN.

WALL ST.

TRINITY PLACE

MILE
0   1/4

York Daily Record

Since 1796 ☐ Wednesday, September 12, 2001

www.ydr.com **35¢**

9/11/01

Vicious attacks stun nation; Enormous death toll feared

Flames explode from the South Tower of the World Trade Center, left, as it is struck by a hijacked jetliner at 9:03 a.m. Tuesday in lower Manhattan, in the midst of an unprecedented terrorist attack on the United States. The North Tower, right, had been struck by another hijacked jetliner minutes earlier. Within 90 minutes, both 110-story towers collapsed upon themselves due to structural damage and intense heat. The unknown terrorists' assault also included a third hijacked jetliner that crashed into and devastated a portion of the Pentagon in Washington, D.C., and a fourth hijacked jetliner that crashed in a wooded area 80 miles southeast of Pittsburgh. There was no estimate on casualties, but President Bush told the nation Tuesday night that 'thousands of lives were suddenly ended.'

■ The date will stand as a memorial to the worst act of terrorism in world history.

By DAVID CRARY and JERRY SCHWARTZ
Associated Press

NEW YORK — In the most devastating terrorist onslaught ever waged against the United States, knife-wielding hijackers crashed two airliners into the World Trade Center on Tuesday, toppling its twin 110-story towers. The deadly calamity was witnessed on televisions across the world as another plane slammed into the Pentagon, and a fourth crashed outside Pittsburgh.

"Today, our nation saw evil," President Bush said in an address to the nation Tuesday night. He said thousands of lives were "suddenly ended by evil, despicable acts of terror."

Said Adm. Robert J. Natter, commander of the U.S. Atlantic Fleet: "We have been attacked like we haven't since Pearl Harbor."

Establishing the U.S. death toll could take weeks. The four airliners alone had 266 people aboard and there were no known survivors. At the Pentagon, about 100 people were believed dead.

In addition, a firefighters union official said he feared an estimated 200 firefighters had died in rescue efforts at the trade center — where 50,000 people worked — and dozens of police officers were believed missing.

"The number of casualties will be more than most of us can bear," a visibly distraught Mayor Rudolph Giuliani said.

No one took responsibility for the attacks that rocked the seats of finance and government. But federal authorities identified Osama bin Laden, who has been given asylum by Afghanistan's Taliban rulers, as the prime suspect.

Aided by an intercept of communications between his supporters and harrowing cell phone calls from at least one flight attendant and two passengers aboard the jetliners before they crashed, U.S. officials began assembling a case linking bin Laden to the devastation.

U.S. intelligence intercepted communications between bin Laden supporters discussing the attacks on the World Trade Center and Pentagon, according to Utah Sen. Orrin Hatch, the top Republican on the Senate Judiciary Committee.

See ATTACK, page 9A

Fear crashes into York County lives

Daily Record staff report

Schools, government offices and businesses that could be the target of terrorist attacks were closed Tuesday as York County was placed on high alert following the apparent coordinated terrorist assault on America.

York County Emergency Management Agency officials declared the alert, asking residents to limit their phone use and putting out a call for residents to donate blood to treat those wounded in the attack.

Emergency services director Patrick McFadden also asked residents to limit travel Tuesday and to stay tuned to the local and national media for updates

"Nothing has occurred so far in York County," McFadden said. "The county commissioners urge people not to panic."

The general of the Pennsylvania Army Reserve met with Gov. Tom Ridge Tuesday to discuss calling reservists to active duty. The threat level for the state was set at "bravo" Tuesday afternoon, the second highest level. Parts of New York were set at a "delta" level, the highest.

Businesses with offices and employees in New York struggled to find out what was happening. All air traffic

See YORK, page 10A

COMPLETE COVERAGE INSIDE

■ Bush goes into hiding, returns to D.C. to address nation. **3A**
■ Osama bin Laden tops most lists of suspects. **3A**
■ Witnesses tell of horror inside the last day of the World Trade Center. **4A**
■ For many, the only escape from New York was on foot. **4A**
■ Plane crashes into Pentagon; chaos paralyzes nation's capital. **6A**
■ Horrified caller reports hijacking over Pennsylvania just before crash. **7A**
■ World leaders react to multi-pronged attack on America. **8A**
■ Palestinians celebrate upon learning the news. **8A**
■ Economists say the teetering economy could suffer. **11A**
■ SEC closes markets after attack. **11A**
■ Professionals offer Yorkers healing messages, advice. **1D**
■ Security procedures anger local airline pilots. **1D**
■ Three Mile Island tightens security bolsters entrance. **2B**

DAILY RECORD / ANGELA GAUL
People across York County watch in horror and disbelief. **2B**

■ Churches open doors for prayers, solace. **2B**
■ Counselor: Allow children to direct talks about tragedies. **4B**

CALL US WITH YOUR THOUGHTS

As the country struggles to cope with Tuesday's tragic events, we'd like to hear your thoughts on what has happened.

■ Please call our reader line at 771-2004, press option 2, and leave a short message before 2 p.m. with your name, phone number and town. Or e-mail us at news@ydr.com.

■ If you have friends or family from York who have been directly affected by Tuesday's attacks, please call the Daily Record this morning at 771-2000.

BUSINESS	8-9C
CLASSIFIEDS	10-16C
LIVING	1-6D
LOCAL	1-2, 5C
MOVIES	3D
NATION	12-15A
OBITUARIES	3C
OPINION	14A
SPORTS	5-7B

308th Year, No. 255 • York, Pa.
© 2001 York Daily Record

COUNSELING

The **York County** chapter of the **American Red Cross** is offering crisis mental health counseling today, beginning at 8:30 a.m. Call 1-800-347-2751 or 717-845-2751.

Contact York, a nonprofit group, offers an ear to those who want to talk or find resources for dealing with things that upset them. The 24-hour hot line is 757-0753.

WellSpan offers counseling by crisis intervention to handle psychiatric emergencies. The 24-hour hot line is 851-5320.

FINDING RELATIVES

The **York County** chapter of the **American Red Cross** can help people find relatives in areas hit by terrorist attacks, but will not begin tracing relatives until Thursday morning. However, the Red Cross will take information from people trying to find out if relatives are safe. Call 1-800-347-2751 or 717-845-2751.

DONATIONS

Blood donations are being accepted at Apple Hill Medical Center, Suite 198, Entrance C. Please call 741-8307 to make an appointment. Donations will be taken each day until 8 p.m.

American Red Cross blood drives are scheduled for 2 to 6 p.m. Friday at Susquehanna Communications, 1050 E. King St., and 9 a.m. to 1 p.m. Saturday at Shiloh Fire Company, 2190 Carlisle Road. Call 1-800-GIVE-LIFE.

The American Red Cross is accepting monetary donations to help the victims. Call 1-800-HELP-NOW (that's 1-800-435-7669). Checks made out to the American Red Cross can be mailed to American Red Cross, Attn: Disaster Relief Fund, 724 S. George St., York 17403.

LEND A HAND

Volunteer physicians may contact the Pennsylvania Medical Society at 1-800-228-7823, 558-7750 or by e-mail at staf@pamedsoc.org.

Volunteer nurses may contact the Pennsylvania Nurses Association at 1-800-569-4762 or the Pennsylvania Department of Health at 1-877-724-3258.

Volunteer firefighters may call 1-800-459-4296.

Other volunteers may call 851-2089 or 851-2091.

AIRPORTS & GOVERNMENT

All airports nationwide are closed, and are not expected to reopen until noon today. For information from Baltimore-Washington International Airport, call 1-800-I-FLY-BWI or call individual airlines. For information from Harrisburg International Airport, call 717-948-3900 or individual airlines.

York County government offices will be open today, a spokesman for the county's Department of Emergency Services said.

All **state government** offices will open on time today, a spokeswoman for Gov. Tom Ridge said late Tuesday.

Federal government offices will be open today, President Bush said.

Wednesday *September 12, 2001 • Vol. 95, No. 13*
University of South Carolina • www.dailygamecock.com

THE GAMECOCK

OUR WORLD

IS CHANGED

U.S. FACES WORST TERRORIST ATTACK IN HISTORY

93

President Bush says United States will 'hunt down' those responsible

BY DAVID CRARY AND JERRY SCHWARTZ
ASSOCIATED PRESS

NEW YORK (AP) — In the most devastating terrorist onslaught ever waged against the United States, knife-wielding hijackers crashed two airliners into the World Trade Center on Tuesday, toppling its twin 110-story towers. The deadly calamity was witnessed on televisions across the world as another plane slammed into the Pentagon, and a fourth crashed outside Pittsburgh.

"Today, our nation saw evil," President Bush said in an address to the nation Tuesday night. He said thousands of lives were "suddenly ended by evil, despicable acts of terror."

Said Adm. Robert J. Natter, commander of the U.S. Atlantic Fleet: "We have been attacked like we haven't since Pearl Harbor."

Establishing the death toll could take weeks. The four airliners alone had 266 people aboard and there were no known survivors. Officials put the number of dead and wounded at the Pentagon at about 100 or more, with some news reports suggesting it could rise to 800.

In addition, a union official said he feared 300 firefighters who first reached the scene had died in rescue efforts at the trade center — where 50,000 people worked — and dozens of police officers were missing.

"The number of casualties will be more than most of us can bear," a visibly distraught Mayor Rudolph Giuliani said.

Police sources said some people trapped in the twin towers managed to call authorities or family members and that some trapped police officers made radio contact. In one of the calls, which took place in the afternoon, a businessman phoned his family to say he was trapped with policemen, whom he named, the source said.

Because of fires and unstable debris, no rescue attempts were going on Tuesday night at the site of the towers, however.

No one took responsibility for the attacks that rocked the seats of finance and government. But federal authorities identified Osama bin Laden, who has been given asylum by Afghanistan's Taliban rulers, as the prime suspect.

Aided by an intercept of communications between his supporters and harrowing cell phone calls from at least one flight attendant and two passengers aboard the jetliners before they crashed, U.S. officials began assembling a case linking bin Laden to the devastation.

U.S. intelligence intercepted communications between bin Laden supporters discussing the attacks on the World Trade Center and Pentagon, according to Utah Sen. Orrin Hatch, the top Republican on the Senate Judiciary Committee.

The people aboard planes who managed to make cell phone calls each described similar circumstances: They indicated the hijackers were armed with knives, in some cases stabbing flight attendants. The hijackers then took control of the planes.

All of the planes were bound for California and thus loaded with fuel. At the World Trade Center, the dead and the doomed plummeted from the skyscrapers, among them a man and woman holding hands.

Shortly after 7 p.m., crews began heading into ground zero of the attack to search for survivors and recover bodies. All that remained of the twin towers by then was a pile of rubble and twisted steel that stood five stories high, leaving a huge gap in the New York City skyline.

"Freedom itself was attacked this morning and I assure you freedom will be defended," said Bush, who was in Florida at the time of the catastrophe. As a security measure, he was shuttled to a Strategic Air Command bunker in Nebraska before leaving for Washington.

"Make no mistake," he said. "The United States will hunt down and pursue those responsible for these cowardly actions."

More than nine hours after the U.S. attacks began, explosions could be heard north of the Afghan capital of Kabul, but American officials said the United States was not responsible. "It isn't us. I don't know who's doing it," Pentagon spokesman Craig Quigley said.

Officials across the world condemned the attacks but in the West Bank city of Nablus, thou-

• ATTACK, SEE PAGE 2

HOW TO FIND, GIVE HELP

Grief counseling
THE USC COUNSELING AND HUMAN DEVELOPMENT CENTER is offering grief counseling at 900 Assembly St. Walk-ins are welcome, or you can call 777-5223 to set up an appointment. Although no specific counseling groups have been set up, the center intends to create one soon.

Religious services
THE CAROLINA CHAPLAINS ASSOCIATION will hold a special prayer meeting at 12 p.m. in Rutledge Chapel. The chapel will be open Wednesday from 12 p.m. to 6 p.m. Staff will be there to offer counseling and other assistance.
PALM will hold an all-campus prayer vigil over the attacks on the U.S. Wednesday at noon in Rutledge Chapel. PALM will also offer a reflection and service Wednesday evening at 5:30 in the Rutledge Chapel.

Blood bank information
Call 540-1214 if you're interested in giving blood. Call 251-6000 for general information and appointments
SOUTH CAROLINA JUDICIAL CENTER, Wednesday from 10 a.m. -3 p.m.
LEXINGTON MEDICAL CENTER, Thursday from 10 a.m.-3 p.m.
THE VISTA COMMONS, Thursday from 3 p.m.-7 p.m.

Airline contact numbers for missing people
AMERICAN AIRLINES:
(800) 245-0999
UNITED AIRLINES:
(800) 932-8555
IMPORTANT WEB SITES:
http://helping.org
http://www.ifccfbi.gov

COMPILED BY LAURA MOSS, STEFANIE PARKER, SEAN WALLER AND KAREN YIP

INSIDE TODAY'S ISSUE

PHOTO BY AARON HARK

Columbia community offers assistance
Citizens line up to donate blood at the Red Cross. ◆ PAGE 5

PHOTO BY AARON HARK

South Carolina reacts to terrorist events
City and state offices remain open under high security. ◆ PAGE 4

PHOTO BY JOSH SKIDMORE

USC community views coverage at GMP
Russell House is center of information on tragedy. ◆ PAGE 5

94

The State

110TH YEAR, NO. 255 • SOUTH CAROLINA'S LARGEST NEWSPAPER Wednesday, September 12, 2001 COLUMBIA, S.C. • SWITCHBOARD (803) 771-6161 • STATE EDITION

PHOTO BY SPENCER PLATT / GETTY IMAGES

A fiery blast rocks one of the World Trade Center towers in New York City after a passenger jet slammed into it on Tuesday. Both buildings collapsed to the ground.

America Under Attack

IT WAS PERHAPS the nation's bloodiest day, replayed again and again on every television screen. The jet crashes that destroyed the twin towers of New York's World Trade Center — the first at 8:45 a.m. Tuesday, the next at 9:03 — began a nightmare that would include an attack on the Pentagon, an airline crash in Pennsylvania and a president's vow to punish those responsible.

Officials were not forthcoming with casualty estimates. But as the toll rose, it was apparent that Sept. 11, 2001, could eclipse any other disaster in national memory: the attack on Pearl Harbor, the casualties of D-Day, the Civil War carnage at Antietam.

"Freedom itself was attacked this morning," President Bush said.

As smoke billowed from the Trade Center towers, workplace of 50,000 people, a third hijacked plane slammed into the Pentagon and a fourth crashed southeast of Pittsburgh.

Manhattan, its cityscape altered forever, was evacuated, as were government buildings around the nation, including the Capitol, the White House and the S.C. State House.

At Pearl Harbor in 1941, about 2,400 died; in the Johnstown Flood in Pennsylvania in 1889, more than 2,200;

in the Galveston, Texas, hurricane in 1900, about 6,000; at Antietam in Maryland in 1862, more than 4,700 soldiers.

They were acts of nature and acts of war. But Tuesday's disaster was quickly termed an act of terrorism. "Today, our nation saw evil," Bush told the nation.

He asked people to pray for the families of the victims and quoted the Book of Psalms: "And I pray they will be comforted by a power greater than any of us, spoken through the ages in Psalm 23. 'Even though I walk through the valley of the shadow of death, I fear no evil, for you are with me.' "

TIMELINE
PAGE A2

NIGHTMARE
Terrorists plunge hijacked planes into the World Trade Center towers in New York and the Pentagon.
PAGE A3

NEW YORK
New Yorkers react with disbelief: 'This is the most horrifying thing I've ever experienced.'
PAGE A4

WASHINGTON
The toll at the Pentagon is 'extensive'. Some lawmakers say U.S. intelligence network has atrophied. .
PAGE A6

IN S.C.
South Carolinians react with shock, anger, worry and compassion for victims of the attacks.
PAGE A11

CHILDREN
How do you explain the tragic events to children? Here are some tips on how to approach each age group.
PAGE A14

0 07770 00001 0

Special Edition

THE ISLAND
PACKET

Volume 31
Founded 1970

25¢

TUESDAY, SEPTEMBER 11, 2001   *Southern Beaufort County's Newspaper*

Terrorists attack

Photos by The Associated Press

An aircraft, at right, is seen today as it is about to fly into the World Trade Center in New York in this image made from television. The aircraft was the second to fly into the tower this morning.

World Trade Center collapses; Washington hit

BY JERRY SCHWARTZ
THE ASSOCIATED PRESS

NEW YORK — In one of the most horrifying attacks ever against the United States, terrorists crashed two airliners into the World Trade Center in a deadly series of blows today that brought down the twin 110-story towers. A plane also slammed into the Pentagon as the government itself came under attack.

Thousands could be dead or injured, a high-ranking New York City police official said, speaking on condition of anonymity.

Authorities had been trying to evacuate those who work in the twin towers when the glass-and-steel skyscrapers came down in a thunderous roar within about 90 minutes after the crashes, which took place minutes apart around 9 a.m. But many people were thought to have been trapped. About 50,000 people work at the Trade Center and tens of thousands of others visit each day.

American Airlines initially said the Trade Center was hit by two of its planes, both hijacked, carrying a total of 156 peo-

People run from the collapse of the World Trade Center Tower today. A police official said thousands could be dead or injure.

ple. But the airline later said that was unconfirmed. Two United airliners with a total of 110 aboard also crashed — one outside Pittsburgh, the other in a location

not immediately identified. Altogether, the planes had 266 people aboard.

Please see **TRADE CENTER**, Page 4

Plane crashes into Pentagon; troops deployed in response

BY RON FOURNIER
THE ASSOCIATED PRESS

WASHINGTON — The Pentagon took a direct, devastating hit from an aircraft and the enduring symbols of American power were evacuated today as an apparent terrorist attack quickly spread fear and chaos in the nation's capital.

President Bush ordered the nation's military to "high-alert status," and vowed to "hunt down and punish those responsible" for the attacks in Washington and New York, where the World Trade Center was devastated with a heavy loss of life.

The president was in Florida at the time of the attacks, and was flown at midday to the safety of a military installation, Barksdale Air Force Base in

Louisiana. The top leaders of Congress were led to the safety of an undisclosed location, and military aircraft were reported patrolling the skies above the capital.

The nerve center of the nation's military burst into flames and a portion of one side of the five-sided structure collapsed when the plane struck in mid-morning. Secondary explosions were reported in the aftermath of the attack and great billows of smoke drifted skyward toward the Potomac River and the city beyond.

At midday, local hospitals reported receiving 40 victims of the attack, with seven patients in critical condition admitted to one facility for treatment of burns.

Please see **WASHINGTON**, Page 5

Security at Beaufort Marine base increased after incidents

GAZETTE STAFF REPORT

Beaufort's military bases were checking identification at the gates on today, and most community events were canceled, as the area reacted to terrorist attacks in New York and Washington.

The Marine Corps Air Station-Beaufort was under Threat Condition Charlie, a

state of increased physical security, based on the terrorist attacks in New York and Washington.

Access to the air station is limited and identification cards are being checked at all gates.

Marine Corps Recruit Depot Parris Island was checking identification cards at the gate, with random ID checks and spot

vehicle searches at the depot.

The recruit depot is coordinating with local police departments to prepare for possible traffic congestion leading from gate.

Beaufort's National Guard Armory has been locked, and no mobilization order had been received for the troops as of 1 p.m. Tuesday, said Staff Sgt. Steven Barnett.

The Beaufort County Emergency Operations Center was partially activated in response to the incidents.

Beaufort County and municipal police departments are on alert, but had not recalled officers. Fire departments across Beaufort County were reviewing their

Please see **BEAUFORT**, Page 5

Beaufort's National Guard Armory has been locked, and no mobilization order had been received for the troops as of 1 p.m. Tuesday, according to Staff Sgt. Steven Barnett.

THE COMMERCIAL APPEAL

162nd Year, Memphis, Tennessee   Wednesday, September 12, 2001   **Final   50¢

'EVIL ACTS'

Hijackers destroy N.Y. towers, rip Pentagon; thousands feared dead in war on America

96

By Spencer Platt/Getty Images

- Terrorism against United States rises to a new level. **A3**

- Beautiful morning in New York turns into inferno. **A6**

By Ernesto Mora/AP

- FedEx's usual wee-hour flights skip a night. **A9**

- Stranded air travelers here 'solemn,' not angry. **A10**

- For continuing coverage, log on to *www.gomemphis.com*

7 49377 10040 0   A B C D
Copyright, 2001,
The Commercial Appeal

WEDNESDAY
September 12, 2001

THE **City Paper**

Nashville, Tenn.   www.nashvillecitypaper.com

Free Publication
support our advertisers

© 2001 • Edge Communications, Inc.

America in shock

97

REUTERS/Shannon Stapleton

24 PAGES OF DISASTER COVERAGE INSIDE

Wednesday, September 12, 2001

NASHVILLE, TENNESSEE

THE TENNESSEAN

A GANNETT NEWSPAPER

VOLUME 97, NO. 255   5 SECTIONS   3   © COPYRIGHT 2001   PERIODICALS POSTAGE PAID IN NASHVILLE, TN

SEPTEMBER 11, 2001: WORLD TRADE CENTER CRUMBLES

Left picture shows the World Trade Center as it appeared before being hit by two planes yesterday. In the next picture, a hijacked plane is seconds away from slamming into the south tower as the north tower burns from an earlier attack. The plane pierces the building, center. Within two hours of the first attack, both towers had collapsed, second from right, leaving the Manhattan skyline in a cloud of smoke. Rescuers work their way through the rubble, right.

AP PHOTOS

Day of terror

World Trade Center, Pentagon attacked by terrorists using airliners; Bush vows punishment by U.S.

**By DAVID CRARY
and JERRY SCHWARTZ**
Associated Press

NEW YORK — In the most devastating terrorist onslaught ever waged against the United States, knife-wielding hijackers crashed two airliners into the World Trade Center yesterday, toppling its twin 110-story towers.

The deadly calamity was witnessed on televisions across the world as another plane slammed into the Pentagon, and a fourth crashed outside Pittsburgh.

"Today, our nation saw evil," President Bush said in an address to the nation last night. He said thousands of lives were "suddenly ended by evil, despicable acts of terror."

Establishing the U.S. death toll could take weeks. The four airliners alone had 266 people aboard and there were no known survivors. At the Pentagon, about 100 people were believed dead. Authorities anticipated a large number of deaths at the World Trade Center although it was possible some people were alive in the rubble.

No one took responsibility for the attacks that rocked the seats of finance and government. But federal authorities identified Osama bin Laden, who has been given asylum by Afghanistan's Taliban rulers, as the prime suspect.

Aided by an intercept of communications between his supporters and harrowing cell phone calls from at least

▶ Please see TERROR, 2A

▶ Please see TERROR, 2A

Chronology of tragedy

7:45 A.M.
American Airlines Flight 11 slams into the north tower of the World Trade Center.

8:03 A.M.
A second plane slams into the south tower of the World Trade Center.

8:43 A.M.
An aircraft crashes into the Pentagon. A portion of one side of the five-sided building collapses.

8:50 A.M.
The south tower of the World Trade Center collapses in a plume of ash and debris.

9 A.M.
United Airlines Flight 93, a Boeing 757 en route from Newark, N.J., to San Francisco, crashes just north of the Somerset County Airport, about 80 miles southeast of Pittsburgh.

9:29 A.M.
The World Trade Center's north tower collapses from the top down as if it were being peeled apart, releasing a tremendous cloud of debris and smoke.

— TENNESSEAN NEWS SERVICES

Military personnel flee the Pentagon after a plane crashed into the building yesterday morning.
GANNETT NEWS SERVICE

A fireball erupts from the south tower of the World Trade Center after a second plane slammed into the complex. Smoke billows from the north tower, which was struck by another aircraft minutes earlier. The Brooklyn Bridge is in the foreground.
NEW YORK TIMES

Nashville native survives attack from 90th floor: 'It was like you were in hell'

▶ A Harpeth Hall graduate was in her office at the World Trade Center when the first plane hit. **On 16A**

Anne Prosser

Prime suspect
▶ Before the smoke cleared from the Pentagon and the World Trade Center, Saudi Arabian terrorist leader Osama bin Laden emerged as the prime suspect. **On 3A**

AP

Witnesses in New York react with horror after the World Trade Center is hit.

New York nightmare
▶ After the initial horror, the city braced itself for more pain: digging through the rubble for the dead and the injured. **On 6-7A**

Readers react
▶ *Tennessean* readers respond to tragedy in the "Letters to the Editor." **On 30A**

Financial worries
▶ Business community left reeling. **On 1-3E**

How you can help
▶ Local Red Cross is seeking extra blood donations for the next two weeks. **On 20A**

0 40901 05606 5

To subscribe call:
242-NEWS
or (800) 342-8237

www.tennessean.com

DYESS: Is the Air Force base safe from terrorist attack? ■ 1AA

WEDNESDAY

Abilene Reporter-News

50 cents   September 12, 2001

NIGHTMARE

Justin Lane/The New York Times

Firefighters tend to a victim following the collapse of the World Trade Center. On Tuesday morning, planes slammed into both towers of the World Trade Center in Manhattan. A short time later another crashed into the Pentagon outside Washington in what appeared to be parallel attacks on quintessential symbols of American financial and military power. Before the day was over, both of the 110-story towers at the World Trade Center collapsed minutes apart.

Havoc rekindles memories

Devastation reminds many of Pearl Harbor surprise attack

By Bill Whitaker
Reporter-News Staff Writer

Alan Chin/The New York Times

A man and an injured woman walk down a street in downtown Manhattan shortly after the collapse of the World Trade Center towers Tuesday.

When World War II pilot Jack Connor broke away from televised reports of the World Trade Center tragedy Tuesday to attend his weekly civic club luncheon, the 82-year-old Abilenian had a word for fellow Rotarians, many also aging veterans of a vanishing era.

"I suggested at Rotary Club that all we retirees report to Dyess for duty," he said, referring to the Air Force base that has long contributed to Abilene's patriotic character. "Some of them said they were going to get their uniforms, too."

However ill-timed Connor's all-American bravado might have seemed, it briefly broke the somber tone that reigned over Abilene on Tuesday. The mood eclipsed outright grief and anger — emotions that will doubtless surface in the days ahead.

For now, numbing disbelief prevails.

For many, that sentiment accompanied an eerie sensation that the havoc in New York and Washington had catastrophic precedents dating all the way back to Pearl Harbor. Yet, at the same time, Tuesday's tragedy represented something new, something even more horrible.

"You know, everyone keeps comparing this to Pearl Harbor, but back then we knew who was responsible," said Dr. John C. Stevens, 83, Abilene Christian University chancellor emeritus and an Army chaplain during World War II. "Right now, nobody seems sure who to blame.

"We need to do our level best to find out who's responsible. But, sure, when it first happened, it seemed like Pearl Harbor again."

H.V. Chapman, 80, a local bookbinder who served in the Naval Air Corps during World War II, conceded it was easy enough to view Tuesday's attack as similar to Pearl Harbor. But on closer examination even the Japanese bombers took a higher road, he said.

"They were after military," he said just before an Abilene Community Band concert Tuesday night, "and this is ordinary people."

With the uneasy feeling that war is in the air — even if it's a war unlike any America has faced — veterans of all eras admit confusion as to how best to respond,

which only contributed further to the somber mood.

"Everybody's kind of awestruck," said 46-year-old Air Force veteran David Jorgensen, a city employee and junior vice commander at VFW Post No. 6873. "There's a lot of talk about this and the Oklahoma City bombing — I mean, the feeling of how this could ever happen here.

"Of course, this is much worse."

Glena Haley, 77, of Buffalo Gap, who served as a Navy aerial machine gun instructor during World War II, admitted she was nearly dumbfounded at what she was seeing on TV — and, she said, she had seen her share of wartime horrors.

"This is a different world from the one I grew up in," she said. "I guess what's so different is that so much of this involves civilians — not necessarily the people who

Please see HAVOC, 2A

Please see HAVOC, 2A

U.S. Under Attack

6:58 a.m. United Airlines flight 175, a Boeing 767, to Los Angeles departs Boston's Logan International Airport, 56 passengers, nine crew.

6:59 a.m. American Airlines flight 11, a Boeing 767, to Los Angeles leaves Boston, 81 passengers, 11 crew.

7:01 a.m. United flight 93, a Boeing 757, to San Francisco takes off from Newark N.J., International Airport, 38 passengers, seven crew.

7:10 a.m. American flight 77, a Boeing 757, to Los Angeles departs Washington's Dulles International Airport, 58 passengers, six crew.

7:51 a.m. One of the Boston-originated planes crashes into north World Trade Center tower.

8:06 a.m. The second Boston-originated plane crashes into south World Trade Center tower.

8:25 a.m. New York Stock Exchange delays trading. U.S. Federal Aviation Administration orders all planes grounded.

8:41 a.m. American flight 77 crashes into the Pentagon in Arlington, Va.

8:44 a.m. White House and Pentagon evacuated.

8:48 a.m. U.S. Capitol evacuated.

9 a.m. South World Trade Center tower collapses.

9:28 a.m. North World Trade Center tower collapses.

9:40 a.m. United flight 93 crashes southeast of Pittsburgh.

9:56 a.m. Securities and Exchange Commission closes all U.S. markets for the day.

Air Force One

12:04 p.m. President Bush speaks via videotape from Barksdale AFB near Shreveport, La. Departs for Offutt AFB in Omaha.

3:33 p.m. Bush leaves Nebraska for Washington.

5:55 p.m. Bush returns to White House via Marine One.

7:30 p.m. President addresses nation.
—Bloomberg News Service,
Photos by Associated Press
*Times converted to Central Daylight Time

INSIDE: Please see page 2A for a complete guide to all the coverage of Tuesday's tragic events.
PLUS: Index of all regular *Reporter-News* features.

SPECIAL REPORT

Austin American-Statesman

50 cents   Final   statesman.com   Wednesday, September 12, 2001

'OUR NATION SAW EVIL'

- **Targets:** Hijacked planes slam into World Trade Center, Pentagon
- **The toll:** Thousands are killed in world's worst terrorist attack
- **Missing:** Nearly 400 NYC firefighters, police feared dead; 266 aboard jets
- **The suspect:** Evidence 'strongly points' to terror mastermind bin Laden
- **Gridlock:** U.S. markets shut down; air travel halted; Austin airport closes
- **The president:** Tragedy fills nation with 'a quiet, unyielding anger'

100

Guinam Samoilova/Associated Press

Covered in dust and debris, people made their way through the layers of destruction on the streets of New York as they walked away from the World Trade Center, where both towers collapsed.

U.S. has 'no blueprint' for how to strike back

BY PAUL RICHTER
Los Angeles Times

WASHINGTON — The terrorist attack on the United States put powerful pressure on President Bush to retaliate swiftly, even as U.S. officials and outside experts warned that any military operation will involve risks and tough choices.

Although U.S. officials said they have no conclusive evidence showing who was responsible, many government officials and terrorism experts consider Saudi dissident Osama bin Laden the prime suspect. If the Bush administration eventually concludes he is to blame, the Pentagon could choose a variety of responses.

The military could launch air attacks on bin Laden's camps in Afghanistan and seek to strike his cells in the Middle East and around the world. As the Clinton administration learned, hitting the bin Laden operation with enough force to deter future terrorism will be tough. Unlike nations with military infrastructures and targets such as tank divisions and air defense batteries,

bin Laden's network is widely dispersed, consisting of relatively mobile terrorist cells with few easily identifiable targets.

Also, the suicide terrorists who carried out Tuesday's attacks have such strong motives that any counterattack may not deter them — and could even strengthen their resolve. Another option for the Pentagon would be to hit the military and command infrastructure of the Taliban government in Afghanistan. The Taliban, which has acquiesced to bin Laden's activities in their country, denied any involvement and condemned Tuesday's attacks.

Explosions shook Afghanistan's capital of Kabul hours after the attacks in the United States, but Bush administration officials denied any responsibility. In a briefing at the Pentagon, Defense Secretary Donald Rumsfeld said that "in no way is the United States government connected to those explosions."

It may be days, weeks or even months before a fuller picture of Tuesday's attacks is assembled. In

See U.S. forces, A20

Carmen Taylor/Associated Press

A fireball spews glass and steel out of the World Trade Center's south tower after an airliner rammed it Tuesday morning. The building later collapsed as the flames gutted the upper floors.

Airliners are turned into weapons of terror

BY SCOTT SHEPARD AND SHELLEY EMLING
American-Statesman Washington Staff

WASHINGTON — Unknown enemies waged the worst terrorist attack in U.S. history Tuesday, flying hijacked airliners into the World Trade Center, collapsing the 110-story buildings into piles of rubble, and into the Pentagon. There was no official count, but President Bush said thousands had perished.

Bush condemned the attacks as the government assumed a war footing.

"Today, our nation saw evil . . . This is a day when all Americans from every walk of life unite in our resolve for justice and peace," Bush said in a national address Tuesday night. "America has stood down enemies before, and we will do so this time."

The horrendous attacks, witnessed on televisions across the world, seemed carefully coordinated. They began when two commercial jetliners that were hijacked within 16 minutes of each other from Boston's Logan International Airport crashed into the

giant World Trade Center towers in New York City. Soon afterward, another hijacked commercial airliner plowed into the Pentagon outside the nation's capital. A fourth hijacked plane crashed 80 miles southeast of Pittsburgh, apparently bound for the presidential retreat at Camp David, Md.

"The search is under way for those who are behind these evil acts," Bush said as rescuers continued combing through rubble of the various targeted sites, searching for survivors.

No one took responsibility for the attacks, but federal authorities pointed to Osama bin Laden, an exiled Saudi millionaire who has been linked to an earlier bombing of the World Trade Center.

Police sources said some people trapped in the twin towers managed to call authorities or family members and that some trapped police officers made radio contact. In one of the calls, which took place in the afternoon, a businessman phoned his family to say he was trapped with policemen,

See Attacks, A19

Today's American-Statesman is being delivered to all weekday and Sunday subscribers.
For the latest breaking news, go to **statesman.com**

For home delivery, call 445-4040. © 2001, Austin American-Statesman

7 65668 20202 8

◆ **EDITORIAL:** Terrorist attacks won't thwart American ideals/**14A** ◆

WEATHER

Today: Partly cloudy.
High: 90s. Low: 70s.

Update, page 2A

THE BEAUMONT ENTERPRISE

WEDNESDAY

SEPTEMBER 12, 2001

VOL.CXX, NO. 311

http://www.SoutheastTexasLive.com ◆ ━━━━ ◆ THE ADVOCATE FOR SOUTHEAST TEXAS SINCE 1880 ◆ ━━━━ ◆ 50 Cents

TERRORIZED

Hijacked planes crash, collapse World Trade Center; coordinated attack also hits Pentagon; thousands die

**By DAVID CRARY
and JERRY SCHWARTZ**
THE ASSOCIATED PRESS

NEW YORK — In the most devastating terrorist onslaught ever waged against the United States, knife-wielding hijackers crashed two airliners into the World Trade Center on Tuesday, toppling its twin 110-story towers. The deadly calamity was witnessed on televisions across the world as another plane slammed into the Pentagon, and a fourth crashed outside Pittsburgh.

"Today, our nation saw evil," President Bush said in an address to the nation Tuesday night. He said thousands of lives were "suddenly ended by evil, despicable acts of terror."

Said Adm. Robert J. Natter, commander of the U.S. Atlantic Fleet: "We have been attacked like we haven't since Pearl Harbor."

Establishing the U.S. death toll could take weeks. The four airliners alone had 266 people aboard and there were no known survivors. At the Pentagon, about 100 people were believed dead.

In addition, a firefighters union official said he feared an estimated 200 firefighters had died in rescue efforts at the trade center — where 50,000 people worked — and dozens of police officers were believed missing.

No one took responsibility for the attacks that rocked the seats of finance and government. But federal authorities identified Osama bin Laden, who has been given asylum by Afghanistan's Taliban rulers, as the prime suspect.

Aided by an intercept of communications between his supporters and harrowing cell phone calls from at least one flight attendant and two passengers aboard the jetliners before they crashed, U.S. officials began assembling a case linking bin Laden to the devastation.

U.S. intelligence intercepted communications between bin Laden supporters discussing the attacks on the World Trade Center and Pentagon, according to Utah Sen. Orrin Hatch, the top Republican on the Senate Judiciary Committee.

The people aboard planes who managed to make cell phone calls each described similar circumstances: They indicated the hijackers were armed with knives, in some cases stabbing flight attendants. The hijackers then took control of the planes.

At the World Trade Center, the dead and the doomed plummeted from the skyscrapers, among them a man and woman holding hands.

Shortly after 7 p.m., crews began

ATTACK, page 5A

Inside

Southeast Texas effects, thoughts
→ PAGES 2-3A

State, Louisiana roundup
→ PAGE 4A

First person account
→ PAGE 6A

Worldwide reaction
→ PAGE 7A

Follow coverage of Tuesday's events at www.SoutheastTexasLive.com

A shell of what was once part of the facade of one of the twin towers of New York's World Trade Center rises above the rubble that remains after both towers were destroyed in a terrorist attack Tuesday. The 110-story towers collapsed after two hijacked airliners carrying scores of passengers slammed into the towers.

The Associated Press

Bush: U.S. will retaliate against 'those behind these evil acts'

THE ASSOCIATED PRESS

WASHINGTON — A grim-faced President Bush mourned the deaths of thousands of Americans in Tuesday's atrocities and vowed to avenge their killings. "Today, our nation saw evil," he said.

In his first prime-time Oval Office address, Bush said the United States would retaliate against "those behind these evil acts," and any country that harbors them.

Bush spoke from the Oval Office just hours after bouncing between Florida and air bases in

President Bush was shuttled around the country Tuesday under protection of the Secret Service.

rity reasons. Fighter jets and decoy helicopters accompanied his evening flight to Washington and the White House.

With smoke still pouring out of rubble in Washington and New York, he said, "These acts shat-

the steel of American resolve."

Bush spoke for less than five minutes from the desk that Bill Clinton and John F. Kennedy used before him.

Beside the door, a TelePromTer operator fed Bush the words that he and his speechwriters hastened to pen just an hour earlier.

He stumbled a couple of times even as he strove to maintain a commanding air.

Aides pushed an American flag and one with the presidential seal behind him for the somber occasion.

Bush said the government offices deserted after the bomb-

He asked the nation to pray for the families of the victims and quoted the Book of Psalms. "And I pray they will be comforted by a power greater than any of us spoken through the ages in Psalm 23. Even though I walk through the valley of the shadow of death, I fear no evil for you are with me."

The United States received no warning of the attacks on the Pentagon and New York's World Trade Center towers, White House press secretary Ari Fleischer said.

U.S. officials privately said they suspected terrorism Osama

INSIDE

26-year-old QB
Mark Farris leads Aggies
→ PAGE 1B

America's fruit
Great season for apples
→ PAGE 1C

EXTRA EXTRA EXTRA

Corpus Christi Caller Times

 50 cents

Serving South Texas since 1883 ❏ Copyright © 2001 Corpus Christi Caller-Times

Tuesday, September 11, 2001

102

TERRORISTS

STRIKE AMERICA

Smoke billows from one of the towers of the World Trade Center as the other tower explodes during a terrorist attack today that destroyed both towers. Two hijacked commercial airliners were crashed into the center.

Associated Press

Copyright © 2001 Caller-Times Publishing Company. Reprinted with permission. All rights reserved.

Trade Center, Pentagon hit; airliners down

Much of D.C. is evacuated; deaths in the thousands

BY JERRY SCHWARTZ

AP National Writer

NEW YORK — In one of the most devastating attacks ever against the United States, terrorists crashed two airliners into the World Trade Center in a closely timed series of blows Tuesday that brought down the twin 110-story towers. A plane also slammed into the Pentagon as the government itself came under attack.

Thousands could be dead or injured, a high-ranking New York City police official said.

A fourth jetliner, apparently hijacked, crashed in

People evacuating the World Trade Center today make their way through dust that obscures colors.

Associated Press

Pennsylvania.

President Bush ordered a full-scale investigation to "hunt down the folks who committed this act."

Authorities had been trying to evacuate those who work in the twin towers when the glass-and-steel skyscrapers came down in a thunderous roar about 90 minutes after the attacks, which took place minutes apart around 9 a.m.

But many people were thought to have been trapped. About 50,000 people work at the Trade Center and tens of thousands of others visit each day.

American Airlines said two of its planes, both hijacked, crashed with a total of 156 people aboard, but said it could not confirm where they went down. Two United airliners with a total of 110 aboard also crashed — one outside Pittsburgh, the other in a location not immediately identified. Altogether, the planes had 266 people aboard.

"This is perhaps the most audacious terrorist attack that's ever taken place in the world," said Chris Yates,

Please see ATTACK/2

ATTACK ON AMERICA: A 32-PAGE SPECIAL REPORT

The Dallas Morning News

Texas' Leading Newspaper   Dallas, Texas, Wednesday, September 12, 2001   DallasNews.com   50 cents

War at home

Shaken nation awaits tally from Pentagon, Trade Center attacks; Bush vows to track down terrorists and 'bring them to justice'

DOUG KANTER/Agence France-Presse

New York's World Trade Center towers were reduced to rubble by hits from two hijacked jets. Another jet smashed into the Pentagon in Washington, and a fourth went down near Pittsburgh. No one immediately claimed responsibility.

'Today our nation saw evil, the very worst,' president says

By VICTORIA LOE HICKS
Staff Writer

Americans found themselves at war Tuesday with a shadowy enemy whose ruthless precision raised fears that more — or even worse — might lie ahead.

A grim-faced President Bush vowed to find those responsible for flying hijacked airliners into the World Trade Center and the Pentagon — claiming perhaps thousands of lives — and to "bring them to justice."

"Today our nation saw evil, the very worst of human nature," Mr. Bush said.

Earlier, at a Pentagon briefing,

Army Gen. Hugh Shelton, chairman of the Joint Chiefs of Staff, said he would not discuss any possible military response, "but make no mistake about it, our armed forces are ready."

The suicide missions by the terrorists left Americans deeply shaken, as they watched the most potent symbols of the nation's financial and military might disintegrate, sickeningly, in billows of

black smoke.

A fourth airliner also crashed Tuesday, going down in a field near Pittsburgh. Some authorities speculated that it had been preparing to hit the presidential retreat at Camp David, Md.

A woman on the streets of New York captured the enormity in a single word: "Armageddon."

See **SYMBOLS** *Page 14A*

A DAY OF TERROR

The four airliners had 266 people aboard; there were no known survivors.

At the Pentagon, about 100 people were believed dead.

An estimated 300 firefighters died in rescue efforts at the World Trade Center — where 50,000 people worked. At least 78 police officers died and about 30 are missing.

Air travel throughout the nation ceased, stranding thousands of passengers.

Trading on Wall Street was shut down.

A guide to *The Dallas Morning News'* full coverage of the tragedy appears on **2A**

For continuing coverage today, visit **DallasNews.com** and tune in to WFAA (Ch. 8) and TXCN.

EDITORIAL

America the resilient

During the early, dark days of World War II, when Britain stood virtually alone against Adolf Hitler's war machine, Prime Minister Winston Churchill took his advisers to a bombed-out quarter of London. Several houses stood amid the rubble. Smoke curled from the houses' chimneys. Mr. Churchill pointed to the smoke and told them that it signified the indomitable spirit of the British people who were still carrying on with their lives despite daunting difficulties, fear and uncertainty. He urged them to take heart from this example of bravery.

By that very same token, Americans must be united, not intimidated, by the terrorist attacks in New York and Washington on Tuesday, in which thousands of people died. The great generosity and spirit of the American people were evident by midday as they rushed to donate blood and attended special prayer services around the country.

In the post-Cold War world, the most likely threat for the United States now comes from enemies operating surreptitiously, employing unconventional means and taking advantage of the openness of American society. With all possible speed, our country should pursue a homeland defense that gives the greatest emphasis to the kinds of attacks that turned the World Trade Center and the Pentagon into fiery hecatombs.

Until then, all citizens should dedicate themselves to addressing the immediate needs of the victims and their loved ones. The nation mourns grievously for the departed and their families; we have only begun to absorb the dimensions of this tragedy.

This moment is a test of our country's character. President Bush and Congress have put aside all partisan interests and now must respond with the same fortitude of Londoners 60 years ago. Our leaders must bind "we the people" together, mend and console the survivors, and call upon our great stock of moral strength.

The United States of America must continue to epitomize the values of democracy. Americans know we are a resilient people. Now, through our courage and resolve, we must remind the world of how precious freedom is and how relentlessly we will defend it.

CARMEN TAYLOR/KHBS/KHOG-TV

CARMEN TAYLOR/KHBS/KHOG-TV

JERRY TORRENS/Associated Press

Left: A jetliner heads toward a World Trade Center tower, about 20 minutes after another plane crashed into its twin. Center: A fireball explodes from the second tower. Right: That tower collapses; 40 minutes later, the other falls.

'The whole world's changed today'

Sadness, anger grip a nation that has lost all sense of security

By TODD J. GILLMAN and MARK WROLSTAD
Staff Writers

Everything changed Tuesday. At work, home and school, Americans struggled to make sense of the horror.

"It's something I just can't

imagine," said 16-year-old Erica Ward, a high school junior in Garland. "It's like the world is coming to an end."

The devastation — of a nation's symbols of security and prosperity — gripped everyone, with a strong undertow of emotions: Shock. Disbelief. Anger. Fear. The flash of explosions, the downing of airliners, the collapse of skyscrapers shook Americans' sense of safety to the core.

In Dallas and across the country, the mood of the people grew

somber, dark and complex. In offices, colleagues gathered in a hush to watch the TV reports. In classrooms, teachers consoled weeping students. In airports, business executives and tourists tried to call home to let loved ones know they were all right.

Parents raced to pull their sons and daughters from school — then wondered how to explain the attacks to them. Others grew outraged and compared the attacks to Pearl Harbor, to the Kennedy assassination, to the Oklahoma City

bombing.

Cindy Smith, a mother in Mansfield, put it simply: "The whole world's changed today."

See **AMERICANS** *Page 15A*

III+
©2001, The Dallas Morning News

ASSAULT ON AMERICA

• Special 16-page section, Pages 21A-36A   • Up-to-the-minute coverage, video, extras: www.houstonchronicle.com

Houston Chronicle

Vol. 100 No. 334   Wednesday, Sept. 12, 2001   50 Cents   ★★★

TERRORISTS SLAM JETLINERS INTO WORLD TRADE CENTER, PENTAGON

DEATH TOLL MAY REACH INTO THOUSANDS; HOSPITALS FLOODED WITH INJURED

BUSH VOWS TO USE 'FULL RESOURCES' OF GOVERNMENT TO TRACK DOWN THOSE RESPONSIBLE

TERROR HITS HOME

104

A second aircraft nears the World Trade Center, top, moments before hitting the south tower Tuesday. Within a span of 18 minutes, both New York landmarks were hit by hijacked airliners in what President Bush called "a national tragedy and an apparent act of terrorism against our country."

Kelly Guenther / The New York Times

By BENNETT ROTH
Houston Chronicle Washington Bureau

WASHINGTON — Terrorists hijacked U.S. commercial jets Tuesday and hurtled them into the Pentagon and New York's World Trade Center in a fiery, coordinated attack that stunned a disbelieving nation and may have killed thousands.

President Bush vowed to bring to justice those who plowed two aircraft into the 110-story twin towers in New York's financial district and slammed another plane into the five-sided military complex across the Potomac River from the White House. A fourth plane was hijacked and crashed in Pennsylvania.

In a hastily arranged televised address from the Oval Office, Bush sought to reassure the nation that the atrocious acts would not intimidate the United States.

"Terrorist attacks can shake the foundations of our biggest buildings, but they cannot touch the foundation of America," he said. "These acts shatter steel, but they cannot dent the steel of American resolve."

About an hour after the planes hit in New York, the skyscrapers collapsed, trapping rescue workers and police still trying to evacuate workers from the buildings.

"All this stuff started falling and all this smoke was coming through. People were screaming, falling, and jumping out of the windows," Jennifer Brickhouse, 34, from Union, N.J., told The Associated Press after the south tower was hit.

The Federal Emergency Management Agency sent eight urban search and rescue task forces from around the nation as the extent of the tragedy became clear. Debris clogged streets, and smoke and dust drifted for blocks as parts of the city shut down.

It was estimated that as many as 50,000 people worked in the World Trade Center complex. After reports of possible cell phone calls from victims, New York Mayor Rudy Giuliani said late Tuesday that some people could be alive but trapped in buildings near the collapsed towers.

While the number of tower workers who died was not known, New York fire officials estimated that more than 100 firefighters who responded to the scene — including a deputy fire chief — are presumed dead. Police officials said at least 78 officers are missing.

Officials said 266 people were on board the four planes that were hijacked and crashed. All of those on board were presumed dead. Fire officials said at least 100 and as many as 800 people may have died at the Pentagon.

The Federal Aviation Administration took the unprecedented action of grounding all commercial flights in the nation until noon today.

See ATTACK on Page 6A.

Vicious attacks shock Houston

By TONY FREEMANTLE
Houston Chronicle

Though deliberately and carefully aimed at the seats of commerce and power, Tuesday's deadly terrorist attacks sent waves of shock and horror across America. In Houston, the most devastating terrorist attack in the nation's history penetrated deep into the psyche.

There were no direct threats, no clear evidence that any of the city's buildings or institutions were targeted, no indications that any great peril was forthcoming. But rush hour in the nation's fourth-largest city was barely over before it began again in the opposite direction. By afternoon, Tuesday felt like Sunday.

Parents pulled their children out of school. Highrise offices and shopping malls were evacuated. Airports, normally bustling and noisy, were quiet and somber as stranded passengers watched the drama unfold on television. The Johnson Space Center was closed to nonessential personnel. Hospitals tightened

See LOCAL on Page 6A.

www.houstonchronicle.com
InfoSource 713-220-2000
Houston's Leading Information Source
©2001 Houston Chronicle Publishing Company

WEATHER

Houston and vicinity: Skies mostly sunny today with hot conditions. High 92. Skies clear tonight. Low 64. More data on **Page 8B.**

TO OUR READERS

The Houston Chronicle has reconfigured today's editions in order to bring our readers complete coverage of Tuesday's terrorist attacks.

There is a separate 16-page special section on the attacks on New York City and Washington, D.C. There is no Metropolitan section; local coverage begins on Page 13A. More stories on the fallout from the attacks, including cancellation of Major League Baseball games and the closing of financial markets, are in the combined Business and Sports section.

Bush expresses nation's grief

By KAREN MASTERSON
Houston Chronicle Washington Bureau

WASHINGTON — A somber President Bush responded Tuesday night to attacks on the World Trade Center and the Pentagon by vowing to hunt down the terrorists responsible and hold those harboring them accountable.

"I've directed the full resources of our intelligence and law enforcement communities to find those responsible and bring them to justice," Bush said. "We will make no distinction between the terrorists who committed these acts and those who harbor them."

The president added: "Today, our nation saw evil, the very worst of human nature."

And he invoked an Old Testament psalm to offer comfort to those who lost loved ones: "Even though I walk through the valley of the shadow of death, I fear no evil, for you are with me."

Neither Bush nor Defense Secretary Donald Rumsfeld would name the terrorist organization

See BUSH on Page 6A.

Associated Press

Two women weep as they watch the World Trade Center burn Tuesday in New York City. "I looked at the Manhattan skyline and thought there's no more beautiful place in the world. And now it's gone," said one New Yorker.

6 37953 11111 0

WEDNESDAY, SEPTEMBER 12, 2001

San Antonio Express-News

M   50¢

SERVING SOUTH TEXAS SINCE 1865

America in agony

4 jetliners hijacked for rain of death

By STEWART M. POWELL
HEARST WASHINGTON BUREAU

President Bush vowed far-reaching U.S. retaliation Tuesday night for the loss of "thousands of lives" in a devastating attack by terrorists who crashed hijacked airliners into the twin 110-story World Trade Center towers in Manhattan and the Pentagon.

The president, moving to reassure the nation in a brief and somber nationally televised address from the Oval Office, said the federal government would resume full operations today after being interrupted Tuesday by the attacks in New York and Washington.

"Thousands of lives were suddenly ended by evil, despicable acts of terror," Bush said after returning to the White House from stops at two military installations en route home from Florida. "These acts of mass murder were intended to frighten our nation into chaos and retreats — but they have failed."

Bush said the search was "under way for those who are behind these evil acts."

Full coverage inside

See Page 2A for a guide to stories and photos

He promised the United States "will make no distinction between the terrorists who committed these acts and those who harbor them."

Bush spoke as authorities in New York City braced for thousands of casualties in the collapse of two 1,350-foot office towers attacked by suicidal terrorists who commandeered and then guided fully fueled aircraft into the symbols of America's global economic and military power.

Authorities reported 300 firefighters and 78 police officers were dead or missing and presumed dead in a sneak attack that could claim far more casualties than the surprise attack on Pearl Harbor in 1941.

There was no immediate credible claim of responsibility by any known terrorist organization, authorities said.

Initial reports showed at least 2,100 people injured in New York City and more than 100 injured at the Pentagon, but the tallies were expected to skyrocket today as emergency workers combed through the debris of two Manhattan skyscrapers that pancaked after being hit by the planes.

Authorities said all of the passengers and crewmembers were believed killed aboard the three hijacked aircraft used in the attacks.

A fourth aircraft hijacked as part of the plot crashed in western Pennsylvania, with the loss of an additional 45 lives. That plane apparently was headed for Camp David, Md., the presidential retreat, according to a congressman.

Camp David was the sight of the signing of the Camp David Accords between Israel and Egypt on Sept. 17, 1978 — a document that has inflamed much of the Arab world.

A shell of what once was part of the facade of one of the twin towers of New York's World Trade Center rises above the rubble that remains after both towers were destroyed. The 110-story towers collapsed after being struck by commandeered airliners.

SHAWN BALDWIN/ASSOCIATED PRESS

See HIJACKED/7A

HIJACKED:
Four jets with 266 people aboard crash along East Coast

NEW YORK:
Two planes destroy World Trade Center's 110-story towers and adjoining 47-story office building

SUSPECT:
Analysts say much of the evidence points to Osama bin Laden

WASHINGTON:
Airliner strikes Pentagon; all bases put on high alert

TERRIFIED:
Passengers frantically use cell phones as planes go down

AIR TRAVEL:
Flights grounded, airports closed at least until noon today

105

Evidence pointing toward bin Laden

PHOTO COURTESY CARMEN TAYLOR

A hijacked airliner crashes into the south tower of the World Trade Center on Tuesday morning, blasting a fireball through the building.

Doomed passengers called home

By KAREN GULLO
AND JOHN SOLOMON
ASSOCIATED PRESS

WASHINGTON — U.S. officials began piecing together a case linking Osama bin Laden to the worst terrorist attack in U.S. history Tuesday.

They were aided by an intercept of communications between his supporters and harrowing cell phone calls from victims aboard the hijacked jetliners be-

fore they were crashed.

Authorities were focusing some of their efforts on possible bin Laden supporters in Florida based on the identification of a suspected hijacker on one of the jets' manifests, law enforcement sources said.

The sources said the FBI was preparing to search locations in Broward County in southern Florida and Daytona Beach in central Florida.

The locations had links to the suspected bin Laden supporter on the jet manifest, the officials said.

U.S. intelligence intercepted communications between bin Laden supporters discussing the attacks on the World Trade Center in New York and the Pentagon,

according to Utah Sen. Orrin Hatch, the top Republican on the Senate Judiciary Committee.

"They have an intercept of some information that included people associated with bin Laden who acknowledged a couple of targets were hit," Hatch said.

He declined to be more specific.

Hatch also said law enforcement has data possibly linking one person on one of the four ill-fated flights to bin Laden.

Government and industry officials said at least one flight attendant and two passengers called from three of the planes as they were being forced down — each describing similar circumstances.

The callers indicated hijackers

armed with knives, in some cases stabbing flight attendants, took control of the planes and were forcing them down toward the ground, officials said.

One of the passengers was Barbara Olson, wife of Solicitor General Theodore Olson, who called her husband as the hijacking was occurring.

She was aboard American Airlines Flight 77 that left Dulles International Airport in Washington and was forced to crash into the Pentagon.

The officials said Olson told her husband the attackers had used knifelike instruments to take over the plane and forced passengers and crew to the back

See EVIDENCE/6A

Today's Weather
Partly cloudy and warm
High 91, Low 68
Full weather report, Page 12B

From the
San Antonio
Express-News
and KENS 5. Get personalized
news and information.

my sa .com

INDEX

Business	15A	Deaths	4B	Movies	3G	Sports	8B	
Classifieds	1C	Editorials	6B	Puzzles	8G	Food	1F	
Comics	6G	Metro/State	1B	S.A. Life	1G	TV listings	5G	

136th year, No. 344,
114 pages. Entire
contents copyright
2001, San Antonio
Express-News.
This newspaper is
recyclable.

The Salt Lake Tribune

Utah's Independent Voice Since 1871 ★

Volume 262 Number 151
©2001, The Salt Lake Tribune   2 3 4

WEDNESDAY, SEPTEMBER 12, 2001

http://www.sltrib.com

143 South Main Street, Salt Lake City, Utah 84111
Telephone numbers listed on A-2

DAY OF
TERROR

UNTHINKABLE

Suzanne Plunkett/The Associated Press

People run from the collapse of one of the World Trade Center Towers on Tuesday. Both towers crumbled to the ground after two hijacked planes were steered into them.

Death toll likely in thousands; U.S. vows retaliation

TRIBUNE STAFF and NEWS SERVICES

In the wake of the worst attack ever on American civilians, the United States is pointing fingers at Islamic radical Osama bin Laden. The exiled Saudi is believed to be hiding in Afghanistan.

"Today, our nation saw evil," President Bush told the nation about 12 hours after three hijacked commercial airliners hit the heart of America's military and financial capitals, killing perhaps thousands, reducing New York's World Trade Center Towers to stumps of rubble and destroying a portion of the national fortress known as the Pentagon.

Bush vowed to "hunt down and punish" those responsible.

A fourth commandeered airliner, which crashed in western Pennsylvania, was believed headed for Washington. None of the 266 people aboard the two American Airlines and two United Airlines planes survived.

"We will make no distinction between the terrorists who committed these acts and those who harbor them," said Bush,

who, for security reasons, spent much of the day in the air aboard Air Force One, escorted by fighter planes from Florida to Louisiana to Nebraska before returning to Washington, D.C., on Tuesday evening. (The complete text of the president's evening address can be found on Page A-2.)

No official death tally had been announced by press time, but the number of casualties includes about 300 firefighters who responded to the initial crash, and the final number will be "more than any of us can bear," said New York Mayor Rudolph Giuliani.

Bin Laden is blamed for masterminding the bombings of U.S. embassies in Kenya and Tanzania in 1998, and is suspected in the bombing of the USS Cole in Yemen last October. He is believed to be based in Afghanistan. He heads the Al-Qaida, a global terrorist network that has targeted the United States repeatedly.

Sen. Orrin Hatch, R-Utah, a member of the Senate Intelligence Committee,

said Tuesday night "just about everything points" to him.

The loss of life from Tuesday's attacks is likely to be horrendous — as many as 50,000 people could have been in the two 110-story skyscrapers, and thousands in the Pentagon.

The grim toll is almost certain to surpass the 2,403 who were killed in the surprise Japanese attack on the U.S. naval base at Pearl Harbor, Hawaii, on Dec. 7, 1941, and already is greater than the 167 who died in a domestic terrorist bomb attack on a federal building in Oklahoma City on April 19, 1995.

The attack is likely to have a similarly jarring effect on a stunned nation, as Americans hunkered down, suddenly unsure of the safety of their skies and the nation's ability to protect them from faceless enemies. Talk turned quickly to retaliation and even war.

"This is an act of war, and we are at war," proclaimed Sen. Bob Bennett,

See ATTACKS, Page A-9

Carmen Taylor/The Associated Press

A jet airliner is lined up on one of the World Trade Center towers in New York on Tuesday. Both towers crumbled to the ground after two hijacked jets were steered into them in an unprecedented act of terrorism.

INSIDE

Weather: Scattered showers and thunderstorms around the state; 70s-80s north, 70s-90s south. **D-10**

Attacks Force Review of Olympic Security

BY MICHAEL VIGH and CHRISTOPHER SMITH

THE SALT LAKE TRIBUNE

Tuesday's fiery terrorist attacks will spur Utah's Olympic security planners to scrutinize their strategy for keeping the 2002 Winter Games safe, but they warn the threat of terrorism can never be eliminated.

During next February's Games, Utahns may feel the uncomfortable effects of increased security measures likely to be implemented in the wake of the suicide bombings at the World Trade Center and the Pentagon.

"There is a country in the world which has learned to live under the same threat of terrorism, and that is Israel," said Utah Sen. Bob Bennett. "I expect that the same kinds of heightened

security we see there will be applied to the Olympics. Utahns will find them inconvenient and unfamiliar."

Olympic security experts say Salt Lake City Games organizers' task of balancing the inherent tension between an open society and adequate safety is now more difficult.

"We should do everything we can to increase security, but we don't want to do it at the risk of losing the values of the rest of the country. Otherwise we're going to be stopping cars at the Utah border," said Jack Greene, Northeastern

University's dean of criminal justice.

"One of the unfortunate prices we pay in a free society is a higher level of risk," said Greene, whose research on Olympic security measures is used by organizing committees and the federal government.

Salt Lake Organizing Committee President Mitt Romney met Tuesday with the U.S. Secret Service, which is in charge of Utah's $200 million Olympic security program.

"I thought the program was a complete and holistic plan, which did not have gaping holes or obvious weaknesses," he told The Associated Press. "I

GAMES AND THREATS
Some Utahns are feeling vulnerable   **A-5**

See SECURITY PLAN, Page A-9

MORE INSIDE

The Free Lance-Star

VOL. 117, NO. 255 FREDERICKSBURG, VA.   SERVING FREDERICKSBURG, SPOTSYLVANIA, STAFFORD, KING GEORGE, CAROLINE AND NEIGHBORING COUNTIES   WEDNESDAY, SEPTEMBER 12, 2001 50 CENTS

U.S. ATTACKED

Trade Center, Pentagon struck by hijacked jets

By DAVID CRARY
and JERRY SCHWARTZ
AP National Writers

NEW YORK—In the most devastating terrorist onslaught ever waged against the United States, knife-wielding hijackers crashed two airliners into the World Trade Center yesterday, toppling its twin 110-story towers. The deadly calamity was witnessed on televisions across the world as another plane slammed into the Pentagon, and a fourth crashed outside Pittsburgh.

"Today, our nation saw evil," President Bush said in an address to the nation last night. He said thousands of lives were "suddenly ended by evil, despicable acts of terror."

Said Adm. Robert J. Natter, commander of the U.S. Atlantic Fleet: "We have been attacked like we haven't since Pearl Harbor."

Establishing the U.S. death toll could take weeks. The four airliners alone had 266 people aboard and there were no known survivors. At the Pentagon, up to 850 people were believed dead.

In addition, a firefighters union official said he feared an estimated 200 firefighters had died in rescue efforts at the trade center—where 50,000 people worked—and dozens of police officers were believed missing.

"The number of casualties will be more than most of us can bear," a visibly distraught Mayor Rudolph Giuliani said.

No one took responsibility for the attacks that rocked the seats of finance and government. But federal authorities identified Osama bin Laden, who has been given asylum by Afghanistan's Taliban rulers, as the prime suspect.

Aided by an intercept of communications between his supporters and harrowing cellphone calls from at least one flight attendant and two passengers aboard the jetliners before they crashed, U.S. officials began assembling a case linking bin Laden to the devastation.

U.S. intelligence intercepted communications between bin Laden

An emergency worker helps a woman after she was injured in the terrorist attacks on New York City's World Trade Center.

supporters discussing the attacks on the World Trade Center and the Pentagon, according to Utah Sen. Orrin Hatch, the top Republican on the Senate Judiciary Committee.

The people aboard planes who managed to make cellphone calls each described similar circumstances: They indicated the hijackers were armed with knives and in some cases stabbed flight attendants. The hijackers then took control of the planes.

At the World Trade Center, the dead and the doomed plummeted from the skyscrapers, among them a man and woman holding hands.

Shortly after 7 p.m., crews began heading into ground zero of the attacks to search for survivors and recover bodies. All that remained of the twin towers by then was a pile of rubble and twisted steel that stood barely two stories high, leaving a huge gap in the New York City skyline.

"Freedom itself was attacked this morning, and I assure you freedom will be defended," said Bush, who was in Florida at the time of the

See TERRORISM, Page A3

Photos by THE ASSOCIATED PRESS

United Airlines Flight 175, hijacked by terrorists, banks toward the south tower of the World Trade Center in New York City yesterday.

INSIDE

ASSAULT ON THE PENTAGON

Terrorists strike heart of nation's defense

Area residents reeling after airliner crashes, heavy toll expected

By ELIZABETH PEZZULLO
and JANET MARSHALL
THE FREE LANCE-STAR

ARLINGTON—Ian Wyatt glanced into the sky just as a commercial airplane roared by about 100 yards off the ground.

"I was so scared I thought it was coming after me and just ducked for cover," said Wyatt, a 1999 graduate of Mary Washington College who was walking to his federal job when terrorists struck at the heart of the nation's defense yesterday morning.

"It was going so fast and it was so low," he said, standing on Army-Navy Drive. "The only intelligent thought that came into my head was, 'Oh my God, they hit the Pentagon.' I could then hear cars squealing all around and people were just stunned."

After the plane struck the west side of the famed five-sided building, thick black smoke billowed from a huge crater as fire

ASSOCIATED PRESS

A priest prays over a wounded man outside the west entrance of the Pentagon as emergency workers from the military services mobilize to help the wounded after yesterday's attack on the building.

raged within.

Inside the Pentagon, Connie Morrow was talking to co-workers in the fourth floor of the Pentagon's Air Force Logistics office at the time of the crash

about 9:30 a.m.

She said employees had been put on heightened alert after the World Trade Center attacks.

"We were trying to figure out what our next move should be,"

Morrow said. "Then, we heard an explosion and people started racing for the doors. There was a lot of fear, but it wasn't total chaos."

Morrow, who rides her bike to work from her Arlington home, said it took a long time to be evacuated from the reinforced concrete building.

"It was just horrible," she said, afterward standing a few blocks from the Pentagon embracing a friend. "And people were trying to get through on their cellphones to notify family, but nothing was working."

Others who witnessed the mayhem around the Pentagon yesterday said it felt like a scene from the movie, "Independence Day." Only in this case it was the Pentagon that erupted into flames, not the White House.

Casualty estimates ranged from 100 to as many as 850.

"This is worse than any disaster movie," said Arlington resident Rob Schickler, who was standing on a hill near the Pentagon with a crowd of onlookers. "You might be able to expect

See PENTAGON, BACK PAGE

EXTRA

50¢

The News & Advance

Lynchburg, Virginia

www.newsadvance.com

Tuesday, September 11, 2001

A Media General Newspaper

ATTACK!

World Trade towers down

Terror attacks hit Pentagon; airliners were hijacked

NEW YORK (AP) — In a horrific sequence of destruction, terrorists hijacked two airliners and crashed them into the World Trade Center in a coordinated series of attacks Tuesday morning that brought down the twin 110-story towers. A plane also slammed into the Pentagon, raising fears that the seat of government itself was under attack.

"I have a sense it's a horrendous number of lives lost," Mayor Rudolph Giuliani said. "Right now we have to focus on saving as many lives as possible."

Authorities had been trying to evacuate those who work in the twin towers, but many were thought to have been trapped. About 50,000 people work at the Trade Center. American Airlines said its two aircraft were carrying a total of 156 people.

"This is perhaps the most audacious terrorist attack that's ever taken place in the world," said Chris Yates, an aviation expert at Jane's Transport in London. "It takes a logistics operation from the terror group involved that is second to none. Only a very small handful of terror groups is on that list. ... I would name at the top of the list Osama bin Laden."

President Bush ordered a full-scale investigation to "hunt down the folks who committed this act."

Within the hour, the Pentagon took a direct, devastating hit from an aircraft. The fiery crash collapsed one side of the five-sided structure.

The White House, the Pentagon and the Capitol were evacuated along with other federal buildings in Washington and New York.

Authorities in Washington immediately began deploying troops, including an infantry regiment. The Situation Room at the White House was in full operation. And authorities went on alert from coast to coast, halting all air traffic and tightening security at strategic installations.

"This is the second Pearl Harbor. I don't think that I overstate it," said Sen. Chuck Hagel, R-Neb.

American Airlines identified the planes that crashed into the Trade Center as Flight 11, a Los Angeles-bound jet hijacked after takeoff from Boston with 92 people aboard, and Flight 77, which was seized while carrying 64 people from Washington to Los Angeles.

In Pennsylvania, United Airlines Flight 93, a Boeing 757 en route from Newark, N.J., to San Francisco, crashed about 80 miles southeast of Pittsburgh with 45 people aboard. The fate of those aboard was not immediately known and it was not clear if the crash was related to the disasters elsewhere. In a statement, United said another of its planes, Flight 175, a Boeing 767 bound from Boston to Los Angeles with 65 people on board, also crashed, but

Please see ATTACK, Page 4

EXTRA! EXTRA! EXTRA! EXTRA! EXTRA!

TUESDAY, SEPTEMBER 11, 2001

Daily Press

Harquin Newport News, Virginia | EXTRA |

AMERICA ATTACKED

TERROR

Smoke, flames and debris erupts from one of the World Trade Center towers as a plane strikes it Tuesday, September 11, 2001. The first tower was already burning following a terror attack minutes earlier.

I n the worst attack on U.S. soil since Pearl Harbor, terrorists crashed two hijacked airliners into the World Trade Center and brought down the twin 110-story towers this morning.

A jetliner also slammed into the Pentagon as the government itself came under attack. The crash collapsed one side of the home of America's military. The White House and the Capitol were evacuated, along with all federal buildings across the United States.

A fourth airliner, also possibly hijacked, crashed in rural Pennsylvania about 80 miles from Pittsburgh.

Thousands could be dead or injured, officials said. No one, as yet, has claimed responsibility for the attacks, but suspicions have been cast on Osama bin Laden, who also has been linked to the attack on the Norfolk-based USS Cole.

COMING WEDNESDAY: 18 PAGES OF COVERAGE FROM TODAY'S ATTACKS

109

110

Richmond Times-Dispatch

VIRGINIA'S NEWS LEADER
A MEDIA GENERAL NEWSPAPER

RICHMOND, VIRGINIA 23293

WEDNESDAY, SEPTEMBER 12, 2001

50¢

ATTACK ON U.S.

AMERICA'S DARKEST DAY

111

INDEX TO MORE THAN 18 PAGES OF COVERAGE A2

ROANOKE, VIRGINIA

Helping out
Western Virginians lined up
Tuesday to donate blood.
Donation centers are listed inside.
VIRGINIA

Workplace 'spirituality'
Linda Ferguson of Hollins University says
happiness at the office is "really about your
own sense of creativity, purpose and passion."
EXTRA

Games postponed everywhere
The sports world shut down Tuesday,
and the UVa-Penn State football
game will not be played Thursday.
SPORTS

THE ROANOKE TIMES

ROANOKE, VIRGINIA   **WEDNESDAY, SEPTEMBER 12, 2001**   SINGLE COPY 50¢

As the World Trade Center towers crumbled Tuesday, Manhattan drowned under a fog of smoke, debris and disbelief. Thousands are feared dead in the apparent terrorist attack there and at the Pentagon in Washington, D.C. The twin towers collapsed not long after they were hit by two airliners, killing hundreds on board and likely hundreds more police and firefighters who were already on the scene.
ASSOCIATED PRESS

112

DAY OF HORROR

Just 18 minutes after the north tower was hit, an airliner smashed into the south tower (left). "All this stuff started falling. . . . People were screaming, falling and jumping out of the windows," said one survivor.
ASSOCIATED PRESS

"Make no mistake — the United States will hunt down and pursue those responsible for these cowardly actions," President Bush said Tuesday.

*KNIGHT RIDDER/TRIBUNE
and ASSOCIATED PRESS*

NEW YORK — A pall of smoke, dust and sadness settled over lower Manhattan at nightfall Tuesday as rescue workers, police and firefighters pressed their desperate search for survivors of the worst terrorist attack in United States history, a coordinated airborne assault that destroyed the twin towers of the World Trade Center and left a portion of the Pentagon in Washington in smoking ruins.

In New York alone, it was feared the death toll could reach the thousands. Officials said at least 200 firefighters and 78 police officers were missing and presumed dead at mid-day. Upwards of 50,000 people worked in the 110-story World Trade Center towers, reduced by explosions and fire to ruins within hours of the initial attack.

More on the attacks. A2-9

Economic impact. A10

Southwest Virginia reacts. B1

Speaking Tuesday night from the White House, President Bush evoked a biblical message in saying the United States was walking "through the valley of the shadow of death" but still feared no evil. He described the attack as a mass murder that had ended the lives of thousands of people and called on the nation to remember the victims in its prayers.

Said Adm. Robert Natter, commander of the U.S. Atlantic Fleet: "We have been attacked like we haven't since Pearl Harbor."

Establishing the U.S. death toll could take weeks. The four airliners alone had 266 people aboard and there were no known survivors. At the Pentagon, about 100 people were believed dead.

In addition, a firefighters union official said he feared half of the 400 firefighters who first reached the scene had died in rescue efforts at the trade center — where 50,000 people worked — and dozens of police officers were believed

PLEASE SEE ATTACK/A4

Two women cling to each other in fear as they watch the twin towers burn. Thousands of gallons of jet fuel stoked the fire.
ASSOCIATED PRESS

An emergency worker helps a woman to safety. As the ruins fell around them, bystanders did what they could to help.
ASSOCIATED PRESS

Valley residents feel the effects of attacks

By KATHY LU
THE ROANOKE TIMES

Despite the chaos in New York and Washington, D.C., just a few hundred miles away, life had to continue for people in the Roanoke and New River valleys.

There was still trash to pick up, people to feed and errands to run.

But many made an effort to take time out to mark the gruesome day or keep up-to-date on the news.

"It's hard to believe the twin towers is gone," said Amos Fair, 38, a sanitation driver for Roanoke Solid Waste Management. Fair, originally from New York, moved to Roanoke in 1990. He believes his relatives in the Bronx are safe, though he had yet to speak with them by phone.

He was taking his afternoon break at the Krispy Kreme Doughnut Co. on Melrose Avenue. There was no television at the shop and the radio was pumping music, not news. Yet, Fair made sure to take his

PLEASE SEE EFFECTS/A5

Sense of security in America damaged

By CALVIN WOODWARD
ASSOCIATED PRESS

WASHINGTON — Any notion of America being invincible died in the monstrous rubble.

With the twin towers crumbled in New York, the Pentagon burning, a jetliner down in Pennsylvania, a morning's cruel work ended the nation's normalcy.

"America is forever changed," said Sen. Chuck Hagel, R-Neb. "America is in for a long fight."

On the confused streets of Washington, where police gazing skyward stood with guns drawn, where much of the nation's leadership went into hiding, where pockets of pedestrians would start running but not know where or even why, the allusion that so many reached for was Pearl Harbor.

But even that great shocker of American history was not completely apt, for this time the invader was unknown.

The enemies were simply "they."

PLEASE SEE SECURITY/A2

News tips?
981-3333
(800) 346-1234
ext. 333

Weather

TODAY: SUNNY
77 **HIGH**
52 **LOW**

Thursday
Partly sunny
with a high
of 77

Index

A10 Business	B2 Deaths	B6 Sports
C1 Classified	A16 Editorial	E2 TV Listings
A17 Commentary	A2 Lottery	A2 Weather
E2 Crossword		

Online 🖱
roanoke.com
BREAKING NEWS The latest news and sports from The Associated Press
and the Roanoke Times staff. Local news updates weekdays by 4 p.m.

6 45527 08554 5

WWW.THESUNLINK.COM

SUN

WEDNESDAY, SEPTEMBER 12, 2001 ■ 50 CENTS

Prayers are whispered.
Tears are shed.
Kitsap joins a nation
reeling from tragedy.
■ A3

Bethany Miner, 15, top, and her sister Andrea, 13, consoled each other during a special service Tuesday night at Port Orchard's Christian Life Center. Andrea said a friend's uncle who worked at the Pentagon died in the attack.

Staff photo
by Carolyn J. Yaschur

We Mourn

113

AP photo by Thomas E. Franklin

New York City firefighters paused to raise the American flag Tuesday in the midst of the rubble of the World Trade Center. Estimates were that 300 firefighters may have lost their lives in the most devastating terrorist onslaught ever waged against the United States. Thousands are presumed dead in New York; several hundred may have lost their lives in the attack on the Pentagon.

■ **Rescuers dig through rubble as thousands feared dead**

■ **Bush vows revenge for attacks on World Trade Center, Pentagon**

■ **Terrorists hijack four airliners in bloody strikes on New York City, D.C.**

■ **Military base security at highest level**

"We had gone to about the 40th floor when our building was hit. People were thrown to the ground, and the building rocked one way and another. For several minutes, the building seemed to keep rocking."
— Ted Peterson, a Bremerton native who narrowly escaped death
■ A5

Coverage of the terrorist attacks on the U.S. appears on Pages A1-8 and B1-3.
For regular updates, see www.TheSunLink.com

Bangor: Destroyer heads in; Trident sub sails out ■ A3

TERROR IN AMERICA: Complete coverage inside, A3-14

Skagit Valley Herald

WEDNESDAY
SEPTEMBER 12, 2001

A locally owned newspaper serving Northwest Washington since 1884

50 CENTS
Copyright 2001. Skagit Valley Publishing Co.

Who did it?

700 leads in probe of terrorist attacks

By JOHN SOLOMON
Associated Press Writer

WASHINGTON — The FBI has received 700 leads in the investigation of the terrorist attacks in New York and Washington but no arrests have been made, a Justice Department official said today.

The government believes the hijackers were trained pilots and that three to five were aboard each of four airliners that crashed Tuesday in the worst terrorist attack ever in the United States, said Justice Department spokeswoman Mindy Tucker. She said the conclusion was based on information gathered from frantic phone calls made by passengers on the doomed jets.

"It appears from what we know that the hijackers were skilled pilots," said Tucker.

Tucker declined to comment on evidence linking the attacks to Saudi exile Osama bin Laden or whether authorities have executed search warrants.

Lawmakers believe bin Laden may have been behind the attacks. "I don't think everyone in Congress has enough information to make those assumptions," said Tucker.

She said investigators are following all credible leads, but declined to comment on whether the government is close to arresting anyone. The 700 tips came from a special FBI Web site seeking information on the attacks.

The FBI interviewed a Venice, Fla., couple today about two men who stayed at their house for a week in July 2000 while the men were taking small-plane flight training at Venice Municipal Airport.

FBI agents "informed me that there were two individuals that were students at Huffman Aviation, my employer, and FBI told me they were involved in yesterday's tragedy," said Charlie Voss, who was interviewed with his wife, Drew Voss, at their home.

The couple accepted the two men as house guests as a favor to the company, Voss said. The men, who stayed just a few days, trained at the

See **PROBE**, Page A13

Three New York City firefighters raise the American flag in the rubble of the World Trade Center late Tuesday afternoon. Both towers of the Trade Center collapsed after being struck by two hijacked jetliners Tuesday morning.

AP

Locally, security remains high on state ferries, Whidbey base

By SCOTT GUTIERREZ
Staff Writer

Life got back to normal for mall shoppers and ferry passengers today, but security at the Whidbey Island Naval Air Station got even tougher.

Naval personnel on their way to work were experiencing traffic delays because the base was under the highest level of security today, said Kim Martin, public affairs officer.

All cars were inspected thoroughly, and in some cases with the aid of dogs trained to sniff for explosives, Martin said.

"We're doing everything to protect our people and our assets here," Martin said.

Only essential personnel were allowed on base and only essential air operations will be performed, Martin said.

The inspections severely congested traffic this morning for those entering the base, Martin said. She said two gates are opened, the Charles Porter and the Saratoga gates.

A shuttle bus from Rocky Point, near Gold Course Road, also will take people onto the base, Martin said.

Meanwhile shoppers and employees returned to Cascade Mall in Burlington, which resumed normal business hours after being closed Tuesday.

The state ferry system returned to carrying automobiles Tuesday after being restricted to passenger-only service through the afternoon in most of the Puget Sound outside the San Juan Islands, said spokesperson Susan Harris.

But state troopers were on hand at both the terminals and on the vessels to inspect any vehicles that appear suspicious, Harris said.

"All vehicles may be subject to a possible search," Harris said.

On the ground, Amtrak trains resumed normal service to the area today after a thorough inspection of the state's railroads, bridges and roadways by Department of Transportation and Amtrak officials.

"Inspections will be running throughout the day and should anything unusual happen, they will take strong precautions," spokesperson Stan Suchan said about service today. " And that could mean some

See **SECURITY**, Page A13

Trade Center fell 'like a house of cards'

By JAMES GELUSO
Staff Writer

Ben Luce was at work Tuesday morning in the Commodities Exchange building, two blocks from the World Trade Center, when a co-worker came in and told people that something had happened.

Luce, a natural gas trader and 1994 Stanwood

High School graduate, joined his colleagues around a television, where they watched live footage of the second airplane crashing into the World Trade Center.

Not long after that, the exchange building was evacuated, and Luce and his colleagues saw the destruction up close.

"We just kind of stood in shock for about 15

minutes," he said.

Two of his colleagues started walking north toward midtown Manhattan, and the rest followed. They had gotten 20 blocks when they heard a low rumble and turned around to see the first tower fall.

See **STANWOOD**, Page A12

Ben Luce in 1994.

Hijackings hit home for school official

By PETER KELLEY
Staff Writer

CONCRETE — As Marie Phillips watched Tuesday's horrific events unfold, she remembered her own days as a flight attendant, and a life-and-death crisis she faced one day, thousands of feet in the air.

Phillips

Phillips is superintendent of the Concrete School District now, but in 1968 she was a 22-year-old flight attendant for Pan American Airlines. She remembers vividly how her crew dealt with a bomb threat on an

See **HIJACKINGS**, Page A13

Alice White of Mount Vernon reacts to the terrorist attack on the United States before the start of noon Mass Tuesday at Immaculate Conception Catholic Church in Mount Vernon.

Frank Varga / Skagit Valley Herald

Worshippers find solace in tune from World War II era

By JIM FEEHAN
Staff Writer

MOUNT VERNON — At the end of a well-attended mass, a spontaneous lone voice singing "God Bless America" quickly was joined by a choir of parishioners seeking spiritual relief from the day's events.

June Hudson didn't plan to start singing the patriotic song at the conclusion of a noontime Mass Tuesday at Immaculate Conception Roman Catholic Church in Mount Vernon.

But as the Rev. Patrick McDermott ended the religious service and turned to walk away from

See **SONG**, Page A12

Inside

Three sections. 28 pages

Baldo	C7	Horoscope	C7
Classified	C5-10	Local	A3
Comics	C4	Lottery	A2
Crossword	C8	Movies	A5
Daily Briefing	A2	Obituaries	A12
Doonesbury	C10	Opinion	A4
Dr. Gott	A10	Spare Time	A10
Healthy Living	C1	Sports	B1-4
Herman	C8	Television	A10

Internet: www.skagitvalleyherald.com

Weather

■ Mostly fair through Friday with highs in the 70s and 80s. **Details, A14.**

114

WEDNESDAY, SEPTEMBER 12, 2001

Seattle Post-Intelligencer

A HEARST NEWSPAPER | WWW.SEATTLEPI.COM

KING, SNOHOMISH, PIERCE CO. & BAINBRIDGE
ISLAND, KITSAP, THURSTON CO. 50¢ | ELSEWHERE 75¢

25¢

ATTACK ON AMERICA: 09/11/2001

'None of us will ever forget'

FULL COVERAGE

'Sadness and . . . unyielding anger'
The text of the speech President Bush gave last night after a day spent on the move **SEE A3, A4**

U.S. military goes into action
Navy ships on both coasts deployed to set up a defensive screen **SEE A3**

Terrorist attack sophisticated
Osama bin Laden's supporters may be to blame, experts say **SEE A3**

Direct hits, then screaming
The Pentagon burst into flames, and the Trade Center looked 'like a war zone' **SEE A5-A7**

MORE INSIDE
▶ How to help, tips for coping **B2**

▶ Photos from the scenes and a timeline of events **A8-9**

▶ Experts disagree on how easily terrorists can fly planes **A11**

▶ Seattle reaches out to help **B1**

▶ Editorial: The United States needs a decisive response — and certainty that it gets to those responsible **B4**

▶ David Horsey: P-I political cartoonist documents the events **B4**

▶ Trading comes to a halt **C1**

▶ Major League Baseball games canceled last night **D1**

seattlepi.com
For the latest developments and photos, see the P-I's Web site

© 2001 SEATTLE
POST-INTELLIGENCER

A fireball erupts from the World Trade Center after it was struck by a hijacked aircraft yesterday. The Brooklyn Bridge is in the foreground.

THE NEW YORK TIMES

▶ Knife-wielding hijackers carried out deadly plan

▶ Death toll could easily be in thousands

▶ At least 300 firefighters may be among dead

▶ Terrorists 'flew the planes themselves'

P-I NEWS SERVICES

NEW YORK – In the most devastating terrorist onslaught ever waged against the United States, knife-wielding hijackers crashed two airliners into the World Trade Center yesterday, toppling its twin 110-story towers. The deadly calamity was witnessed on televisions across the world as another plane slammed into the Pentagon, and a fourth crashed outside Pittsburgh.

"Today, our nation saw evil," a grim-faced President Bush said last night in a televised address to the nation. He said thousands of lives were "suddenly ended by evil, despicable acts of terror."

With the country on a war footing, the nation's aviation system was shut down, government buildings around the country were closed, along with major skyscrapers and a variety of other sites, ranging from Disney theme parks to the Golden Gate Bridge and U.N. headquarters in New York.

In his first prime-time Oval Office address, Bush asked the nation to find comfort in Scripture as he mourned the deaths and vowed to avenge their killings. He said the United States would find and punish "those behind these evil acts," and any country that harbors them.

Establishing the U.S. death toll could take weeks. The four airliners alone had 266 people aboard and there were no known survivors. Officials put the number of dead and wounded at the Pentagon at about 100 or more, with some news reports suggesting it could rise to 800.

In addition, a union official said he feared 300 New York firefighters had died in rescue efforts at the trade center and dozens of police officers were missing.

"The number of casualties will be more than most of us can bear," a visibly distraught Mayor Rudolph Giuliani said.

An army of 10,000 workers brought in dogs and lights last night as they began heading into ground zero to search for survivors and recover bodies.

All that remained of the twin towers by then was a pile of rubble and twisted steel that stood barely five stories high, leaving a huge gap in the New York City skyline and making the Empire State Building once again the city's tallest structure.

No one took responsibility for the attacks. But federal authorities identified Osama bin Laden, who has been given asylum by Afghanistan's hard-line Taliban rulers, as the prime suspect. The Taliban denied such suggestions.

Investigators descended on Logan International Airport in Boston yesterday, trying to determine how terrorists commandeered two nearly identical jets that took off moments apart and then crashed them into the trade center.

SEE TERRORISTS, A12

7 59423 99999 5

WEDNESDAY MORNING
SEPTEMBER 12, 2001

Weather
Mostly sunny after morning fog. High, 75; low, 53. D 8

The Seattle Times

25¢
KING, SNOHOMISH AND PIERCE COUNTIES AND BAINBRIDGE ISLAND
50¢ IN ISLAND, KITSAP AND THURSTON COUNTIES
75¢ ELSEWHERE

Terrorist attacks horrify nation

AMERICA IN SHOCK
14 PAGES INSIDE

Thousands of lives lost

4 jets crashed; Trade Center, Pentagon hit

'I looked down . . . I saw the horror'
A 3

Bush vows to avenge deaths
A 2

Suspect: Osama bin Laden
A 5

How intelligence, security failed
A 5, 6

Dire economic effects predicted
A 4

Frantic relatives search for loved ones
A 11

Resources for coping
A 15

For continuing coverage, see
seattletimes.com
www.seattletimes.com

Copyright 2001
Seattle Times Company

25¢ IN KING, SNOHOMISH, PIERCE
COUNTIES AND BAINBRIDGE ISLAND;
50¢ IN ISLAND, KITSAP AND THURSTON
COUNTIES; 75¢ ELSEWHERE

70% of The Seattle Times newsprint contains
recycled fiber. The inks are also reused.
Please recycle when you are finished with it.

A fiery blast *rocks the World Trade Center in New York City yesterday after it was hit by two airplanes. Officials said casualties will be in the thousands.*

SPENCER PLATT / GETTY IMAGES

Closely timed attacks leave America in warlike state

BY DAVID CRARY AND JERRY SCHWARTZ
The Associated Press

NEW YORK — In the most devastating terrorist onslaught ever waged against the United States, knife-wielding hijackers crashed two airliners into the World Trade Center yesterday, toppling its twin 110-story towers.

The deadly calamity was witnessed on televisions across the world as another plane slammed into the Pentagon and a fourth crashed outside Pittsburgh.

"Today, our nation saw evil," President Bush said in an address to the nation last night. Bush said thousands of lives were "suddenly ended by evil, despicable acts of terror."

Establishing the death toll could take weeks but is believed to be in the thousands.

No one took responsibility for the attacks that rocked the nation's seats of finance and government. But federal authorities identified Osama bin Laden, who has been given asylum by Afghanistan's Taliban rulers, as the prime suspect.

Aided by an intercept of communications between his supporters and harrowing cellphone calls from at least one flight attendant and two passengers aboard the jetliners before they crashed, U.S. officials began assembling a case linking bin Laden to the devastation.

U.S. intelligence intercepted communications between bin Laden supporters discussing the attacks on the World Trade Center and the Pentagon, according to Utah Sen. Orrin

PLEASE SEE **Terror** ON A 2

A shell of what *was once part of twin 110-story towers at the World Trade Center rises above the rubble, leaving a huge gap in the New York skyline.*

SHAWN BALDWIN / THE ASSOCIATED PRESS

Destruction and death far away felt close to home

BY ALEX TIZON
Seattle Times staff reporter

It happened on the other coast, yet yesterday's terrorist attacks reverberated like an underground quake through the region, uniting us with the rest of the country in a profound state of grief and apprehension.

As the magnitude became known yesterday, scenes of ordinary bustle mixed with somber realization that we as a nation had entered a new era. War was no longer a thing that happened elsewhere.

Even as the sun shone brightly through a cloudless sky — what soggy Northwesterners usually live for — many people stayed indoors, in homes and offices and restaurants and taverns, hovering around television sets, watching replays of the destruction of one of the nation's most important economic symbols — the World Trade Center — and wondering aloud at the death toll, what it all means, and what's next.

'It's on everybody's mind and in everybody's heart.'
CONNIE GODMAN

"I mostly feel its nearness rather than its farness," said Seattle author Jonathan Raban. "Insofar as terrorism sends a message, this message was not directed at New York or Washington, D.C., or Pittsburgh, but at the very idea of America, and Seattle is a part of that idea."

Much of Seattle appeared to go about busi-

PLEASE SEE **Northwest** ON A 10

116

THE SPOKESMAN-REVIEW

A jetliner hijacked by terrorists bears down on one of the towers of the World Trade Center in New York. The other tower had already been struck by another jet Tuesday morning.

A NEW DAY OF INFAMY

Firefighters comb through the rubble of the World Trade Center, which collapsed Tuesday after being struck by two hijacked jetliners as the nation and the world watched in horror.

Photos by Associated Press

117

INSIDE 13 PAGES OF COVERAGE

An icon reduced to rubble

Fire, not crash impact, suspected of bringing down New York's twin towers./**A3**

SPECIAL SECTION

Hijackers were trained pilots

Aviation experts say airline crews would die before flying jetliner into a building./**A13**

'Rogue state' aid suspected

Splinter group working alone not capable of such an elaborate operation./**A13**

Disbelief, shock, fear, anger

Every American will have to confront attack's psychological effects./**A16**

'Overtaken by concern'

Spokesman-Review readers share their thoughts on the terrorist attacks./**A16**

How you can help victims

Where you can donate blood, financial assistance; local services scheduled./**A17**

Local Muslims cautious

Police concerned about possibility of backlash against Islamic community./**A18**

BUSINESS

Region's retailers react

Many stores close their doors Tuesday; air-dependent businesses crippled./**A11**

Recession on traders' minds

Financial analysts divided on how attack will affect the struggling economy./**A11**

SPORTS

Events across U.S. postponed

Baseball schedule on hold; major college football games postponed./**C1**

Associated Press

An emergency worker helps a woman after she was injured in the terrorist attack on the World Trade Center.

119th year, No. 94
© Copyright 2001,
The Spokesman-Review

Spokane, Wash.,
Coeur d'Alene, Idaho,
and the Inland
Northwest

U.S. suffers worst act of terror in its history

Terrorists struck at the symbols of America's wealth and might Tuesday, flying hijacked airliners into the World Trade Center and the Pentagon, killing untold thousands.

As a horrified nation watched, the twin towers of the World Trade Center in lower Manhattan collapsed into flaming rubble after two Boeing 767s rammed their upper stories. A third airliner, a Boeing 757, flattened one of the Pentagon's famed five sides.

A fourth hijacked jetliner crashed in western Pennsylvania.

The assaults which evoked comparisons to Pearl Harbor, were carefully planned and coordinated, occurring within 50 minutes. No one claimed responsibility, but official suspicion quickly fell on Saudi fugitive Osama bin Laden.

President Bush vowed to "find those responsible and bring them to justice." This country, he said, would retaliate against "those behind these evil acts" and anyone harboring them.

Altogether, the four downed planes carried 311 people. All were killed. Scores jumped to their deaths or died in fire and the collapsing superstructure of the towers.

Bush placed U.S. forces around the world on highest alert after the worst siege of terrorism waged against the United States in its history.

Full coverage begins on page A2.

For home delivery: (509) 747-4422; (800) 338-8801   Contact The Spokesman-Review: (509) 459-5000; fax (509) 459-5482; e-mail editor@spokesman.com   Online news: www.spokesmanreview.com

THE POST~CRESCENT

www.postcrescent.com

WEDNESDAY, SEPTEMBER 12, 2001   SERVING WISCONSIN'S FOX RIVER VALLEY SINCE 1853   50¢

U.S. UNDER ATTACK: 10-PAGE SPECIAL SECTION

'UNYIELDING ANGER'

President Bush says America will not falter in face of horrific terrorist assault / Page 2

Inside

■ Establishing
U.S. death toll
could take
weeks
Page 2

■ Investigation
targets five
terrorist
groups, Osama
bin Laden
Page 3

■ Leaders in
Congress make
a show of unity
Page 3

■ U.S. air
defense not
prepared for a
suicide attack
Page 3

■ Tragedy
could plunge
weak economy
into a recession
Page 4

■ New Yorkers
with Fox Valley
connections
weigh in
Page 4

■ Attack stirs
emotions in Fox
Valley
Page 5

■ Lines form
amid fears of
rising gas prices
Page 5

■ Editorials,
columns
Pages 8, 9

■ Photos
recount a day
of horrors
Page 10

AP photo by Thomas E. Franklin

FIREFIGHTERS RAISE A FLAG at the remains of the World Trade Center Tuesday in New York City. A coordinated terrorist attack sent two hijacked jetliners straight into the landmark skyscrapers, toppling them. Thousands of people could be dead or trapped in the rubble, and Lower Manhattan was evacuated as the nation coped with a similar attack on the Pentagon in Washington, D.C.

We use recycled paper

A Gannett Newspaper

118

■ Journal Sentinel reporter Catherine Fitzpatrick reports on the scene in New York City after the attack. ■ Financial markets in the U.S. and around the world are disrupted. Trading at the New York Stock Exchange and Chicago Board of Trade is halted. ■ Washington struggles to come to grips with the terror attacks on the United States. ■ President Bush vows to "hunt down and to find" the terrorists responsible for the deadly hijackings. ■ Military and police agencies in Wisconsin tighten security in response to the disaster. ■ This special edition is wrapped around this morning's Final Edition of the Journal Sentinel.

EXTRA

MILWAUKEE
JOURNAL SENTINEL

EXTRA EDITION 2 ★ TUESDAY, SEPTEMBER 11, 2001 ★ WWW.ONWISCONSIN.COM

TERROR

Bush tells stunned nation freedom will be defended

RICK WOOD / STAFF PHOTOGRAPHER

One of World Trade Center towers burns out of control after being struck by a hijacked commercial aircraft Tuesday in New York City. Both of the 110-foot towers collapsed shortly after being hit by planes.

119

COMPLETE COVERAGE INSIDE

HORROR IN STREETS
■ Journal Sentinel reporter Catherine Fitzpatrick reports on the scene in New York City after the attack.
Page 3

MARKETS IN TURMOIL
■ Financial markets in the U.S. and around the world are disrupted. Trading at the New York Stock Exchange and Chicago Board of Trade is halted.
Page 3

CAPITAL STUNNED
■ Washington struggles to come to grips with the terror attacks on the United States.
Page 4

BUSH'S PROMISE
■ President Bush vows to "hunt down and to find" the terrorists responsible for the deadly hijackings.
Page 5

SECURITY TIGHTENS
■ Military and police agencies in Wisconsin tighten security in response to the disaster.
Page 5

EXTRA EDITION
■ This special edition is wrapped around this morning's Final Edition of the Journal Sentinel.

'To injure no man,
but to bless all mankind'

BOSTON · WEDNESDAY
SEPTEMBER 12, 2001

VOL. 93, NO. 202   COPYRIGHT © 2001 THE CHRISTIAN SCIENCE PUBLISHING SOCIETY - All rights reserve

Strategic target *The reported assassination of the Taliban's chief enemy in war-torn Afghanistan.*

Homefront *Some black and white churches are bridging the racial divide by merging.*

11

75

120

From London to Los Angeles, the world stood still

By Ann Scott Tyson
Special correspondent of
The Christian Science Monitor

WASHINGTON – America – and indeed the world – stopped still Tuesday to watch what seemed like a horrific movie that no one ever wanted to see.

From a coffee shop on Ventura Boulevard in Los Angeles to the chaos of a Washington street, Americans across the country entered a state of altered reality. Much as with the 1963 assassination of President John Kennedy, or the 1986 explosion of the space

'Mommy, it looks just like Pearl Harbor on TV.'

– An 11-year-old boy, leaving
for school in Los Angeles

shuttle Challenger, the nation screeched into slow motion as people took in a tragic intersection of life and history.

But while those shocking events were seared into the American psyche – never letting us forget exactly where we were and what we were doing when they happened – Tuesday was different.

As images of destruction flooded TV screens in homes, businesses, and schools everywhere – and it became clear that the US was under the most massive, coordinated terrorist attack in the nation's history – there was a jarring, collective realization that this is not just about history. It's about the future.

"It's the end of innocence," says Robert Goldman, an
See WORLD page 3

For the Monitor's view, see Page 8.

csmonitor.com
For current updates, maps, and timelines, visit our site:
www.csmonitor.com

THE NATION REELS

Terrorist attacks against the World Trade Center and Pentagon challenge aspects of America's core identity

By Peter Grier
Staff writer of The Christian Science Monitor

WASHINGTON – On a Tuesday like any other, with fall coming on and the kids settling into school, the United States of America was struck a series of terror blows so searing they could change the nation's sense of itself as profoundly as did Pearl Harbor or the worst days of the Vietnam War.

The US is used to feeling invulnerable. Bombs, smoke, and a banshee chorus of rescue vehicles were for other, weaker, less prosperous places.

Now the very idea of America, as expressed in its symbolic buildings, has been successfully attacked. Going forward, one overarching debate will likely involve how that idea – of openness, of freedom of movement, of confidence in itself – may change.

"The big issue here is how much we will feel forced to close down our society now," says Stansfield Turner, former director of the Central Intelligence Agency.

The scale of the attacks was such that they were difficult to put into perspective. They created a whole new historical context of their own.

The terrible efficiency with which they were executed astounded even hardened terrorist experts. Two hijacked airliners slammed into the twin towers of the World Trade Center within minutes of each other. Shortly thereafter, another hijacked craft hit the Pentagon.

"To be able to make these attacks within an hour [of each other] – that shows an incredible degree of organization or skill," says Stanley Bedlington, a retired senior analyst at the CIA counterterrorism center.

The terrorist organization responsible must have been planning the attack for some

time. That makes it unlikely the hijackers entered the country recently.

The implication: terrorist cells of long-standing organization are likely at work within the United States.

"They were seeded here and waiting," says a former CIA counterintelligence officer who asked not to be named.

See ATTACKS page 2

ARI DENISON

ABC//

SYMBOL OF VULNERABILITY: One of World Trade Center towers in New York collapses as another one burns in this still image from TV. Above, Kim Dyer watches television covers of the disasters in the student center at Northeastern University in Boston.

Who could have done it? A very short list

■ Terrorism experts say that only Osama bin Laden is known to have the capacity for an attack of this scale.

By Faye Bowers and Scott Peterson
Staff writers of The Christian Science Monitor

BOSTON AND MOSCOW – Only one man, say counterterrorism experts, had the motive – and capability – to carry out terrorist attacks of this magnitude: Osama bin Laden.

"From the scale and obvious coordination, it seems clear that a major group is re-

sponsible – and like most people, I'm betting on Osama bin Laden," says a former analyst who worked in the CIA's counterterrorism unit. "The fact that he signaled a major hit three weeks ago suggests his organization is responsible."

Stanley Bedlington, a retired CIA officer who also worked in counterterrorism, agrees: "What really points to Osama bin

Laden is the similarity to the attacks i Nairobi, Kenya, and Dar es Salaam, Tanza nia, in 1998," says Mr. Bedlington. "Ther are some direct correspondences – the fac that two attacks in two different countrie were carried out at the same time which re sulted in enormous casualties, and nov there are these attacks in New York an Washington which occurred within an hour.

There are other groups, of course, wh could be responsible. There are man groups in the Mideast angry with the US ove
See SUSPECT page .

Copyright © 2001 *The Christian Science Monitor* (www.csmonitor.com). All rights reserved. Reproduced with permission.

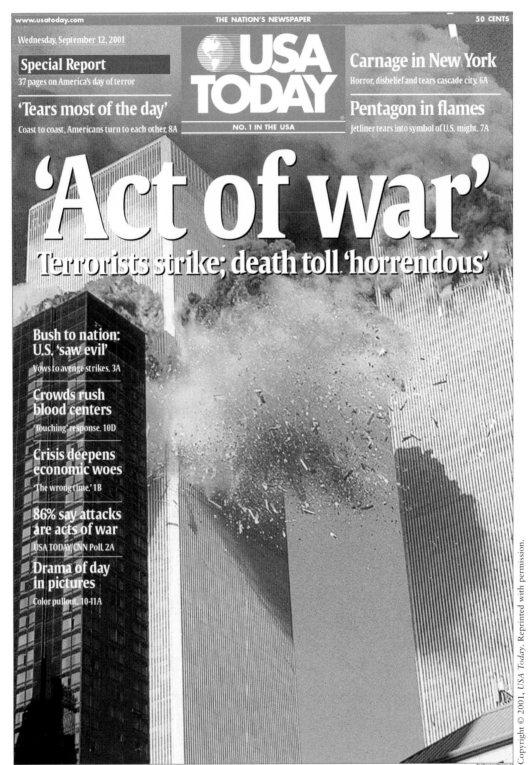

Copyright © 2001, *USA Today*. Reprinted with permission.

www.usatoday.com — THE NATION'S NEWSPAPER — **50 CENTS**

Wednesday, September 12, 2001

USA TODAY
NO. 1 IN THE USA

Special Report
37 pages on America's day of terror

'Tears most of the day'
Coast to coast, Americans turn to each other. 8A

Carnage in New York
Horror, disbelief and tears cascade city. 6A

Pentagon in flames
Jetliner tears into symbol of U.S. might. 7A

'Act of war'
Terrorists strike; death toll 'horrendous'

Bush to nation: U.S. 'saw evil'
Vows to avenge strikes. 3A

Crowds rush blood centers
'Touching' response. 10D

Crisis deepens economic woes
'The wrong time.' 1B

86% say attacks are acts of war
USA TODAY/CNN Poll. 2A

Drama of day in pictures
Color pullout. 10-11A

Second impact: Flames and debris explode from a World Trade Center tower as a jetliner slams into the structure Tuesday. Both towers in Manhattan collapsed into a pile of rubble shortly thereafter.

By Chao Soi Cheong, AP

Minute by minute, fear envelops the country
As jetliners strike U.S. landmarks, America's sense of security is shattered

It may have been the bloodiest day in U.S. history, when our two biggest office towers were obliterated and the Pentagon, symbol of our military authority, was ripped open like an egg carton.

Our commercial jetliners were turned into weapons of mass murder, and we had to stop doing things we always do, from trading stocks to going to Disney World.

People ran through the ash-covered streets of lower Manhattan like extras in a nuclear winter fantasy, chased by a mighty cloud of dust and debris from the office towers they once occupied. Others, some on fire, jumped from 30, 40, 80 stories. One couple held hands as they leapt.

Even if Sept. 11, 2001, was not our deadliest day, it was surely our worst. Americans talked of "a second Pearl Harbor" and "an act of war," but the comparisons faltered.

This time it was civilians dying in the nation's political and financial centers, not soldiers and sailors in a distant Pacific territory. This time the targets were not outdated battleships, but buildings familiar to every schoolchild.

And if this really was war — 86% of Americans in a USA TODAY/CNN/Gallup Poll Tuesday said it was — who was the enemy? What did he want? When was the next battle?

Suspicion focused on an individual, indicted Saudi terrorist Osama Bin Laden, not a nation.

As some called for a congressional declaration of war, Rep. Jim Moran of Virginia asked, "Who do you declare war on?"

History will find that something about America changed at 9 a.m. Tuesday, predicted John Morton Blum, a retired Yale historian and World War II scholar.

"Americans aren't used to being in a war zone," he said. "From here on,

Cover story
By Rick Hampson
USA TODAY

they are. No superpower has ever been hit like this."

Sen. John McCain, R-Ariz., struck an apocalyptic note: "I don't think our lifestyles will be the same for a long time."

The prime casualty was America's sense of safety. When Arab terrorists bombed the World Trade Center 8 years ago, six people died, and the complex came back better than ever.

But by noon Tuesday, the Trade Center looked like a smoldering dump and America looked like a nation in retreat — office workers ran up Broadway, and men and women in uniform walked from the Pentagon past Arlington National Cemetery and the Iwo Jima Marine Memorial. They glanced fearfully behind them, as though afraid of what

"Pearl Harbor brought us together to face a problem. Maybe this can do the same."
—Former Secretary of State Lawrence Eagleburger.

See COVER STORY next page ▶

©COPYRIGHT 2001
USA TODAY, a division
of Gannett Co., Inc.
Subscriptions, customer
service
1-800-USA-0001
www.cs.usatoday.com

THE WALL STREET JOURNAL.

© 2001 Dow Jones & Company, Inc. All Rights Reserved.

DOWJONES VOL. CCXXXVIII NO. 51 EE/PR ★★★★ WEDNESDAY, SEPTEMBER 12, 2001 WSJ.com ★★★★ $1.00

TERRORISTS DESTROY WORLD TRADE CENTER, HIT PENTAGON IN RAID WITH HIJACKED JETS

Nation Stands In Disbelief And Horror

Streets of Manhattan Resemble War Zone Amid Clouds of Ash

A WALL STREET JOURNAL News Roundup

They were like scenes from a catastrophe movie. Or a Tom Clancy novel. Or a CNN broadcast from a distant foreign nation.

But they were real yesterday. And they were very much in the U.S.

James Cutler, a 31-year-old insurance broker, was in the Akbar restaurant on the ground floor of the World Trade Center when he heard "boom, boom, boom," he recalls. In seconds, the kitchen doors blew open, smoke and ash poured into the restaurant and the ceiling collapsed. Mr. Cutler didn't know what had happened yet, but he found himself standing among bodies strewn across the floor. "It was mayhem," he says.

Around the same time, Nestor Zwyhun, the 38-year-old chief technology officer of Tradecard, an international trading firm, had just stepped off the New Jersey commuter ferry and was walking toward the World Trade Center when he heard a sound "like a jet engine at full throttle," he says, then a huge explosion. Smoke billowed in the sky and sheets of glass were falling everywhere. "I stood there for two seconds, then ran," Mr. Zwyhun said.

More than 100 floors above him at the Trade Center offices of Cantor Fitzgerald, someone put a call from the company's Los Angeles office on the speaker phone. What was happening there? The Los Angeles people heard someone say, "I think a plane just hit us." For more than five minutes, the Los Angeles people listened in horror as the sounds of chaos came through the speaker phone, people screaming, "Somebody's got to help us. ... We can't get out. ... The place is filling with smoke." Then the phone went dead.

Three hundred miles to the south, in Washington, D.C., a jet swooped in from the west and burrowed into the side of the Pentagon building, exploding in a tower of flame and smoke. Mark Thaggard, an office manager in the building, was there when the plane hit. People started running this way and that, trying to get out. "It was chaotic," Mr. Thaggard says. "It was unbelievable. We could not believe this was happening."

The nation stood in shock and horror yesterday after three apparently hijacked jetliners, in less than an hour's time, made kamikaze-like crashes into both towers of the World Trade Center and the Pentagon, killing hundreds, maybe thou-

Please Turn to Page A12, Column 1

The Eye of the Storm: One Journey Through Desperation and Chaos

* * *

A Nightmare of Falling Bodies, Acrid Smoke and Heroism; 'It's Coming Down! Run!'

By JOHN BUSSEY
Staff Reporter of THE WALL STREET JOURNAL

NEW YORK—If there's only one sight I'll remember from the destruction of the World Trade Center, it is the flight of desperation—a headlong leap from the topmost floors by those who chose a different death than the choking smoke and flame. Some fell swinging their arms and legs, looking down as the street came up at them. Others fell on their backs, peering upward toward the flames and sky. They dropped like deadweight, several seconds, hopeless and unhelpable.

And always the same end. Some crashed into the plastic awning over the entrance to the North Tower. Others hit a retaining wall. Still others landed on lampposts and shrubbery. After the 80-floor drop, the impact left small puffs of pink and red vapor drifting at ground level. Firefighters arriving on the scene ran for cover.

In the movie "Armageddon," the asteroids pierced New York buildings sending shrapnel out the other side. That, remarkably, is exactly what it looked like from the street, when the first plane hit the north tower of the World Trade center.

The first warning was the sound of jet engines, flying low over the island of Manhattan. A second or two later, what seemed like a sonic boom.

From the sidewalk, behind the building that houses The Wall Street Journal's offices just across the street from the World Trade towers, I didn't see the first plane dive into its target. But I saw the result: an arc of debris, aflame against the blue

Please Turn to Page A4, Column 1

What's News—

* * *

Business and Finance

ALL MAJOR U.S. FINANCIAL markets closed yesterday and remain closed today in the wake of the terrorist attack on the World Trade Center. The near-panic reaction in the global markets that remained open suggested that substantial damage was done to the psyche of a world financial system already on edge from prospects of an international recession. In Tokyo, the Nikkei stock index fell below 10000 early Wednesday for the first time since 1984.

(Article on Page B1)

* * *

The World Trade Center housed many Wall Street and banking firms, law offices, technology companies, trading firms and other businesses. Many escaped before the destruction of the buildings yesterday, but the toll of dead and injured is unclear.

(Article on Page B1)

* * *

The attacks threaten to push a fragile global economy into widespread recession, smashing consumer confidence and disrupting basic commercial functions such as air travel.

(Article on Page A1)

* * *

The dollar tumbled in global markets following the attacks. In late London trading, the euro stood at 91.44 U.S. cents, up from 89.95 cents late Monday in New York. The dollar tumbled to 119.16 yen from 120.93 yen and the British pound rose to $1.4751 from $1.4579.

(Article on Page B3)

* * *

Energy prices soared on fears the attacks might have originated in the Middle East and any retaliatory action could disrupt supplies. U.S. companies went on heightened alert to safeguard the nation's energy supplies.

(Articles on Page A2)

* * *

Telecom systems were strained as the terrorist attacks on New York and Washington knocked out telephone and wireless service across the Northeast.

(Article on Page A3)

* * *

The Internet proved the most reliable way to communicate following the attacks, as the phone system sagged from severed lines and an extraordinary volume of calls. Corporate executives used e-mail to find employees across town or across the country.

(Article on Page A3)

* * *

Insurers are facing what is certainly the largest man-made and possibly the largest-ever disaster they have dealt with in yesterday's destruction, with the price tag estimated at over $10 billion.

(Article on Page B1)

* * *

Xerox reached an equipment-financing agreement with GE Capital that will let Xerox erase about $5 billion of debt.

(Article on Page A16)

* * *

Treasury Secretary Paul O'Neill left China yesterday persuaded that authorities in Beijing already are planning to adopt a significantly more flexible currency system—at their own pace.

(Article on Page A16)

* * *

After months of reviewing the Clinton-era money-laundering crackdown, President Bush's Treasury Department has completed a set of revisions that would slightly ease rules in one area and tighten them in another.

(Article on Page A16)

Markets—

Stocks: Market closed.
Bonds: Market closed.
Commodities: Dow Jones-AIG futures index 101.329, up 0.168.
Dollar: 119.16 yen, off 1.77; 1.0936 euros, off 0.0181; 2.1389 marks, off 0.0355.

World-Wide

BUSH PROMISED action against terrorist attacks in the Eastern U.S.

The death toll from the hijacked-jet attacks that destroyed the World Trade Center's towers in New York and damaged the Pentagon outside Washington was impossible to gauge immediately. But the president said "thousands of lives were suddenly ended." A fourth hijacked plane crashed near Pittsburgh. Another commercial jet went down in western Pennsylvania. It wasn't immediately clear who was responsible for the attacks, but the president told the nation the U.S. "would make no distinction" between terrorists and "those who harbored them." He virtually promised armed response earlier yesterday. "Make no mistake: The United States will hunt down and punish those responsible for these cowardly acts," he said. (Articles on pages A1 and A15)

Sen. McCain, a Vietnam War veteran, expressed the incidents' gravity: "These were not just crimes against the United States, they are acts of war."

* * *

HEALTH TEAMS launched efforts to treat thousands of injured victims.

Health workers mobilized a nationwide effort to treat the thousands of injured taken to hospitals, identify the dead and supply tens of thousands of units of blood in the wake of the terrorist attacks. More than 2,000 people were reported injured in New York City, and hospitals expected to see more. Blood-center officials said immediate needs would be met by available supplies, but they worried that they would run short in coming days as they face the need to replenish supplies. (Article on Page A6)

The Health and Human Services chief activated all of the nation's 80 special disaster teams. It was the first general mobilization of the teams.

* * *

The FAA shut the national air-traffic system, leaving air travelers stranded, following the crashes of the four hijacked commercial jets in New York, Washington and Pennsylvania. While the FAA said it might lift its ban on flying as early as noon today, the impact of the suspected hijackers appears permanent. (Article on Page A3)

* * *

World leaders reacted with revulsion to the attacks in the U.S. and demanded war on international terrorism, but in the Middle East some people supported the actions. The U.N.'s Annan said the "deliberate acts of terrorism" traumatized the world, but he called for reasoned judgment.

* * *

New York called off its primary election after the attack on the World Trade Center. Mayor Giuliani said he called off the election after consulting with the governor of New York, and they will decide later when it will be rescheduled. The mayor said all available police and fire personnel had been deployed to Lower Manhattan to aid in rescue operations.

* * *

Congressional Republicans are crafting standby spending cuts meant to showcase support for Social Security while they push for new tax cuts to spur the economy. The GOP lawmakers appear unwilling to wait for clear guidance from Bush.

* * *

Afghanistan's ruling Taliban launched a fresh offensive as the chief of the rival forces against it said their military chief Masood had been seriously wounded in an assassination attempt. Amid rumors Masood had been killed in Sunday's attack, officials said doctors were recommending Masood be taken to Europe for treatment.

* * *

Israeli tanks encircled the Palestinian-ruled city of Jenin in a West Bank operation that Israel's army said was intended to prevent suicide bombers from reaching Israel. That prompted fighting in which two Palestinians died. Truce talks fell through amid arguments over a venue and Palestinian condemnation of the tank operation.

* * *

Powell arrived back in Washington from Peru after cutting short a South American trip because of the attacks in New York and Washington. The secretary of state had attended a meeting of the Organization of American States. Foreign ministers began the meeting with a moment of silence for the American victims.

A Day of Terror

The World has become a different place in the wake of yesterday's terrorist attacks as a new kind of war has been declared on the world's democracies. Review & Outlook on page A18.

Elsewhere:

- **Just as Japan on Dec. 7, 1941, destroyed America's historic belief in its ocean-guarded invulnerability, now Sept. 11, 2001, joins that date to live in infamy—for obliterating Americans' sense that terrorism was something that happened somewhere else, A20.**
- **Although the perpetrators of the terrorist attacks have yet to be identified, Islamic-Americans in many U.S. cities have already begun grappling with an angry backlash. Islamic groups in this country condemned the attacks, A15.**
- **Health workers mobilized an unprecedented nationwide effort to treat the thousands of injured taken to hospitals, identify the dead and supply tens of thousands of units of blood, A6.**
- **An anxious waiting took hold in many suburban towns that dot the train lines that carry tens of thousands of commuters into lower Manhattan each day, and word of who was still missing filled neighborhoods, A2.**
- **Their Internet sites swamped, many American newspapers turned to an old-fashioned device—the special edition—to disseminate news quickly on the terrorist attacks, A3.**
- **The closure of the New York exchanges shut down the Chicago futures markets, creating a situation in the Farm Belt not seen since the Chernobyl nuclear plant explosion in April 1986: Nobody knew the price of a bushel of U.S. grain, B3.**

Death Toll, Source of Devastating Attacks Remain Unclear; U.S. Vows Retaliation as Attention Focuses on bin Laden

By DAVID S. CLOUD
And NEIL KING
Staff Reporters of THE WALL STREET JOURNAL

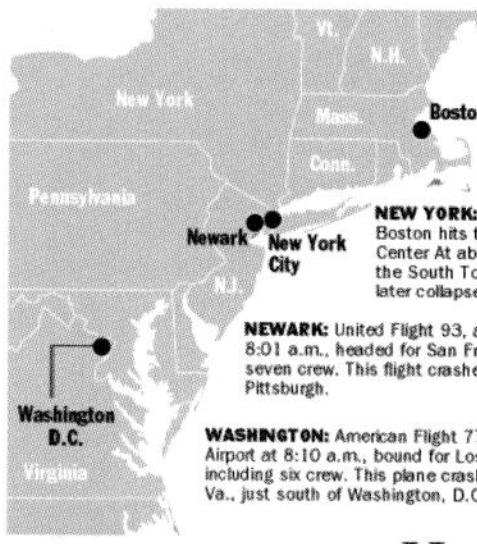
Vt.
N.H.
New York
Mass.
Conn.
Pennsylvania
N.J.
Virginia
Boston
Newark
New York City
Washington D.C.
BOSTON: American Airlines Flight 11, a Boeing 767, leaves Boston at 7:59 a.m. EDT for Los Angeles. This flight, with 92 people aboard, including 11 crew, becomes the first plane to hit the World Trade Center.
NEW YORK: At about 8:50 a.m., Flight 11 from Boston hits the North Tower of the World Trade Center At about 9:03 a.m., a second plane hits the South Tower of the trade center. Both towers later collapse.
NEWARK: United Flight 93, a Boeing 757 aircraft, leaves Newark at 8:01 a.m., headed for San Francisco with 45 people, including seven crew. This flight crashes at about 10 a.m. southeast of Pittsburgh.
WASHINGTON: American Flight 77, a Boeing 757, departs Dulles Airport at 8:10 a.m., bound for Los Angeles with 64 people aboard, including six crew. This plane crashes into the Pentagon in Arlington, Va., just south of Washington, D.C.

By successfully attacking the most prominent symbols of American power—Wall Street and the Pentagon—terrorists have wiped out any remaining illusions that America is safe from mass organized violence.

That realization alone will alter the way the U.S. approaches its role in the world, as well as the way Americans travel and do business at home and abroad.

The death toll from the hijacked jets' attacks that destroyed the World Trade Center in lower Manhattan, and damaged the Pentagon, was impossible to gauge immediately. But it could eclipse the loss of life the country suffered in the Japanese attack on Pearl Harbor, when more than 2,300 perished.

It wasn't immediately clear who was responsible for the attack, though official attention focused on Middle East terrorist Osama bin Laden and his organization. One U.S. official said intelligence agencies already had gathered "strong information" linking Mr. bin Laden to the attacks. If the bin Laden organization isn't directly responsible, U.S. officials suspect, it could have sprung from a network of Islamic terror groups he supports and finances.

The gravity of the challenge to the country was summarized by Sen. John McCain, a Vietnam War veteran, who said: "These were not just crimes against the United States, they are acts of war."

Yet a war against terrorism is unlike a conventional war, and in some ways is far scarier. As a traumatized nation saw in gruesome detail on its television sets, terrorists attack civilians, not soldiers. And while the wars of the past century involved nation-states that could ultimately be defeated, a war against terrorism involves a less distinct enemy, whose defeat will be hard to ensure.

President Bush nearly promised armed response in his response to the tragedy. "America has stood down enemies before, and we will do so this time," he said in nationally televised address from the Oval Office. In a pointed warning to terrorists as well as to nations such as Afghanistan, which hosts Mr. bin Laden, the president declared: "We will make no distinction between the terrorists who committed these acts and those who harbored them."

Leaders of the House of Representatives and the Senate—shuttered yesterday amid the threat—plan to reconvene today in a special session to consider a bipartisan resolution condemning the terrorist attacks.

The sheer sophistication of the terrorists was remarkable. The FBI is operating on the assumption that there were multiple hijackers on each of the flights that struck New York

Please Turn to Page A12, Column 5

Hour of Horror Forever Alters American Lives

Attacks Will Force People To Make Adjustments In Ways Large and Small

An hour of terror changed everything.

Far from the World Trade Center or the Pentagon, Florida shut down its state universities yesterday. San Francisco closed its schools, as well as the TransAmerica building and pedestrian access to the Golden Gate Bridge. Major league baseball games were canceled.

The popular, needlelike Stratosphere

By Wall Street Journal staff reporters June Kronholz in Washington, Christina Binkley in Los Angeles and Clare Ansberry in Pittsburgh.

tower on the north end of the Las Vegas strip was closed; so was the Paris casino's mock Eiffel Tower. University of Virginia psychologist Dewey Cornell canceled his lecture on student threats and violence inside the schools—so his audience of principals could go back to their schools to deal with the violence outside.

"You just thought America was the safest country," said Jesse Strauss, a 13-year-old eighth-grader at Pelham Middle School, a Manhattan suburb. His mother added, "Our world as we know it isn't going to return to normal for a long time."

Yesterday's terrorism darkened, marked and forever altered the way Americans live their lives.

"We are going to have to learn what a

Please Turn to Page A6, Column 4

U.S. Airport Security Screening Long Seen as Dangerously Lax

New Measures Are Likely To Add Inconvenience And Costs for Passengers

Government agencies have long warned about lax U.S. airport security screening, something that frequent fliers see on a regular basis. Yesterday, that crucial system failed in the most tragic and spectacular way.

Commandeering four airplanes yesterday and using them as giant jet fuel bombs, suicidal hijackers apparently made it through airport security screening in Boston, Newark, N.J., and Washington, armed but not detected. Investigators will

By Wall Street Journal staff reporters Scott McCartney in Seattle, J. Lynn Lunsford in Los Angeles and David Armstrong in Boston.

undoubtedly look at whether the attackers might have had fellow terrorists working at particular metal detectors and X-ray machines, or planted weapons aboard the planes through catering or other service trucks, but authorities have long raised alarms about security, with little action taken to tighten airport procedures.

Just last year, in an almost prophetic warning, the General Accounting Office said airport security hadn't improved, and in many cases had worsened. Even though airport security screening stops an average 2,000 weapons a year, "the security of the air transport system remains at risk," the GAO said.

"People are very creative," says Viola Hackett, a security guard at Houston's George Bush Intercontinental Airport, who said she wasn't surprised that the attackers could bypass airport security. "There are all sorts of things they're trying to hide."

One passenger aboard a doomed jet called her husband from the air, federal officials said, and said two hijackers were armed with box-cutting knives, which often have retractable blades.

The Federal Aviation Administration was already moving to tighten screening standards; in fact, new rules were supposed to be issued next week.

The metal detectors and X-ray machines so familiar at airport concourses are basically the only line of protection for U.S. airliners. With more than 10,000 commercial flights a day, airliners don't carry security personnel, and airline crews are armed with little more than plastic handcuffs to corral unruly customers and an ax for pilots to escape in the event of a crash.

Pilots and airline officials believe it is likely the hijackers disabled or killed both pilots in each of the three planes that struck the twin towers of the World Trade Center and the Pentagon, and then flew the planes themselves into the structures. A fourth airline crashed near Pittsburgh. The two American Airlines flights and the two United Airlines flights involved were all large Boeing Co. two-pilot jets heavily loaded with fuel for transcontinental flights.

Pilots are able to lock their cockpit door, but the lightweight door, built with breakaway panels so pilots can escape a

Please Turn to Page A10, Column 1

NOTICE TO READERS

Because delivery of The Wall Street Journal may be delayed for many readers due to repercussions from yesterday's terrorism attacks, the entire online edition of the Journal can be accessed free of charge, at WSJ.com. U.S. financial markets were closed on Tuesday and there are no U.S. stock listings in the paper today. Abbreviated statistical coverage begins on page B3.

38216>
0 78908 63140 4

Attacks Raise Fears of a Recession

By GREG IP AND JOHN D. MCKINNON
Staff Reporters of THE WALL STREET JOURNAL

WASHINGTON—Yesterday's terrorist bombings threaten to push an already fragile global economy into widespread recession, smashing consumer confidence and disrupting basic commercial functions such as air travel and financial markets.

"A full-blown global recession is highly likely," Sung Won Sohn, chief economist at Wells Fargo & Co., predicted in a report yesterday afternoon.

Economic policy makers did their best to ensure calm. Shortly after noon, the Federal Reserve issued an emergency statement stating that the central bank's system was "open and operating" and that officials were "to meet liquidity needs" of the global financial system, echoing a similar declaration issued during the 1987 stock-market crash.

Treasury Secretary Paul O'Neill issued a statement from Tokyo, saying: "In the face of today's tragedy, the financial system functioned extraordinarily well, and I have every confidence that it will continue to do so in the days ahead." No major problems were reported in the banking system, though branches did close in New York. The stock, bond, and commodity markets all closed and will remain closed today.

'Everything Possible'

"I'm sure that central bankers everywhere will do everything possible to maintain calm and seek to ensure the world economy functions smoothly in the face of this horrendous deed," Federal Reserve Bank of New York President William McDonough told Dow Jones Newswires by telephone from Basel, Switzerland, where he was attending meetings at the Bank of International Settlements. Fed Chairman Alan Greenspan was on his way back to the U.S. from those meetings, but his airplane returned to Switzerland after the attacks.

Economists groped in vain for historical precedents to help evaluate the potential impact of such a shocking, tragic event on the economy. "I don't know where to look for analogies," said Alan Blinder, economics professor at Princeton University. "Confidence-shaking events usually have transitory negative effects on consumer spending. But we've never seen anything like this that I can think of."

The most recent comparable event was the 1990 Gulf War, involving a spike in oil prices and dispatch of U.S. troops to the Middle East, which depressed confidence and played a decisive role in bringing about the 1990-91 recession.

But many economists said this event is likely to be more severe because of the much greater loss of life on U.S. soil. In 1990, travel was depressed by fears of a terrorist attack. This time, the entire air-travel system has been shut down by actual attacks. "One might expect [confidence]) ... will plunge much like they did when the Gulf crisis began in August of 1990. The weakness might be more severe because this impacts Americans more directly, it's on our soil," said Ray Stone, economist at Stone & McCarthy Research Associates.

In addition, he said, "the economy looks more fragile going into this episode than it did back in 1990." Business investment and exports are falling, unemployment has risen sharply and stock prices are sinking. The impact of the tragedy on confidence could severely undermine consumer spending, which had been the economy's remaining bulwark.

Consumers, Mr. Stone added, will likely "spend less on big-ticket items such as autos, as well as things directly affected. Air traffic likely will be lower, people less willing to visit Washington or New York City or other large cities, less likely to visit sporting events where they're worried about a terrorist attack."

But others played down any long-term consequences. "There's always speculation that these disasters have extreme economic consequences, but they rarely do,"

Please Turn to Page A6, Column 1

WAR ON AMERICA

Thursday September 13, 2001

First published 1831   No. 51,176 $1.10 (incl GST)

The Sydney Morning Herald

Apocalypse now . . . a group of firefighters gaze through dust filled air at the shattered remains of the World Trade Centre, destroyed by two hijacked aeroplanes on Tuesday. There is no casualty toll yet. 'It will be more than we can bear,'' said New York's mayor Rudi Giuliani.   Photo: Reuters/Shannon Stapleton

Bush: this means war

● Aircraft carriers guard coasts　　　　● Six survivors found in rubble　　　　● Fears for 50 Australians

Mark Riley and Gay Alcorn
Herald Correspondents
in the United States

The United States has moved onto a war footing against a still hidden enemy, as estimates of the death toll from Tuesday's catastrophic terrorist assaults on the World Trade Centre and the Pentagon climb into the thousands.

Aircraft carriers with missile defence systems were positioned off both the east and west US coasts and in the Arabian Gulf as President Bush's National Security Council and intelligence services tried to determine who was responsible and how to retaliate.

Mr Bush, facing the first crucial test of his leadership, vowed to hunt down those responsible for the "evil, despicable acts of terror", and all countries which harboured terrorists.

He made it clear that he expected friends and allies to "join forces for a war on terrorism".

The White House said it had received no warning before two hijacked aircraft slammed into the twin towers of the World Trade Centre in New York, another into the Pentagon, and another into a field in Pennsylvania.

The Minister for Foreign Affairs, Mr Downer, said 50 Australians were unaccounted for.

He said the assault would constitute an act of terrorism against Australia if any of its citizens had been killed.

No official tally of Australians

'Half an hour into the flight to Los Angeles, the passengers must have known something was wrong. Somewhere near Albany the plane took a sharp turn and headed straight to New York City.' MARIAN WILKINSON reconstructs the fatal flights **Page 5**

'The two implosions – and a third at the Pentagon – reduced the Bush Administration to a wobbly attempt to demonstrate it still had a grip on the levers of power.' PAUL McGEOUGH on the mood in New York and America **Page 11**

working in the World Trade Centre was made available, but New York officials said they suspected it would be 100 or more.

The sophisticated and coordinated act of terror lasted less than 90 minutes but fear quickly spread throughout the country.

All flights were grounded for the first time in US history, government buildings were shut, and Mr Bush criss-crossed the country aboard Air Force One because the Secret Service feared for his safety.

The Commander of the US Atlantic Fleet, Admiral Robert Natter, said: "We have been attacked like we haven't since Pearl Harbour."

Republican and Democratic politicians said the attack was an act of war, and vowed swift revenge.

No creditable claim of responsibility had been made by yesterday, although FBI and intelligence

officials said they suspected it was the work of the Saudi extremist Osama bin Laden.

"This apparently was well-planned over a number of years, planned by real pros and experts," Republican Senator Orrin Hatch said in Washington after a security briefing.

"Their belief is, at least initially, that this looks like Osama bin Laden's signature."

He said intelligence services had intercepted communications between bin Laden operatives discussing the attacks.

Bin Laden is thought to be hiding in Afghanistan, where the Taliban regime denied any knowledge of those behind the attacks.

The Taliban militia said it would consider requests for the extradition of bin Laden but would need evidence from US investigators.

A Palestinian journalist re-

ported in Islamabad that bin Laden had congratulated the terrorists who carried out the deadly strikes, but had denied being involved.

The scenes of terror were worst in New York, the largest city in the US and the financial capital of the world.

Six survivors were found as a massive rescue operation began amid the rubble of the World Trade Centre. Emergency services reported receiving several mobile telephone calls from people trapped in the ruins.

Rescuers said they could hear screams from under the rubble. They hoped further survivors would be found in large airpockets between the slabs of broken buildings.

Mr Bush estimated the total dead to be in the thousands.

The Mayor of New York, Mr Rudolph Giuliani, said: "I have a sense it's a horrendous number

of lives lost. Right now we have to focus on saving as many lives as possible." Estimates of the death toll from the attack on the Pentagon, where 20,000 people work, ranged from 100 to 800. The 266 people in the four hijacked planes all died.

Mr Bush addressed the nation from the Oval Office late on Tuesday, declaring that the US would find and punish "those behind these evil acts", along with any country that harbours them.

"These acts shattered steel, but they cannot dent the steel of American resolve," he said.

Economists warned that the effect of the attacks on international markets could tip the already flagging US economy into recession, taking the rest of the world with it.

Regional financial markets descended into chaos, with billions of dollars wiped off the value of sharemarkets as investors

rushed away from shares, corporate bonds and the US dollar in favour of government-backed bonds, gold and oil.

US stock exchanges were expected to remain closed on Tuesday. All airports in the country remained closed.

Fifteen US warships were sent to protect the west coast and Hawaii, while USS Kennedy and USS George Washington were off the east coast, protecting New York City and Washington, DC. USS Enterprise was ordered to remain in the Gulf.

As many as 50,000 people worked in the two 110-storey towers at the World Trade Centre, and an unknown number of visitors, business guests and shoppers were also inside.

The Australian property group Westfield Holdings had recently signed a $US3.2 billion, 99-year lease on the centre's shopping precinct. The company said one US-based employee remained missing from its 10-person office.

US reports said five Arabic men had been identified as suspects and that a rental car containing Arabic-language flight training manuals had been seized at Boston's Logan International Airport.

The men had boarded the two aircraft that crashed into the World Trade Centre – an American Airlines 767 and a United Airlines 767, which left Logan Airport bound for Los Angeles.

The American Airlines plane

crashed into one of the towers at 8.45 am local time on Tuesday, and the other plane hit the second tower about 15 minutes later.

People ran from the towers, others were trapped inside, and some hurled themselves from the windows, before both buildings and a smaller adjoining building collapsed.

An American Airlines 757 en route from Dulles Airport near Washington to Los Angeles was flown into the Pentagon at 9.40 am.

The fourth aircraft, which crashed outside Pittsburgh – a United Airlines 757 flying from Newark, New Jersey, to San Francisco – was believed to have been heading for the White House, the Congress or the presidential retreat at Camp David.

Security officials in Massachusetts identified the five Arab men as suspects, The Boston Herald reported.

Two of the men, whose passports were traced to the United Arab Emirates, were brothers, one of whom was a trained pilot, said the paper. At least two other suspects had crossed from Canada and flown to Logan airport.

The paper said the suspects had no guns, but used shaving kits and other carry-on luggage to smuggle knife-like weapons.

Once in the air, the hijackers in one plane reportedly began killing flight attendants in order to lure a pilot from the cockpit.

9 770312 631049

ISSN 0312-6315

Select your **FREE** handset,   1   then **TAILOR** your included calls to suit you   2   plus only **OPTUS** gives you   3

NOKIA 3330
$0
On Optus Tailored 33

Call **133 999** over 145 stores Australia wide

OPTUS World
THE 'yes' SHOP

OPTUS MOBILE. YES YOU CAN'

Conditions apply including: Tailored 33 – 24 months connection with a monthly access fee of $33. Minimum total cost over 24 months is $792 for the Nokia 3330. If connection is not maintained for 24 continuous months an additional $530 is payable. All Plans – New and credit approved customers only. While stocks last. Offer ends 24/09/01. 'yes' Time and 'yes' Weekend are special promotions available until 31/12/02. †Included call options exclude some call and message types depending on the plan and option selected. Unused included voice/voicemail calls expire at the end of three months. Unused included SMS and WAP calls expire at one month.   Ad Town Z634367   www.optusworld.com.au

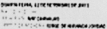

O DIA

R$0,75

11

O DIA ONLINE: www.odia.com.br

CADERNO ESPECIAL

Presidente dos EUA, George W. Bush, promete vingança. Terroristas destruíram com aviões de passageiros o World Trade Center, em Nova Iorque, e explodiram o Pentágono, em Washington, na maior onda de atentados da História. Foi o mais grave ataque aos Estados Unidos desde a ação japonesa contra a base de Pearl Harbor, em 1941, durante a 2ª Guerra Mundial. Cabul, a capital do Afeganistão, foi bombardeada ontem.

GUERRA

MUTILADO pela destruição das torres gêmeas, um dos cartões-postais mais famosos do mundo, a visão dos prédios de Nova Iorque, ficou coberta de fumaça e poeira

INSTANTE em que o Boeing com 65 pessoas a bordo é lançado contra a segunda torre do World Trade Center

DESESPERADO, um homem se atira do prédio de 110 andares

HOJE É DIA DE INTERNET

3.040 OFERTAS CLASSIFICADAS

ARNALDO CÉSAR
Atentados dessam o Brasil de novo na mira dos especuladores internacionais.

CLÁUDIO HUMBERTO
Médium brasileira garante que avisou a George Bush sobre o terror contra os EUA.

JOÃO B. FREITAS
Simples aviões de carreira destruíram o coração da nação até então inatingível.

O medo toma conta da Terra. Às 8h53, um avião de passageiros seqüestrado foi lançado contra uma das torres do World Trade Center, símbolo do capitalismo mundial. Dezoito minutos depois, um outro avião explodiu contra o segundo prédio. Menos de duas horas depois, as construções viraram pó. Em Washington, orgulho das forças militares mais poderosas do planeta, o Pentágono, foi alvo de outro ataque aéreo kamikaze. O número de mortos é superior a 10 mil. As suspeitas dos atentados recaem sobre o bilionário líder terrorista Osama Bin Laden, que vive no Afeganistão. De madrugada, Cabul, capital do país, foi bombardeada. O presidente Fernando Henrique ficou chocado: "Isso é loucura, pode ser a 3ª Guerra Mundial".

EDITORIAL "HORROR À VIOLÊNCIA NÃO TEM FRONTEIRAS" • PÁGINAS 6 E 7

EDIÇÃO EXTRA

O GLOBO

undador: **IRINEU MARINHO**   RIO DE JANEIRO, TERÇA-FEIRA, 11 DE SETEMBRO DE 2001 • ANO • Nº • www.oglobo.com.br   Presidente: **ROBERTO MARINH**

Terror sem limites
Atentados suicidas deixam milhares de mortos nos EUA

AVIÃO SE APROXIMA da segunda torre do World Trade Center...

...e explode, formando uma bola de fogo, após colidir com o prédio

O MOMENTO EXATO do desabamento de uma das torres do mais alto edifício de Nova York, um dos principais símbolos da cidade

Aviões destroem World Trade Center

Presidente Bush promete reação

Mercados param no mundo inteiro

HELICÓPTERO DE SALVAMENTO sobrevoa o Pentágono, momentos depois da explosão causada pela queda de um avião suicida

www.ledevoir.com

LE DEVOIR

VOL. XCII Nº 206 ◆   LE MERCREDI 12 SEPTEMBRE 2001   87 ¢ + TAXES = 1 $

126

FRAPPÉS AU CŒUR

■ *Les États-Unis essuient la pire attaque terroriste de l'histoire*

■ *Des avions civils détournés détruisent le World Trade Center et frappent le Pentagone*

JEAN DION
LE DEVOIR

Une tragédie sans nom, inimaginable, épouvantable au-delà de tout entendement, a frappé hier les États-Unis en plein cœur alors que des attentats terroristes à répétition ont touché New York et Washington, entraînant dans la mort des milliers de personnes et déclenchant une vague de fond d'horreur, de psychose, voire de panique, d'incrédulité et de réprobation tant chez les Américains qu'à travers le monde.

La série d'attaques, la plus vaste opération terroriste jamais lancée dans l'histoire, a visé deux symboles de la puissance des États-Unis, le World Trade Center, dans le quartier des affaires de Manhattan, et le Pentagone, siège principal de l'armée américaine, à Washington. Son caractère démentiel mais aussi la formidable minutie de son organisation ont évidemment suscité toute une série de conjectures quant à son ou ses auteurs, qui ne l'ont pas revendiquée.

Les attentats, qualifiés d'«actes lâches» par le président George W. Bush, ont commencé à 8h56 hier matin lorsqu'un avion de la compagnie American Airlines au départ de Boston et à destination de Los Angeles, détourné par des pirates de l'air, est allé percuter l'une des tours jumelles du World Trade Center. Dix-huit minutes plus tard, un second appareil, le transporteur United Airlines celui-là, s'écrasait contre l'autre tour du complexe de 110 étages.

VOIR PAGE A 12: **CŒUR**

■ **Dix pages sur la catastrophe**

Qui ?

Ben Laden, suspect nº 1

SERGE TRUFFAUT
LE DEVOIR

Échaudées par les accusations formulées hâtivement dans la foulée de l'attentat commis à Oklahoma City en 1995, les autorités américaines se sont abstenues d'avancer quelque information que ce soit concernant les auteurs de ces attentats. Il reste qu'au moment de mettre sous presse, plusieurs experts avançaient, au conditionnel il est vrai, que les actes commis pourraient bien avoir été conçus par Oussama ben Laden et réalisés par les membres de son groupe Al-Qaeda, ou «La Base».

En fait, trois possibilités ont été évoquées: ben Laden figure en haut de la liste, suivi de le Front populaire de libération de la Palestine (FPLP) et, en troisième position, de l'Irak. Ni ce dernier pays ni le réseau Laden ne se sont manifestés. Par voie de communiqué, le FPLP, qui avait perdu son secrétaire général Abou Ali Mustafa lors d'un attentat perpétré il y a deux semaines de cela par l'armée israélienne, a formellement condamné les gestes commis.

VOIR PAGE A 12: **LADEN**

Une image apocalyptique en plein quartier des affaires à New York. Les ruines des deux tours du World Trade Center transparaissent dans la fumée à travers les véhicules d'urgence détruits. Trois avions civils ont été détournés et lancés délibérément hier contre le World Trade Center et le Pentagone à Washington.

PETER MORGAN REUTERS

«J'ai vu le World Trade Center s'effondrer»

STÉPHANIE TREMBLAY
LE DEVOIR À NEW YORK

Mardi matin, 8h45. Je suis assise devant mon ordinateur et je commence ma journée de travail en buvant mon café. J'allume la radio et c'est à ce moment que j'apprends qu'un avion vient de s'écraser sur le World Trade Center.

Je me précipite sur le téléviseur et, instantanément, je vois la tour en flammes. Il faut que ce soit un accident. J'essaie de croire qu'un mauvais pilote s'est écrasé contre la tour. C'est tout. À la télé, une femme, témoin oculaire de «l'accident», décrit ce qu'elle a vu et entendu: le grondement de moteur de l'appareil, l'avion qui volait trop bas et ensuite le crash. Elle est bouleversée. La télé diffuse des images en direct et, pendant que cette femme parle, un autre avion s'approche, trop bas lui aussi, et fonce dans la deuxième tour. La thèse de l'accident ne tient plus. Je suis en train d'assister à un attentat terroriste. J'arrive à peine à y croire.

J'habite Brooklyn, à quelques coins de rue de l'East River et pratiquement en face du quartier des affaires de Manhattan et à 10 minutes du World Trade Center. Déjà, on annonce à la télé que toutes les voies d'accès vers Manhattan sont fermées, donc je décide de prendre mon vélo et de voir jusqu'où je peux me faufiler.

Au centre-ville de Brooklyn, tout le monde est dans la rue. Il y a une circulation monstre et les gens ont tous un air hébété. Ils regardent en direction de Manhattan à l'énorme nuage de fumée. La ville, normalement bruyante, est cacophonique ce matin. On entend des sirènes d'ambulances et de voitures de police venant de toutes les directions.

Avec mon vélo, j'espère réussir à monter sur le pont de Brooklyn, d'où on a une excellente vue sur le World Trade Center, mais quand j'y arrive, le pont est déjà fermé. Je me dirige donc vers l'East River et je m'arrête sous le pont de Brooklyn, sur un petit quai situé juste en face du quartier des affaires. J'ai le World Trade Center juste devant moi. Il est 9h30.

Le spectacle qui se déroule devant mes yeux tient presque de la science-fiction. Il y a deux énormes brèches dans le haut des tours, ça flambe et il y a une fumée

VOIR PAGE A 12: **J'AI VU**

Des Montréalais inquiets

Des centaines de personnes ont fui leur lieu de travail

FRANÇOIS CARDINAL
LE DEVOIR

À la suite des attaques terroristes menées aux États-Unis, hier matin, des centaines de personnes ont fui volontairement leur lieu de travail à Montréal alors que les autorités appelaient au calme, refusant d'appliquer des mesures d'urgence particulières.

C'est plus précisément la destruction, par des avions de ligne détournés, des gigantesques tours jumelles du World Trade Center à New York qui a semé l'inquiétude au centre-ville de Montréal. À la suite des explosions, plusieurs travailleurs craignant que la proximité de New York et de Montréal

(595 km) fasse de cette dernière une cible potentielle ont déserté leur lieu de travail. Certains employeurs ont même donné congé à leurs employés pour la journée. Ainsi, les plus importants gratte-ciel — la Place Ville-Marie, le 1000 de la Gauchetière et la Tour de la Bourse — ont été vidés en tout ou en partie de leurs occupants.

Cela dit, les événements se déroulant chez nos voisins du Sud n'ont pas inquiété outre mesure les forces de l'ordre de Montréal, qui n'ont pas jugé bon d'augmenter leurs effectifs réguliers. Tout au plus les autorités ont-elles mis sur pied un comité de vigie afin de se tenir prêt en suivant à la minute ce qui se déroule aux États-Unis. Le ministère de

la Sécurité publique, la Sécurité civile, la police de la Communauté urbaine, les pompiers et la Gendarmerie royale du Canada (GRC), entre autres, composent ce comité.

«Nous prenons les événements au sérieux mais nous considérons qu'il n'y a aucune menace à l'heure actuelle, affirmait en début d'après-midi le porte-parole du SPCUM, André Durocher. *En ce sens, rien n'indique que l'on doive évacuer les édifices. [...] It's business as usual.»* Certains édifices, dont les noms n'ont pas été divulgués, ont tout de même fait l'objet d'une surveillance particulière hier.

VOIR PAGE A 12: **INQUIETS**

C'est toujours la même histoire.

La Bible, mieux écrite que jamais.

Traduction entièrement nouvelle par 47 écrivains et spécialistes de la Bible. Six années de travail. 3 200 pages. En librairie 59,95 $.

la bible

MÉDIASPAUL

Bayard

OTTAWA  CITIZEN

WEDNESDAY, SEPTEMBER 12, 2001 | ESTABLISHED IN 1845 | 50 CENTS / 65 CENTS IN OUTLYING AREAS

48 PAGES OF COVERAGE

'An evil act'

AMY SANCETTA, THE ASSOCIATED PRESS

127

Published by the proprietor, Ottawa Citizen Group Inc.,
at 1101 Baxter Road, Box 5020, Ottawa, Ont. K2C 3M4. Russell Mills, Publisher and President.
A division of Southam Publications, a CanWest company.

128

THE GLOBE AND MAIL
SPECIAL 12-PAGE SECTION

'We are survivors'

STAN HONDA/AFP

www.elmercurio.com

EL MERCURIO

EDICIÓN DE 56 PÁGINAS

L, II, XI Y XII REGION $430 $300

FUNDADO EN VALPARAÍSO EL 12 DE SEPTIEMBRE DE 1827 / AÑO CLXXV Nº 59.800 / MCR   ★ SANTIAGO DE CHILE, MIÉRCOLES 12 DE SEPTIEMBRE DE 2001   FUNDADO EN SANTIAGO EL 1 DE JUNIO DE 1900 / AÑO CII Nº 36.603 (ES PROPIEDAD)

Nueva York y Washington:

Aterrador ataque a EE.UU.

Terroristas estrellan aviones con pasajeros contra las Torres Gemelas y el Pentágono.

Alcalde de Nueva York: cifra de muertos "podría ser algo más de lo soportable".

Las bolsas mundiales cierran para controlar el desplome de las acciones.

129

IMPACTOS EN LAS TORRES GEMELAS.— Una enorme bola de fuego y de humo emerge de la segunda torre atacada, en el instante en que el avión secuestrado estalla en el interior del edificio. Atrás se ve el humo de la otra torre impactada minutos antes.

SEGURIDAD:
Estados Unidos pone en alerta máxima a las FF.AA. dentro y fuera del país.
A 6

MUNDO:
Aliados europeos y Rusia, entre otros, efectúan reuniones de emergencia.
A 6

CHILE:
Policía refuerza la vigilancia en embajadas de EE.UU., Israel y Arabia Saudita.
C 1

ECONOMÍA:
Los expertos pronostican un retraso en la recuperación mundial.
B 1

Internet: La red funcionó pese a la alta demanda. A 16
Cultura: El arte cerró sus puertas en señal de duelo y temor. C 18
Sociedad: A la distancia, la angustia invade a los chilenos. A 12

FRASE DEL DÍA
"No se equivoquen: Estados Unidos cazará y castigará a los responsables de esta cobardía".
GEORGE W. BUSH
Presidente de Estados Unidos

FYNS AMTS AVIS

Onsdag

Onsdag den 12. september 2001 • Uge 37 • SVENDBORG AVIS • LANGELANDS AVIS • FAABORG AVIS • ÆRØ AVIS • NYBORG AVIS • 139. årgang • Nr. 184 • Løssalg kr. 11.00

Foto: Carmen Taylor

Over 10.000 dræbte i angreb

Ufattelig tragedie ramte New York og Washington i går

2. SEKTION - SIDE 1-3

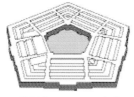

Uvist hvor mange døde i Pentagon

2. SEKTION - SIDE 1

Foto: Jørgen Outzen

Dyb medfølelse

På retsbygningen i Svendborg - som på alle andre offentlige bygninger - gik flaget på halv i dyb medfølelse med de mange ofre

1. SEKTION - SIDE 2

Foto: Nordfoto

Uhyggeligt nemt at kapre fly

-100 timer bag simulator er nok, siger formand for dansk pilotforening

2. SEKTION - SIDE 3

Verden i chok efter terror

Tusinder er dræbt i historiens værste terrorangreb på USA. Præsident George Bush lover at finde de skyldige og straffe dem. Arabiske terrorgrupper mistænkes

■ NEW YORK: Verdens befolkning i almindelighed og 270 millioner amerikanere i særdeleshed er i chok.

Historiens værste terrorangreb skønnes med baggrund i oplysninger i dag ved 11-tiden at have kostet ikke under 10.000 mennesker livet. Langt de fleste opholdt sig i det 110 etagers verdenskendte World Trade Center, der med 18 minutters mellemrum blev ramt af to kaprede fly.

Præsidenten truer

USAs præsident George W. Bush lovede i en tv-tale til nationen, at alt vil blive gjort for at fange de ansvarlige.

Præsidenten truede direkte alle de lande, der giver husly til terrorister.

-Terrorhandlinger kan ryste vore største bygningers fundament, men de kan ikke ramme USAs fundament, sagde præsidenten.

Fire kaprede fly med 266 ombordværende deltog i angrebet, som indledtes kort før kl. 9.00 amerikansk tid.

Udover World Trade Center i New York, der ramtes af to af flyene, blev det amerikanske forsvarsministerium Pentagon i Washington angrebet. Det fjerde fly styrtede ned i delstaten Pennsylvania.

I følge flere amerikanske tv-stationer er antallet af dræbte i Washington op mod 800. Allerede nu skønnes knap 300 brandfolk at være omkommet, og knap 100 politifolk er savnet.

Det sydlige Manhattan i bølgende røgskyer efter de to skyskrabere i World Trade Center brød sammen.
Foto: Daniel Hulshizer

Et gigantisk oprydningsarbejde er igang på Manhattan i New York - redningsfolkene ved, der er overlevende i ruinerne - de ringer fra deres mobiltelefoner.
Foto: Peter Morgan

Bush lover gengæld

Alle anstrengelser vil blive gjort for at finde de skyldige, sagde USAs præsident George W. Bush i sin natlige tv-tale til nationen.

- Angrebene på World Trade Center i New York og forsvarsministeriet Pentagon i Washington har »sluttet tusindvis af liv«, sagde Bush og fortsatte:

- Disse massemord havde til hensigt at føre vores land ud i kaos og på tilbagetog, men de har slået fejl. Vores land er stærkt, fastslog præsidenten.

George W. Bush.
Foto: Larry Downing

Fjende nr. 1

Alverdens eksperter enige om et, nemlig at der er tale om verdens alvorligste og bedst koordinerede terrorangreb. Hvem, der stod bag, er derimod uvist, men kilder i den amerikanske kongres og flere eksperter i antiterror har den opfattelse, at angrebet bærer den saudiarabiske rigmand Osama bin Ladens fingeraftryk. bin Laden menes at opholde sig i Afghanistan.

Osama bin Laden.

2. SEKTION - SIDE 3

Terrorangreb på USA

FYN & ØER 1. SEKTION - SIDE 2

2. SEKTION - SIDE 1- 3

LEDER 2. SEKTION - SIDE 4

FYNS AMTS AVIS mener:

66 ...der er næppe tvivl om, at den tendens, som i præsident Bushs første regeringstid har vist sig, nemlig et mindre engagement i verdensproblemerne, vil ændre sig. Simpelthen fordi amerikanerne har opdaget, at ikke engang verdens eneste supermagt kan stå alene. 99

DEBAT 2. SEKTION SIDE 4

Resten af ugen...

1/1 FORENDE

PR. 1/2 KG

9⁹⁵

føtex SVENDBORG

DISKRET TILBUD!

HØREAPPARAT

Så længe lager haves, sælges diskret "i-øret" model med klar lyd og automatisk lydregulering.

Pris fra 4.995,-
÷ offentlig tilskud 3.096,-
÷ tilskud fra "Danmark" op til 1000,-

Din tilbudspris fra 899,-

DANSK HØRECENTER
Kongegade 14
5700 Svendborg
TH. 62 800 848

RING OG BESTIL TID NU!

Libero Baby Comfort eller Up & Go
Flere varenumre 38-70 stk. Stk-pris 3,16-1,7 l
Frit valg

Bleer
Spar 45,-

Libero

Kvickly

Betal som det passer dig
med et brilleabonnement

Vælg præcis den brille, du vil have og betal den over 12 eller 24 måneder. Uden rente eller gebyrer.

RAVN

PROFIL OPTIK

50p
Wednesday
September 12 2001
Published in London
and Manchester
guardian.co.uk

The Guardian

A declaration of war

PHOTOGRAPH: SPENCER PLATT

131

Libération

11 SEPTEMBRE 2001

1,14 euro France métropolitaine
www.liberation.com

M 0135 - 912 - 7,50 F - 1,14 €

133

The sensation of Womenhood & the regularity of 3 Generations in Silk Sarees..
SARATHA'S
(THE MOST AUSPICIOUS PLACE FOR WEDDING SAREES)
Dhun Building, 827, Mount Road, Chennai-2. Ph: 8521177
32, N.S.B. Road, Trichy-620 002. Ph: 702077

THE HINDU

INDIA'S NATIONAL NEWSPAPER

Printed at Chennai, Coimbatore, Bangalore, Hyderabad, Madurai, Delhi, Visakhapatnam, Thiruvananthapuram and Kochi

✻ Air Blowers
✻ ID Fans
✻ PA/FD Fans
NADI INDUSTRIAL FANS
ISO 9002 COMPANY
NADI Airtechnics Pvt. Ltd.
26, G.N.T. Road, Erukkancherry, Chennai-600 118.
Ph: (044) 5570873, 5570264 Fax: (044) 5371149
E-mail: chennadi@md2.vsnl.net.in, http://www.nadiindia.com

32 Pages Rs. 3

CHENNAI, WEDNESDAY, SEPTEMBER 12, 2001

ISSN 0971 - 751X Vol. 124. No. 217
Internet: www.hindugrouponnet.com & www.hinduonnet.com

DIGEST

All SP MLAs in U.P. quit

LUCKNOW, SEPT. 11. All Samajwadi Party legislators resigned from the Uttar Pradesh Assembly today in a bid to build pressure on the Rajnath Singh Government to hold early elections. Of the 102 members, 94 handed over their resignations to the Vidhan Sabha Secretary this morning. They are understood to have alleged in their letters that the step is to protest against the alleged move by the BJP-led Government to continue even after the completion of its five-year-term next month. — UNI

— Details on Page 15

Woman without veil attacked

SRINAGAR, SEPT. 11. Just a day after the expiry of the deadline, two suspected Lashkar-e-Jabbar militants attacked a woman in the heart of the city for not covering herself with a veil as demanded by the outfit.

The ultras stopped the woman at Nai Sarak and threw coloured water on her face. Policemen deployed in the area immediately arrested a suspected youth, identified as Fayaz Ahmad.— PTI

— Details on Page 13

Assembly dissolved

IMPHAL, SEPT. 11. The seventh Manipur Legislative Assembly, which had been kept under suspended animation since early June, has been dissolved by the President, Mr. K. R. Narayanan, with immediate effect.

The dissolution notice was issued by the State Law Secretary after the receipt of a Central Government notification in this regard, official sources said. — PTI

INTERVIEW

The Afghan leader, Mr. Ahmad Shah Masood, whose fate is unknown, had warned in a recent interview that the Taliban and Osama bin Laden represented a threat to world stability.

— Details on Page 12

NATIONAL
● Jayalalithaa counsel's arguments — Page 13

BUSINESS
● Imports of sensitive items fall — Page 18

SPORT
● Rebecca shuts out Sheetal — Page 24

TAMIL NADU
● Talk of The Town — Page 2
● T.N. to move SC on Cauvery issue — Page 4

OPPORTUNITIES
— 8 Pages

ALL IN THE GAME

Keshav-
NOTHING TO WORRY–JUST MAKE SURE THE POVERTY REKHA DOESN'T CROSS THE LAKSHMAN REKHA..

134

America under attack

● World Trade Center collapses ● Part of Pentagon destroyed ● White House evacuated ● Thousands feared killed

NEW YORK, SEPT. 11. In one of the most horrifying attacks ever against the United States, terrorists crashed two airliners into the World Trade Center in a deadly series of blows on Tuesday that brought down the twin 110-storey towers. A plane also slammed into the Defence Department as the Government itself came under attack.

Thousands could be dead or injured, a high-ranking New York City police official said, speaking on condition of anonymity.

Authorities had been trying to evacuate those who work in the twin towers when the glass-and-steel skyscrapers came down in a thunderous roar within about 90 minutes after the crashes, which took place minutes apart around 9 a.m. But many people were thought to have been trapped. About 50,000 people work at the Trade Center and tens of thousands of others visit each day.

American Airlines initially said the Trade Center was hit by two of its planes, both hijacked, carrying a total of 156 people. But the airline later said that was unconfirmed. Two United airliners with a total of 110 aboard also crashed — one outside Pittsburgh, the other in a location not immediately identified. Altogether, the planes had 266 people aboard.

"This is perhaps the most audacious terrorist attack that's ever taken place in the world,'' said Mr. Chris Yates, an aviation expert at Jane's Transport in London. "It takes a logistics operation from the terror group involved that is second to none. Only a very small handful of terror groups is on that list... I would name at the top of the list Osama bin Laden.''

The U.S. President, Mr. George W. Bush, ordered a full-scale investigation to "hunt down the folks who committed this act.''

Within the hour, the Defence Department took a direct, devastating hit from a plane. The fiery crash destroyed one side of the five-sided structure.

The White House, the Defence Department and the Capitol were evacuated along with other federal buildings in Washington and New York.

Authorities in Washington immediately called out troops, including an infantry regiment. The Situation Room at the White House was in full operation. Authorities went on alert from coast to coast, the U.S. and Canadian borders were sealed, all air traffic across the country was halted, and security was tightened at strategic installations.

In June, a U.S. judge had set this Wednesday as the sentencing date for a bin Laden associate for his role in the 1998 bombing of U.S. embassies in Africa that killed more than 200 people. The sentencing had been set for the federal courthouse near the World Trade Center. No one from the U.S. attorney's office could be reached on Tuesday to comment on whether the sentencing was still on.

Afghanistan's hardline Taliban rulers condemned the attacks and rejected suggestions that bin Laden was behind them, saying he does not have the means to carry out such well-orchestrated attacks. Osama bin Laden has been given asylum in Afghanistan.

Mr. Abdel-Bari Atwan, editor of the Al-Quds al-Arabi newspaper, said he had received a warning from Islamic fundamentalists close to bin Laden, but had not taken the threat seriously. "They said it would be a huge and unprecedented attack but they did not specify,'' Mr. Atwan said in a telephone interview in London.

In the West Bank city of Nablus, thousands of Palestinians celebrated the attacks, chanting "God is Great'' and handing out candy.

American Airlines initially identified the planes that crashed into the Trade Center as Flight 11, a Los Angeles-bound jet hijacked after takeoff from Boston with 92 people aboard, and Flight 77, which was seized while carrying 64 people from Washington to Los Angeles.

In Pennsylvania, United Airlines Flight 93, a Boeing 757 en route from Newark, New Jersey, to San Francisco, crashed about 130 km southeast of Pittsburgh with 45 people aboard. United Airlines said another of its planes, Flight 175, a Boeing 767 bound from Boston to Los Angeles with 65 people on board, also crashed, but it did not say where. The fate of those aboard the two planes was not immediately known.

United's pilots union said United Flight 175 crashed into the Trade Center. But the airline had no immediate comment.

An emergency dispatcher in Westmoreland County, Pennsylvania, received a cell phone call at 9:58 a.m. from a man who said he was a passenger locked in the bathroom of United Flight 93, said the dispatch supervisor, Mr. Glenn Cramer.

"We are being hijacked, we are being hijacked!'' Mr. Cramer quoted the man as saying. The man told dispatchers the plane "was going down. He heard some sort of explosion and saw white smoke coming from the plane and we lost contact with him,'' Mr. Cramer said.

Evacuations were ordered at the United Nations in New York and at the Sears Tower in Chicago. Los Angeles mobilised its anti-terrorism division, and security was intensified around the naval installations in Hampton Roads, Viginia. Walt Disney World in Orlando, Florida, was evacuated.

The planes blasted fiery, gaping holes in the upper floors of the twin towers. About an hour later, the southern tower collapsed with a roar and a huge cloud of smoke; the other tower fell about a half-hour after that, covering lower Manhattan in heaps of gray rubble and broken glass. Firefighters trapped in the rubble radioed for help.

"I have a sense it's a horrendous number of lives lost,'' the Mayor, Mr. Rudolph Giuliani, said. "Right now we have to focus on saving as many lives as possible.''

The toll on the crashed planes alone could surpass that of the Oklahoma City bombing on April 19, 1995, which claimed 168 lives in what was the deadliest act of terrorism on U.S. soil.

The crashes at the World Trade Center happened minutes apart, beginning just before 9 a.m.

Heavy black smoke billowed into the sky above one of New York City's most famous landmarks, and debris rained down on the street, one of the city's busiest work areas. When the second plane hit, a fireball erupted, leaving a huge hole in the glass and steel tower. — AP

Israel, India next?

By Kesava Menon

MANAMA (Bahrain), SEPT. 11. Israel has evacuated all diplomatic missions around the world fearing that the attacks in the U.S. might not mark the end of today's tragedies. The Palestinian Authority President, Mr. Yasser Arafat, has been amongst the first to issue a statement condemning the incident. There are stray reports of signs of celebration in the Arab world accompanied with statements to the effect that "Israel and India should be next".

India shocked: Page 13
Osama hand suspected: Page 16

DIRECT
WORLD TRADE CENTER, NEW YORK (ETATS

The second tower of the World Trade Center as it caves in. *(Right):* A TV grab shows clouds of smoke and dust spreading over New York as the tower comes down after having an aircraft crash into it on Tuesday. Both the towers of the Center have since come down. — Reuters, AFP

Video-grabs taken from Russian TV channel NTV and US Fox TV showing the second plane that smashed against one of the twin towers of the World Trade Center in New York on Tuesday in an apparent terrorist attack. — AFP

Did terrorists have their own pilots?

NEW YORK, SEPT. 11. The terrorists, who apparently hijacked four planes and attacked the World Trade Center and Pentagon, could only have succeeded by using their own trained pilots in a scheme that defied all scenarios envisioned by national security officials, terrorism experts said.

"They flew the planes themselves,'' Mr. Gene Poteat, president of the Association of Former Intelligence Officers, said on Tuesday. "No pilot, even with a gun to his head, is going to fly into the World Towers.'' The hijackers used the airplanes as weapons, Mr. Poteat said, adding that they may also have had the ability to disable communications systems used to alert authorities to trouble. "This has been an enormously long-planned and obviously carefully planned operation.''

That massive planning effort was far beyond anything conceived by counter-terrorism officials, who have focused on preventing individual attacks, said Mr. Steven Emerson of the Investigative Project, a research group focused on international terrorism. "No one thought there was a capability of doing simultaneous attacks so none of the counter-terrorism scenarios ever envisioned this.''

Authorities had examined the chances of individual attacks on high-profile targets such as the World Trade Center and the Pentagon, including an attack on a large building using a commandeered plane.

But most research examining the potential for attacks causing devastating loss of life had focused on chemical or biological means, he said. "To the extent we know now, this is relatively low technology.'' — AP

Smoke, shock spread over New York

By Sridhar Krishnaswami

NEW YORK, SEPT. 11. The scene is truly tense in this city which has had its share of terrorism eight years ago. In 1993 an attack on the World Trade Center left six dead and more than 1000 injured. But this time around, no one is even tempted to make a guess.

The twin towers of the World Trade Center are gone; only smoke is filling the air and one that can be seen miles away. Thousands are moving away from the scene which the authorities have blocked to facilitate rescue efforts. And with the nation's airports shut down, thousands are stranded and the authorities are trying to talk people into getting out of Lower Manhattan.

People are milling around television sets in hotel lobbies or listening to radios on street corners. Some of the shops in this busy part of town that hardly goes to sleep have downed their shutters. And telephones and cell phones do not seem to be working. The frustration is very visible as one strolls down the street. In a time when roadside telephone booths seemed to be a thing of the past, there are actually lines of people wanting to use them, if a connection could be made. The hotel lines are not any different.

If the authorities in Washington D.C. have declared a State of Emergency and called out the army to patrol sensitive areas, the National Guard in New York has got the call to augment the 40,000 police and 15,000 fire fighters.

What has stunned intelligence and law enforcement agencies, as also the common man, is the kind of coordination and precision the terrorist acts had been executed. In a span of 18 minutes two planes rammed the World Trade Centre; shortly thereafter the Pentagon was hit. And at least two other civilian aircraft went down, for reasons that are now being determined. At least 110 people are said to have died in these two crashes.

The first impression here and elsewhere is where intelligence went wrong; and some are already talking about the colossal intelligence failure. There will be a lot of soul searching on what it was that actually went wrong.

Equally stunning is that terrorists have been able to target the actual nerve centres of the government, the Pentagon in particular. For a long time, the worst case scenario planning was a group of terrorists crashing or blowing up a plane filled with deadly explosives over a crowded city. Very close to this happened in New York on Tuesday.

AMERICA IN AGONY: Women unable to control themselves, console one another, as they watch the Word Trade Center crashing down on Tuesday. — AP

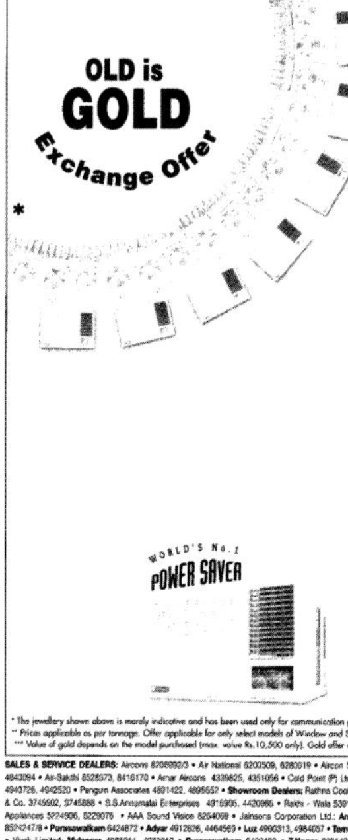
OLD is GOLD
Exchange Offer
*
WORLD'S No. 1
POWER SAVER

YOUR RUSTY, OLD AC FOR A NEW NATIONAL AC AND GOLD!

It's a truly golden opportunity!
Exchange your old AC for a brand-new, top-of-the-line National AC** and get
GOLD WORTH Rs. 10,500!***
Or you may opt for a phenomenal price-off, upto Rs. 10,500 off on a National AC, in exchange for your old AC. No contests. No confusing details. No waiting.
Rush to any of our National showrooms or call any of the phone numbers given below for more details.
Offer valid for a limited period only.

AIR CONDITIONERS

* The jewellery shown above is merely indicative and has been used only for communication purposes
** Prices applicable as per tonnage. Offer applicable for only select models of Window and Split ACs
*** Value of gold depends on the model purchased (max. value Rs.10,500 only). Gold offer available in select cities only. Conditions apply.

SALES & SERVICE DEALERS: Aircons 8206992/3 • Air National 6200509, 6280019 • Aircon Shoppe 4332591, 4339794 • Airmad Marketing Services (P) Ltd. 4732705, 4843094 • Air-Sakthi 8528973, 8416170 • Amar Aircons 4339825, 4351056 • Cold Point (P) Ltd. 8413322, 8553355 • Hi-Tech Air Systems 4326007/8 • Iceberg Engineers 4940726, 4942520 • Penguin Associates 4801422, 4895552 • Showroom Dealers: Rathna Cools & Co. 8226535, 8211266 • Jayam & Co. 6211576, 6211310 • Chellaman & Co. 3745502, 3745888 • S.S.Annamalai Enterprises 4915906, 4420965 • Rakhi - Wala 5391775/6 • Geebal Associates 4330267 • S.P.Electronics 8526925 • Pee Pee Appliances 5224906, 5229076 • AAA Sound Vision 8264069 • Jainsons Corporation Ltd.: Anna Nagar 6261841, 6212107 • T.Nagar 8732020, 8233005 • Royapettah 8524247/8 • Purasawalkam 6424872 • Adyar 4912626, 4464569 • Luz 4990313, 4984067 • Tambaram 2261479 • Perambur 6614586 • Valasaravakkam 4868222, 4868333 • Vivek Limited: Mylapore 4985011, 4982012 • Purasawalkam 6422482 • T.Nagar 8281421, 8284129 • Vadapalani 4845444, 4845454 • Adyar 4422268, 4413323 • Tambaram 2362081, 2362077 • Anna Nagar(W) 6200132, 6200133 • Nanganallur 2316970, 2318970.

HTA.8560.2001

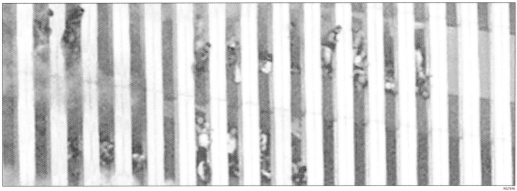

Personas que se encontraban en los pisos superiores de la torre norte del World Trade Center, en Nueva York, se colocan en las ventanas con la esperanza de recibir ayuda. Poco después, la construcción se desplomaba

EL UNIVERSAL

EL GRAN DIARIO INDEPENDIENTE DE MÉXICO

Año LXXXV - Tomo CCCXXXVIII/Número 30,639   MÉXICO, D.F., MIÉRCOLES 12 DE SEPTIEMBRE DE 2001   Internet: www.eluniversal.com.mx $ 7.00

Alerta mundial

135

Miles murieron; cazaremos a los culpables: Bush

Terrorismo: secuestran comandos 4 aviones; impactan 2 contra torres gemelas de NY y 1, que iba dirigido a la Casa Blanca, en el Pentágono

Sobrevivientes: vida entre los escombros. Entran Fuerzas Armadas en alerta máxima. Protegen barcos de guerra la costa este de ese país

Condena: rechazo internacional. Se deslindan agrupaciones extremistas. Sospechan de dirigente musulmán. Hoy, reunión de emergencia de UE

Mercados: impera el nerviosismo. Suben oro, metales industriales y el crudo. Se deprecia el peso 2.6%. Fox ofrece apoyo; "en México hay calma"

▶ **Más información** páginas A4 a A20

EDITORIAL

Destino incierto

El más grave y catastrófico hecho terrorista en la historia universal fue concebido y realizado como un golpe demoledor contra Estados Unidos, pero objetivamente está dirigido contra la paz mundial y entraña riesgos de incalculables consecuencias.

Repudiamos los terribles acontecimientos ocurridos en Nueva York y Washington tanto como si hubieran ocurrido en nuestro propio territorio. Los condenamos, asimismo, porque parecen anunciar el advenimiento de una era de incierto destino mundial. La dimensión de los hechos hace pensar en efectos y reacciones casi apocalípticos, aunque todavía no se conocen con puntualidad la magnitud de los estragos ni la autoría del ataque terrorista, que personajes de la Casa Blanca y gobernantes occidentales consideran como "actos de guerra".

Vea **EDITORIAL**
página A28

Una bola de fuego, polvo y humo surge de la torre gemela sur del World Trade Center después de que un avión fuera impactado contra el edificio

136

Miércoles 12 de septiembre
del 2001
México, D.F.

94 Páginas
7 Secciones
$ 7.00

SECCIÓN A

CORAZÓN DE MÉXICO

Año 8, Número 2830
www.reforma.com

TRES ataques en NUEVA YORK y WASHINGTON dejan MILES de muertos

Aterrorizan a EU

TERROR EN EU

Acaban con Torres Gemelas en hora y media; sospechan de Osama bin Laden

POR REFORMA/REDACCIÓN

LOS ESTADOUNIDENSES AMA-necieron ayer aterroriza-dos con una guerra no de-clarada en sus propias ca-lles, mientras la pesadilla del ataque sorpresa japo-nés contra Pearl Harbor, ocurrido 60 años atrás, se adueña del corazón de la nación más poderosa del mundo.

Tres atentados terroristas en cadena contra los centros neurálgicos del poder político, económico y militar en Nueva York y Washington desnudaron la fragi-lidad de prácticamente todos los sistemas de seguridad de aeropuertos e instalacio-nes militares y civiles estadounidenses.

Cuando se reportó, a las 08:45 de la mañana (hora de Nueva York; 07:45 ho-ra del centro de México) el choque de un Boeing 767-200 de American Airlines con la Torre Norte del World Trade Cen-ter, inicialmente se pensó en una trage-dia producto de un error aeronáutico.

Pero, 18 minutos más tarde, en me-dio de la huida desesperada de cientos de personas del edificio en llamas de 110 pisos, millones vieron en vivo por televi-sión cómo otro avión civil, ahora un Boe-ing 767-200 de United Airlines, se im-pactaba directamente contra la Torre Sur. La sospecha de error se disipó por la certeza de un ataque terrorista.

La agonía del símbolo por excelencia del capitalismo norteamericano duró po-co más de una hora. Ambos rascacielos se vinieron abajo, en un intervalo de 30 mi-nutos, sepultando bajo toneladas de es-combros a tantas personas que el Alcalde neoyorquino, Rudolf Giuliani, definió co-mo un "número horrendo de imaginar".

Mientras los ojos de las autoridades y del mundo se centraban sobre la tra-gedia que convulsionaba a Manhattan, y el Presidente George Bush lamentaba los hechos desde un colegio de Florida, una enorme columna de humo negro comenzaba a elevarse desde el Pentágo-no, producto del choque de otro avión, un Boeing 757-200 de American Airli-nes. El estandarte indestructible del po-derío militar estadounidense también estaba herido.

Otra aeronave de United, que su-puestamente atacaría Campo David, ca-yó cerca de la ciudad de Pittsburgh.

Los cuatro aviones —que en total lle-vaban 266 personas— habían sido se-cuestrados con minutos de diferencia mientras cubrían rutas de ciudades de la Costa Este con destino en California.

Las autoridades ordenaron el cierre de todas las operaciones aéreas en el te-rritorio al tiempo que American Airlines y United daban cuenta de la desapari-ción de varios de sus aparatos. Las co-municaciones telefónicas en las ciuda-des colapsadas se hicieron extremada-mente difíciles.

El Presidente George W. Bush trans-currió gran parte de su día a bordo del avión presidencial Air Force One mo-viéndose entre bases militares. En una escala en Louisiana, prometió "cazar y castigar ejemplarmente" a los culpables de las estocadas, advertencia que repi-tió en un mensaje al regresar a la Casa Blanca.

Fuentes de inteligencia especularon que todas las pistas conducen al líder terrorista árabe Osama bin Laden.

En Nueva York, desde la bahía de Manhattan, el perfil de la ciudad ilumi-nada era diferente al de la noche ante-rior: había un enorme hueco, faltaban las miles de luces de las Torres Gemelas.

Estados Unidos es, desde ayer, una potencia herida y vulnerable.

Internacional (20A)
Negocios • Ciudad
Cultura • Gente!

cobertura especial

Manténgase informado y siga todos los detalles con nuestros gráficos anima-dos, videos, audios y fotogalerías.

reforma.com

Panorama de guerra. *Con aviones llenos de pasajeros como proyectiles, ayer le quitaron a Estados Unidos su símbolo del éxito económico: las Torres Gemelas ubicadas en el corazón de Manhattan. Los 110 pisos se vinieron abajo. Los edificios construidos en 1972 eran utilizados diariamente por 100 mil personas, entre trabajadores y visitantes.*

PEARL HARBOR NEOYORQUINO

AVIÓN 1 American Airlines 011
(De Boston a Los Ángeles)
Objetivo: **TORRE NORTE, WTC**
🕐 **07:45** Un Boeing 767-200 de American Airli-nes se impacta contra la Torre Norte del WTC. Llevaba 81 pasajeros, 2 pilotos y 9 sobrecargos.
Todos los tiempos son hora de México.

AVIÓN 2 United Airlines 175
(De Boston a Los Ángeles)
Objetivo: **TORRE SUR, WTC**
🕐 **08:03** Un Boeing 767-200 de United se im-pacta contra la Torre Sur del WTC. Llevaba 56 pasajeros, 2 pilotos y 7 sobrecargos.

AVIÓN 3 American Airlines 077
(De Washington Dulles a Los Ángeles)
Objetivo: **PENTÁGONO**
🕐 **08:43** Un Boeing 757-200 de American Airli-nes se impacta contra el Pentágono. El avión lle-vaba 58 pasajeros, 2 pilotos y 4 sobrecargos.

AVIÓN 4 United Airlines 093
(De Newark a San Francisco)
Objetivo: **DESCONOCIDO**
🕐 **09:10** Un Boeing 757-200 se estrelló al sureste de Pittsburgh. Llevaba 38 pasajeros, 2 pilotos y 5 sobrecargos.

El impacto. *El vuelo 175 de United Airlines va directo a la Torre Sur del WTC. El aparato se impacta en seco contra el edificio. El Boeing se introduce en las oficinas, estalla y causa el desplome.*

Las consecuencias

■ **Estados Unidos y el resto del mundo han tomado medidas adicionales de seguridad**

EN EU
Se ordenó cerrar todos los aeropuertos del país hasta las 12:00, hora del este, de hoy. Las medi-das de seguridad se incrementarán tanto en ter-minales aéreas como en las estaciones de tren.

EN MÉXICO
Se suspenden los vuelos a EU y Europa hasta nuevo aviso. Se cancelaron 480 vuelos y se incrementó la vigilancia en los 55 aeropuertos. En vuelos naciona-les se redobló la seguridad y los pasajeros deben identificarse. Se intensificó la vigilancia de edificios públicos y diplomáticos. El Gabinete de Seguridad se declaró en sesión permanente.
En los mercados:

Bolsa Mexicana	Oro (centenario)	Dólar en ventanilla
Baja 5.55%	**Sube 6.06%**	**9.80 pesos**

EN EUROPA
La OTAN ordenó evacuar sus instalaciones en Bru-selas y llamó a "formar un frente común contra el terrorismo". Rusia puso en estado de alerta a sus Fuerzas Armadas para prevenir actos terroristas.

Dónde duele. *Uno de los cuatro atentados fue dirigido contra el centro del orgullo estadounidense: el Pentágono.*

APOCALIPSIS AHORA

POR ENRIQUE KRAUZE

Nueva York - Pearl Harbor en el Río Hudson. Un rascacielos ardía en llamas. ¿Aquí?, pregunté. Sí, aquí. De pronto, en vivo, vimos volar sobre el Hudson al segundo avión e incrustarse en el cuerpo su-perior de la segunda torre. Era obvio que se trataba de un ataque terrorista.

Salí a la calle, llegué a la zona del Lincoln Center y vi caravanas de gente en marcha hacia el norte. Con los te-léfonos públicos inservibles, las personas intentaban co-municarse con sus familias a través de los celulares. Las ambulancias vienen y van, y no hay taxis en Nueva York. Camino un trecho a contracorriente, veo los carteles ci-nematográficos. El primero, previsiblemente, tenía que ser *Apocalypse now redux*.

Llamo a mi amigo Pete Hamill, quien estuvo en la lí-nea de fuego. Vio una persona tirarse de ochenta pisos, la vio desaparecer en el horizonte: prefería morir en el vacío que en el fuego. Hamill sostiene que éste es el mayor de-sastre en la historia de Nueva York: "Lo peor es la sensa-ción de que la tragedia de muerte apenas comienza".

Internacional (21A)

Un hombre mayor *es auxiliado después de que se derrumbaron los edificios del WTC.*

610972000016

OPINIÓN Y COLUMNAS: /// Miguel Ángel Granados Chapa y Manuel J. Jáuregui *(7A)* /// Gustavo Esteva, Jorge Ramos y Sergio Sarmiento *(8A)* /// Froylán M. López Narváez y Sergio Aguayo Quezada *(9A)* /// Alberto Aguilar *(3Neg.)* /// Alberto Barranco *(8Neg.)*

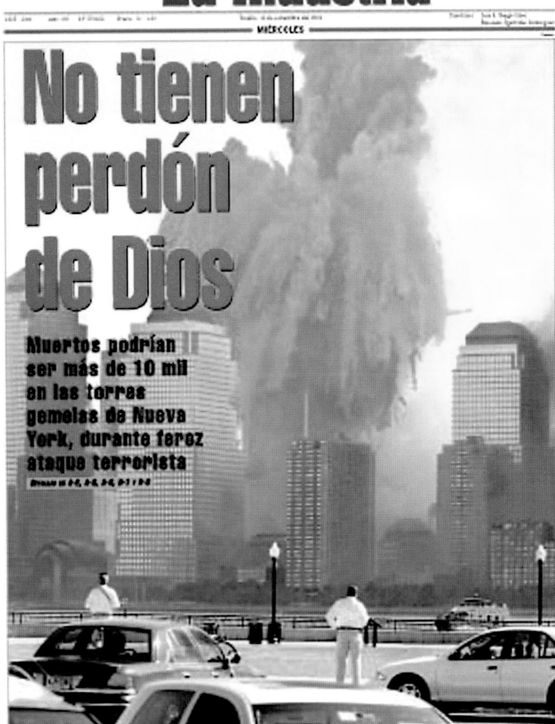

La Industria

No tienen perdón de Dios

Muertos podrían ser más de 10 mil en las torres gemelas de Nueva York, durante feroz ataque terrorista

Procesarán a funcionarios del Pronaa por pérdida de arroz

Grandes anlegos afectan a familias en La Esperanza

PAL cancels flights to crisis-ridden U.S. 2

Extra Extra

Special Edition

SUN ● STAR
CEBU

NO. 1 IN READERSHIP

| Cebu City, Philippines | Vol. XIX, No. 286-A | September 12, 2001 | 8 Pages / P4 |

'THOUSANDS DEAD, HURT'
U.S. 90% sure 'twas bin Laden

A PART OF A TOWER can be seen after the collapse of the first World Trade Center tower in New York. The two towers collapsed when two hijacked planes smashed into them one after the other. Left: U.S. President Bush vows no one will keep the light of America as beacon for freedom and opportunity from shining.　(AFP FOTOS)

- President Bush tells American nation and the world it will make no distinction between terrorists and those harboring them
- Afghanistan also under fire but U.S. denies there were counterstrikes against it
- Casualty figures could be "very high," says New York mayor; thousands and thousands, says President Bush
- American Airlines security "lax since last month"; 2 of 4 hijacked and crashed planes belong to AA (8)

NEW YORK—"It will be more than we can bear."

That's what New York City Mayor Rudolph Giuliani said of the death toll from Tuesday's terrorist attacks, with the figure estimated to hit 10,000 in the New York area alone.

The New York City firefighters' union said at least 200 of its members were feared to have been killed as they tried to evacuate injured people from the twin towers

▶ **THOUSANDS DEAD, 7**

World econ may dip further: Japan

▶ **More stories, photos inside**

JAPANESE Finance Minister Masajuro Shiokawa said terrorist attacks in the United States would worsen the world's economy and have a major negative impact on share prices here.

"This terrorist attack is terrible and intolerable.

Each country should consider how to protect peace and prevent the recurrence of such a disaster," Shiokawa told reporters at an impromptu briefing at the finance ministry.

"It will worsen the world's economy much further," he said. "The world's leading economies

▶ **WORLD ECONOMY, 7**

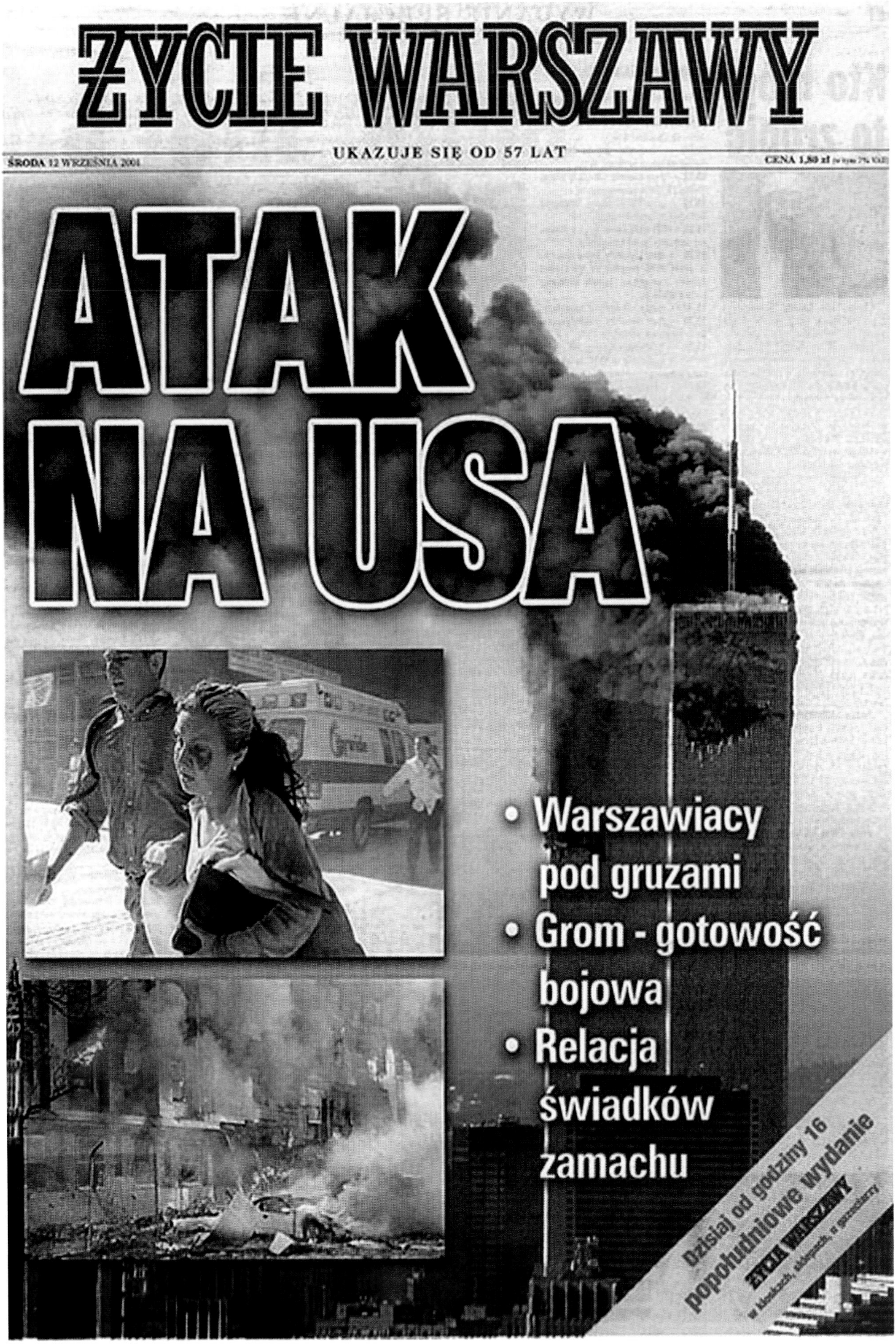

ŻYCIE WARSZAWY

UKAZUJE SIĘ OD 57 LAT

ŚRODA 12 WRZEŚNIA 2001

CENA 1,80 zł (w tym 7% VAT)

ATAK NA USA

- **Warszawiacy pod gruzami**
- **Grom - gotowość bojowa**
- **Relacja świadków zamachu**

Dzisiaj od godziny 16 popołudniowe wydanie ŻYCIA WARSZAWY w kioskach, sklepach, u gazeciarzy

139

Scotland's Business, Financial & Political Daily
Wednesday 12 September, 2001   www.businessam.co.uk
SCOTTISH NEWSPAPER OF THE YEAR

business
a.m.

141

Attack on America

Terror from the skies
Hijackers strike at the heart of
the US with attacks on the Twin
Towers and the Pentagon Page 4

Markets in turmoil
Fears about the impact of the
attacks on the global economy
send shares plunging Page 2

Ian Bell
For America or against? That
could become the only question
relevant in the 21st century Page 3

Profile of a terrorist
The world's most wanted man,
Osama bin Laden, has emerged
as the chief suspect Page 14

Security failures claim
Security at US airports has a
alarming failure rate, according
to a Congress investigation Page 35

Subscriptions Tel 084504 55355

80p

No 246

EL PAIS

MIÉRCOLES 12 DE SEPTIEMBRE DE 2001 · **DIARIO INDEPENDIENTE DE LA MAÑANA** · EDICIÓN **MADRID**

Año XXVI. Número 8.877 · www.elpais.es · Precio: 150 pesetas - 0,90 euros

EE UU sufre el peor ataque de su historia

El mundo en vilo a la espera de las represalias de Bush

142

Momento en el que se cae una de las dos Torres Gemelas de Nueva York. Posteriormente, se desplomó también la segunda a consecuencia de los ataques aéreos.

Miles de muertos entre los escombros de las Torres Gemelas y el Pentágono
Una pasajera contó por el móvil el secuestro de uno de los aviones

George Bush garantizó ayer a los norteamericanos que se han tomado todas las medidas adecuadas para proteger la vida de los ciudadanos y prometió que "EE UU agarrará y castigará a los responsables de estos actos cobardes". A la espera de la proporción y las consecuencias de ese castigo, el mundo entero contiene la respiración ante la peor crisis desde la II Guerra Mundial. Bush cifró esta madrugada en "miles" el número de muertos entre los escombros de las Torres Gemelas y el Pentágono. En el edificio militar, las víctimas son más de 800. El ataque, no reivindicado todavía de forma creíble por ningún grupo, pero con el sello inconfundible del conflicto árabe-israelí, fue perpetrado con cuatro aviones de pasajeros secuestrados por terroristas suicidas y lanzados después contra los objetivos, dos de los edificios más característicos del poder económico y militar norteamericano. Una pasajera relató por un teléfono móvil que su avión estaba siendo pilotado por los piratas. **Páginas 2 a 25 y última**

DEL 1		DEL 2	
LEDARE	2	ALLMÄNT	32
DEBATT	3	UTLAND	34
POLITIK	14	GÖTEBORG	36
EKONOMI	14	LOKALT	38
NAMN	27	VÄSTSVERIGE	43
VÄRLDENS GÅNG	29	SPORT	45
		KONSUMENT	50

Göteborgs-Posten

www.gp.se

ONSDAG 12 SEPTEMBER 2001 • NR 248 • VECKA 37 • 143:E ÅRGÅNGEN • PRIS 12 KRONOR • VÄXEL 031-62 40 00 • PRENUMERATION 031-80 47 00 • PRIVATANNONSER 031-80 06 00

New York 2001-09-11

143

Bild: DOUG KANTER

WORLD TRADE CENTER I RUINER. Förödelsen vid World Trade Center var i det närmaste total. Först kollapsade de två Twin Tower-byggnaderna sedan flygplan kraschat rakt in i dem. Senare på kvällen rasade även ett 47-våningshus i området.

Historiens värsta terrordåd hittills

Tre skyskrapor i ruiner efter attacken i New York

■ USA är ett land i chock. Gårdagens terrorattack är den värsta som världen hittills skådat. Klockan nio lokal tid i går morse kraschade ett trafikflygplan rakt in i World Trade Centers norra skyskrapa på Manhattan. 18 minuter senare kom ett betydligt större trafikflygplan, och kraschade mot den södra skyskrapan. En dryg timma senare hade de båda 110 våningar höga byggnaderna kollapsat.

En stund senare kom nästa attack, denna gång mot försvarshögkvarteret i Pentagon. Även här var det en självmordsattack med flygplan och fem våningar rasade samman på byggnaden.

Senare under kvällen rasade en tredje byggnad, 47 våningar hög, vid World Trade Center. Ytterligare ett höghus på Manhattan höll på rasa i morse sedan det brunnit i tio timmar.

Totalt kapades under gårdagen minst fyra trafikflygplan av terrorister, ett vapen som användes var kniv.

Hur många offer dåden krävde var i natt oklart men det handlar om tusentals offer bara i New York.

Omkring 200 brandmän och uppemot 100 poliser, som deltog i räddningsarbetet på Manhattan, befarades ha omkommit eller saknades tidigt i morse.

EXTRA
Bush lovar leta upp de skyldiga

Halv tre i natt, svensk tid, höll president George W Bush ett kort, men känsloladdat tv-tal till det amerikanska folket.

Han betonade att USA inte låter sig knäckas av terrordåd.

Alla officiella institutioner ska i dag hålla öppet som vanligt.

Han lovade också att leta upp terroristerna och ställa dem inför rätta.

– Jag gör ingen skillnad på de som utförde dådet och de som skyddar dem, sade han.

Folk kastade sig ut i panik

■ Fruktansvärda scener utspelade sig i samband med självmordsattackerna mot World Trade Center. Folk kastade sig i panik ut från skyskraporna, samtidigt som ett regn av glassplitter föll ner mot marken.

Ett sjukhus i närbelägna Greenwich Village sade sig ha "tagit emot hundratals människor med brännskador från topp till tå".

Reino Björk från Göteborg blev ögonvittne till katastrofen.

– Efter ett tag hördes ett enormt dunder och ett av tornen kollapsade. Det följdes av ett stort rökmoln och människor på gatan skrek rakt ut.

Han pekas ut som ansvarig

■ Vem ligger bakom terrorattackerna i USA?
Det är frågan som hela USA nu ställer sig. De starkaste misstankarna riktas mot den saudifödde Usama bin Ladin.

Den omkring 45-årige bin Ladin har fått skulden för att ha organiserat och finansierat bombningarna av de amerikanska ambassaderna i Kenya och Tanzania i augusti 1998. Då dog över 200 människor. Som bestraffning bombade USA påstådda utbildningsläger för terrorister i Afghanistan samt en fabrik i Sudan, som bin Ladin sades vara delägare i.

I natt skakades Afghanistans huvudstad Kabul av en robotattack. USA förnekade dock att de har något med robotanfallet att göra.

Terrorattacken mot USA, sidorna 2, 3, 4, 5, 6, 7, 8, 9, 10, 11, 12, 13 och www.gp.se

7 388111 001202

EXTRA • EXTRA • TERRORISTDÅDEN MOT USA • EXTRA • EXTRA

Norrköpings Tidningar

GRUNDAD ÅR 1758   ÖSTERGÖTLANDS DAGBLAD

Tipsa NT om nyheter 📞 011-13 16 16   NT på Internet www. **nt**.se

nr 211 • onsdag 12 september 2001 • årgång 243 • pris 10 kr inkl moms

Världen i chock efter attacken

Tisdagen den 11 september 2001.

Den mörkaste dagen sedan världskriget.

Plötsligt stannar en hel värld. Minuterna går: World Trade Center i brand efter attack, sedan Pentagon.

World Trade Center rasar. Vita Huset evakueras. Bilbomb utanför amerikanska UD. Sändningarna och rapporteringen fortsätter. Snart räcker orden inte till längre.

Vi får besked om mått och steg långt utanför Amerikas gränser. Plötsligt inser vi att världen försöker försvara sig. Är det möjligt? Vad har hänt? Kan det bli värre? Kommer det att fortsätta? Finns, undrar vi, någon trygg vrå i denna grymma värld?

I dag gör vi Norrköpings Tidningar på ett annat sätt än vanligt. Självklart dominerar katastrofen i USA. I vår huvudledare finns fler frågor än svar. Vi försöker närma oss det ofattbara som hänt.

Vi upplever tragisk världshistoria och Norrköpings Tidningar är sig inte lik.

KARL-ÅKE BREDENBERG
chefredaktör

144

Foto: SCANPIX

Kl 08.48 lokal tid: Ett passagerarflygplan flyger rakt in i det norra tornet på den 110 våningar höga byggnaden World Trade Center i New York. 18 minuter senare kraschar ännu ett passagerarflygplan i byggnaden (bilderna), denna gång i det södra tornet. Allt tyder på en väl planerad terrorattack.

Historiens värsta terroristattack

Åbybo hade kontor i skyskrapan

Norrköpingspolis ögonvittne

Sverige ökar säkerheten

OS-högkvarteret evakuerades

Sidorna 2, 4, 5, 6, 8 och 17

Manhattan. Tisdagen den 11 september 2001. Människor flyr World Trade Center i panik efter terroristdåden mot de jättelika skyskraporna.

Foto: AMY SANCETTA, New York/PRESSENS BILD

SVERIGES STÖRSTA DAGSTIDNING

EXTRA UPPLAGA

AFTONBLADET

GRUNDAD 1830
AV LARS JOHAN HIERTA

254
X

Telefon: 08-725 20 00

TISDAG 11 SEPTEMBER 2001

Pris: **8 kr** Med en bilaga: **13 kr**
Med två olika bilagor: **18 kr**

TERROR-KRIG MOT USA

145

WORLD TRADE CENTER UTPLÅNAT *Det andra av de två tornen på World Trade Center i New York exploderar efter att ett flygplan kört in i det.*

● *Vita huset evakuerat – Pentagon brinner*

● *Hundratals döda – tusentals skadade*

● *World Trade Center rasade* SIDORNA 6, 7, 8, 9

Tipsa om nyheter: 08-411 11 11   ettan@aftonbladet.se

7 388107 000806

146

EXPRESSEN

SENASTE
NYTT PÅ
.SE

Onsdag 12 september 2001

Expressen 8:-   Med TV-guiden 13:-

World Trade Center 11 september 2001

7 388108 000805

ACKNOWLEDGMENTS

Front pages are the end product of hundreds of reporters, artists, photographers, editors, and even a few bosses working for the most part in concert despite chaotic conditions. Such pages are designed every day by journalists who exercise, under intense deadline pressure, a mix of news judgment and artistry. Some of the pages printed here are Extras, that rare form of newspapering that rushes news to the street without regard for business as usual. The other pages were published the day after the attacks, chronicling the events of September 11, 2001, in ways we won't soon forget.

Within the limits of deadline and form, front pages take a wide range of expression. Some are stark and declarative, their black backgrounds creating what Monica Moses of Poynter calls "funereal posters." Others are more traditional, delivering even horrific events in as straightforward a manner as possible under abnormally large headlines. A few newspapers revived an all-but-forgotten custom of the Page One editorial to give voice to the condemnation and grief that would otherwise be tucked inside.

We received no front pages from some parts of the world, including the Middle East and much of Asia. Faced with a practical need to winnow those we did receive, we strove for geographic, corporate, and stylistic variety.

The book is itself a result of the collaborative deadline skills at The Poynter Institute, especially staff of Poynter Online, who spent many hours gathering and posting these and other front pages that can be viewed at www.poynter.org. They are Anne Conneen, Billie Keirstead, Larry Larsen, Bill Mitchell, Ellen Sung, and Cary Pérez Waulk.

James M. Naughton
President, The Poynter Institute